Pythagoras and the Pythagoreans

A Brief History

Pythagoras as representative of music, from the sculptures of the seven liberal arts on the Portail Royal of the cathedral of Chartres. For the indentification as Pythagoras, see Émile Mâle, *L'art réligieux du XIIIe siècle en France*, 5th ed. (Paris, 1923), 87. (Photograph courtesy of Roger-Viollet, © Collection Viollet.)

Pythagoras and the Pythagoreans

A Brief History

Charles H. Kahn

Hackett Publishing Company, Inc.
Indianapolis/Cambridge

Copyright © 2001 by Hackett Publishing Company, Inc.

11   10   09   08   07   06   2   3   4   5   6   7

For further information, please address:

Hackett Publishing Company, Inc.
P. O. Box 44937
Indianapolis, IN 46244-0937

www.hackettpublishing.com

Cover and interior design by Abigail Coyle
Cover photograph of Pythagoras from the cathedral of Chartres
reprinted by permission of Roger-Viollet, copyright © Collection Viollet.

Library of Congress Cataloging-in-Publication Data

Kahn, Charles H.
    Pythagoras and the Pythagoreans : a brief history / Charles H. Kahn.
        p. cm.
    Includes bibliographical references and index.
    ISBN 0-87220-576-2 (cloth) — ISBN 0-87220-575-4 (paper)
        1. Pythagoras and Pythagorean school.   I. Title.

B243 .K34 2001
182'.2—dc21   2001024119

ISBN-13: 978-0-87220-576-5 (cloth)
ISBN-13: 978-0-87220-575-8 (pbk.)

The paper used in this publication meets the minimum requirements
of American National Standard for Information Sciences—Perma-
nence of Paper for Printed Library Materials, ANSI Z39.48–1984.

To the memory of my mother

CONTENTS

PREFACE

As conceived here, the Pythagorean tradition, which begins in the sixth century B.C., stretches down to the seventeenth century A.D. and includes major developments in religion, science, and philosophy. A full history of this movement would be a staggering enterprise, and no one has addressed such a task since A. E. Chaignet's two volumes, *Pythagore et la philosophie pythagoricienne*, published in 1873. What is attempted here is something more modest: a survey of the whole tradition, period by period, reflecting contemporary scholarship.[1]

Naturally enough, most of the work in twentieth-century scholarship has been devoted to Pythagoras and to the early history of the school. It is peculiarly difficult to obtain a reliable picture of Pythagorean thought for the period before Plato. Pythagoras himself became a legendary figure in his own lifetime, while our fullest accounts of the early school come from much later documents, above all from two Neoplatonic "Lives" of Pythagoras composed almost a millennium after his death. The most fundamental work here has been done by Walter Burkert, who (in the 1962 book translated in 1972 as *Lore and Science in Ancient Pythagoreanism*) showed how radically the traditional account of Pythagorean doctrine was altered or invented by Plato's immediate followers. All of us who work on the Pythagoreans

---

[1] For a useful survey, with an up-to-date bibliography, see Bruno Centrone, *Introduzione a i pitagorici* (Roma-Bari: Editori Laterza, 1996).

stand in Burkert's debt. At the same time, because there is so little reliable information concerning early Pythagoreanism, there is room for wide scholarly disagreement in evaluating the personal contribution of Pythagoras himself and the intellectual level attained in the early school. Burkert sees Pythagoras as essentially a religious and cultural leader, a guru rather than a scientist or philosopher, and he has been followed here by Carl Huffman in his important studies of Philolaus (1993) and Archytas (forthcoming). By contrast, a defense of the more traditional picture of Pythagoras as a great intellectual innovator has been presented in Leonid Zhmud's learned book, *Wissenschaft, Philosophie und Religion im frühen Pythagoreismus* (Berlin, 1997). The position to be argued for here reaches conclusions closer to those of Zhmud, although I do not share Zhmud's confidence in our knowledge of Pythagorean thought for the earliest period. In the absence of earlier documentation, the history of Pythagoreanism before Philolaus, like the history of Greek mathematics before Hippocrates of Chios, must remain an area for informed speculation.

It is, however, not only the history of the early Pythagorean school that has been the subject of important scholarly advance in the last generation. The pseudonymous Pythagorean texts of the Hellenistic and Roman periods have been made available in editions by Holger Thesleff (1965), Thomas Szlezak (1972), and others. There has been major work on Eudorus, Philo, and Middle Platonism, including studies of three so-called Neopythagorean philosophers: Nicomachus, Moderatus, and above all Numenius, who has received special attention as a precursor of Plotinus and a remarkable thinker in his own right. Renewed interest in Neoplatonism has also led to important studies of Porphyry and Iamblichus, our two principal sources for Pythagoras. In this connection I want to acknowledge my debts to John Dillon's book *The Middle Platonists* (1977), to Michael Frede's monograph on Numenius (1987), and to Dominic O'Meara's *Pythagoras Revived* (1989).

Finally, I have drawn on studies in early modern science that recognize the importance of the Pythagorean and Neoplatonic traditions for Copernicus and Kepler. These include Thomas Kuhn's classic *The Copernican Revolution* (1957) and much recent work on Kepler. This modern revival of Pythagorean thought is a phenomenon that has not received much attention from students of ancient Pythagoreanism—not even from Chaignet, who did discuss the reappearance of the Pythagorean tradition in the Renaissance. That tradition includes so many elements of wild, almost superstitious speculation, for example in numerology, that it is sometimes difficult to remember that there is also a solid basis for numerical harmonics. So Copernicus and Kepler, with their fundamental contributions to modern science and to the modern world view, may be regarded as providing the Pythagorean story with a happy ending.

This survey originally took shape as a short monograph commissioned by the Istituto della Enciclopedia Italiana and published by them in Italian translation as *Pitagora e i pitagorici* (71 pages, 1993), in the format of the Enciclopedia Multimediale delle Scienze Filosofiche. I am grateful to the Istituto della Enciclopedia Italiana for permission to use here that same title and much of the earlier text, which forms the backbone of the present study.

I want also to mark my gratitude to friends and colleagues who have encouraged me in this project and improved it with their criticism. Paul Kalligas, Michael Frede, and John Dillon have all been immensely helpful. Deborah Wilkes, for Hackett Publishing, has not only been patient and supportive but has also provided me with two superlative readers of the manuscript for the press: Walter Burkert and Carl Huffman, whose comments have helped to make this work less imperfect. Huffman has also generously shared with me much of his forthcoming study of Archytas. And Daniel McLean has served as an outstanding research assistant to prepare the manuscript and indices for the press. To all of them, my thanks.

Charles H. Kahn
Philadelphia, January 2001

ABBREVIATIONS

ANWR	*Aufstieg und Niedergang der römischen Welt*
CP	*Classical Philology*
CQ	*Classical Quarterly*
D. L.	Diogenes Laertius, *Lives of the Eminent Philosophers*
DK	H. Diels and W. Kranz, *Die Fragmente der Vorsokratiker*, 7th ed., Berlin, 1954
REG	*Revue des Études Grecques*
RE	*Realencyclopädie der classischen Altertumswissenschaft*, eds. G. Wissowa, W. Kroll, et al., Stuttgart and Munich, 1894–1978
Iamblichus *VP*	*Vita Pythagorica*
Porphyry *VP*	*Vita Pythagorae*

I

THE PYTHAGOREAN QUESTION

PYTHAGORAS IS NOT ONLY THE MOST FAMOUS NAME IN THE HISTORY OF philosophy before Socrates and Plato; he is also one of the most fascinating and mysterious figures of antiquity. Pythagoras was celebrated in the ancient tradition as a mathematician and a philosopher of mathematics, and his name is still linked to a major theorem in plane geometry. Aristotle claims that Plato's own philosophy was profoundly influenced by Pythagorean teaching,[1] and later authors regard Pythagoras as the creator of the Platonic tradition in philosophy. In the literature of late antiquity Pythagoras appears as a unique genius, the founding father for mathematics, music, astronomy, and philosophy. A modern Platonist, the twentieth-century mathematician and philosopher A. N. Whitehead, has described Pythagoras as the first thinker to appreciate the function of mathematical ideas in abstract thought: "He insisted on the importance of the utmost generality in reasoning, and he divined the importance of number as an aid to the construction of any representation of the conditions involved in the order of nature."[2] Whitehead is echoing the ancient reports that credit Pythagoras with inventing the very notion of philosophy, with the first description of nature as a cosmos or ordered whole, with discovering the sphericity of the earth, developing

---

[1] Aristotle, *Metaphysics* A.6.

[2] A. N. Whitehead, *Science and the Modern World* (New York, 1925), 41.

the theory of proportionals in mathematics, identifying the five regular solids, and discovering the numerical ratios that underlie the basic musical concordances.[3] Since he is represented as the greatest scientific mind of early Greece if not of all antiquity, his ancient admirers came to look upon him as the source of all wisdom, "the prince and father of divine philosophy" in the words of Iamblichus.[4]

But there is another side to the picture. Some of the earliest references to Pythagoras are ambiguous or satirical. Heraclitus attacks him as a clever charlatan: his learning is great, but his wisdom is fraudulent.[5] Eduard Zeller, in his great nineteenth-century history of Greek philosophy, recognized that the Pythagorean community was primarily a religious sect or cult, and that in the first century after his death, Pythagoras was known above all for his teaching of immortality and reincarnation.[6] Zeller was skeptical in regard to Pythagoras' scientific achievements, and his skepticism has been reinforced by the critical work of several more recent scholars. The most extreme judgment was that of Erich Frank, who claimed that "all the discoveries attributed to Pythagoras himself or to his disciples by later writers were really the achievement of certain South Italian mathematicians of Plato's time," a full century later than Pythagoras, and that these mathematicians had no essential connection with the "genuine Pythagoreans who are attested . . . since the sixth century as a religious sect similar to the Orphics."[7] A much more moderate conclusion, but leaning in the same direction, was reached by Walter Burkert in his monumental study *Weisheit und Wissenschaft*, published in 1962 (with a revised translation into English in 1972), which has transformed our understanding of the ancient tradi-

---

[3] See, e.g., Diogenes Laertius VIII. 8 and 48, Iamblichus *Vita Pythagorica* 58, 115–21, 159.

[4] Iamblichus *VP* 2.

[5] Heraclitus fr. 129: "Pythagoras son of Mnesarchus pursued inquiry (*historiê*) further than all other men and, choosing what he liked from these compositions, made a wisdom of his own, much learning (*polymatheiê*), artful knavery (*kakotechniê*)."

[6] E. Zeller, *Die Philosophie der Griechen in ihrer geschichtlichen Entwicklung* (Leipzig, 1892), I.i, 325.

[7] E. Frank, *Platon und die sogenannten Pythagoreer* (Halle, 1923), vi.

tions surrounding Pythagoras and his school.[8] Burkert traces the Pythagorean cosmology and number-philosophy reported by Aristotle back to Philolaus in the middle or late fifth century, but he finds no evidence connecting it to the founder of the school. Pythagoras himself, on Burkert's view, is a shamanistic figure, a charismatic spiritual leader and organizer (like Moses, perhaps) who exercised a great influence on the civic life of Magna Graecia, but who contributed nothing to mathematics or philosophy.

There are two distinct problems here. One is the strictly historical question concerning the extent of our knowledge or ignorance of Pythagoras and his school. The other is a more complex philosophical question concerning the Pythagorean concept itself and its reverberation down through the ages. Why did the figure of Pythagoras achieve such prestige? And in what sense are certain influential aspects of Plato's work peculiarly "Pythagorean"? Burkert has conclusively shown that the conception of Pythagorean philosophy that is taken for granted in later antiquity is essentially the work of Plato and his immediate disciples. But why were these thinkers drawn to Pythagoras, and why is it precisely the Pythagorean element in Plato's thought that prevailed so powerfully in antiquity and that reappears again in so many modern developments in science and the arts?

Let us briefly sketch an answer to this broader question before proceeding to survey the historical record in detail. There are two quite different clusters of ideas that account for the enduring vitality of the Pythagorean tradition. The first, emphasized in our quotation from Whitehead, is the attempt to understand and explain the nature of things in mathematical terms. As Aristotle reports, the Pythagoreans began by observing the numerical ratios of the musical consonances or *harmoniai* and, finding many other points of correspondence between numbers and the world, they concluded that "the whole heaven is *harmonia* and number."[9] This notion of a network of connections between music, mathematics, and celestial phenomena, which is summed up in the notion of

---

[8] *Lore and Science in Ancient Pythagoreanism* (Cambridge, Mass., 1972), the English translation by E. L. Minar, Jr., revised by the author, of *Weisheit und Wissenschaft: Studien zu Pythagoras, Philolaos, und Platon* (Nürnberg, 1962).

[9] *Met.* A.5, 986a3.

the music of the spheres, constitutes one of the two fundamental principles of Pythagorean thought. The other cluster of ideas is the conception of the soul as immortal and hence potentially divine, since in the Greek tradition deathlessness is the distinctive attribute of the gods. In Pythagorean thought, immortality is conceived both in terms of the transmigration of souls (with the related notion of kinship between all living beings) and also in the possibility of purification and escape from the cycle of rebirth, from the bondage of bodily form. (It is this conception of the afterlife that is common to the Orphic and Pythagorean traditions.) This Pythagorean view of the soul is most systematically developed in Plato's *Phaedo*, but it also appears in the doctrine of recollection in other dialogues and in the Platonic myths of judgment and preexistence in the *Phaedo*, *Republic*, and *Phaedrus*. On the other hand, the mathematical-musical conception of the cosmos receives its definitive expression in Plato's *Timaeus*, where the world soul is structured by the musical ratios and the world body is organized out of elementary triangles. The cunning geometry and elaborate arithmetic of the *Timaeus* are certainly Plato's own invention, just as his reinterpretation of recollection and immortality in terms of the cognitive grasp of eternal Forms is Plato's own. But in both cases, Plato is working with themes that are, in their origin, unmistakably Pythagorean. And it is primarily by way of these two dialogues, the *Phaedo* and the *Timaeus*, that Pythagorean ideas became such a powerful influence on the thought of later centuries, not only in antiquity but again in the Renaissance and beyond, down to our own time.

The mutual involvement of the Platonic and Pythagorean traditions is much more complex and extensive than this, as we shall see. But the *Phaedo* and the *Timaeus* may serve as emblems for what is most vital and lasting in the Pythagorean contribution to Western thought: on the one hand, a mathematical understanding of the world of nature; on the other hand, a conception of human destiny that points beyond the visible world and beyond the mortal body to a higher form of life. It is the combination of these two conceptions that is distinctively Pythagorean, but also distinctively Platonic.

Before pursuing these larger themes, we first turn back to the question of historical origins. How much do we know of Pythagoras and his school?

II

PYTHAGORAS AND THE PYTHAGOREAN WAY OF LIFE

THE HISTORICAL FIGURE OF PYTHAGORAS HAS ALMOST VANISHED behind the cloud of legend gathered around his name. We have three lives of Pythagoras from late antiquity, by Diogenes Laertius, Porphyry, and Iamblichus, in that order; and each one is more marvelous than its predecessor. (It was Zeller who first pointed out that the further a document is from Pythagoras' own time, the fuller the account of Pythagoras becomes.) Pythagoras is described as something more than human, as the god Apollo in human form. His supernatural status was confirmed by a golden thigh and the gift of bilocation: he was seen in Croton and Metapontum at the same time.[1] There are surprising reports of his educational success with animals. Thus he is said to have persuaded a greedy bull to abstain from eating beans. In another story Pythagoras made a dangerous bear swear not to harm living things; and the bear kept his oath.[2] Above all, Pythagoras could recall his previous incarnations, including the Trojan hero Euphorbus mentioned by Homer.[3] His learning was universal. He first studied geometry and astronomy with Anaximander,

---

[1] The golden thigh: D.L. VIII.11, Porphyry *Vita Pythagorae* 28. For bilocation, see DK 14.7 (= Aristotle fr. 191 Rose). In Porphyry *VP* 27 and 29 (and Iamblichus *VP* 136), bilocation has become even more miraculous, crossing the straits of Messina from Metapontum to Tauromenium.

[2] Porphyry *VP* 23–4, Iamblichus *VP* 60.

[3] D.L. VIII.4–5, Porphyry *VP* 28, Iamblichus *VP* 63.

then hieroglyphic symbolism with the priests of Egypt and the science of dreams with Hebrew masters. He studied also with the Arabs, with the Chaldaeans of Babylon, and finally with Zoroaster, who taught him the ritual of purification and the nature of things.[4] In the late tradition Pythagoras' life thus assumes mythic form; he becomes the paradigm of the *theios anêr*, the "divine man" who absorbs all forms of wisdom in order to become a sage, a seer, a teacher, and a benefactor of the human race. (The Pythagoreans are said to have distinguished three kinds of rational animals: gods, humans, and beings like Pythagoras.)[5] And the formation of this legendary picture begins very early. The story of Pythagoras' studies with the priests of Egypt is mentioned by Isocrates in the early fourth century B.C. and hinted at even earlier by Herodotus.[6] However, if we thrust aside this curtain of myth and legend, we are able to recognize some outlines of a more factual report.

Pythagoras, son of Mnesarchus, was born on the island of Samos sometime in the middle of the sixth century B.C. He came to maturity then just as the earliest Greek science and natural philosophy was developing in Miletus, on the nearby coast of Asia Minor. This synchronism is significant. Pythagoras was a contemporary of Anaximenes and Xenophanes, and, if he had any contact at all with the new science, it would have been a cosmology of the Milesian type that was familiar to him. Like Xenophanes, Pythagoras left Ionia and settled in southern Italy in the latter half of the sixth century. We know nothing of his life before his arrival in Croton, in approximately 530 B.C. It was in Magna Graecia, and originally in Croton, that he founded the sect or community that bore his name, and that seems to have played an important role in the political affairs of South Italy for the next two or three generations. Croton was defeated by Locri at the Sagras river, perhaps about the time that Pythagoras arrived. But in 510 B.C., Croton defeated and destroyed its proverbially rich and luxurious neighbor Sybaris; and from then until about 450 B.C., Croton seems to have

---

[4] Porphyry *VP* 11–2, Iamblichus *VP* 11–9.

[5] Iamblichus *VP* 31 = Aristotle fr. 192, DK 14.7.

[6] See below, pp. 12f.

been the dominant city in the region. Historians both ancient and modern have credited Pythagoras, and the moral training he initiated, with a decisive influence on the revival and military success of Croton.[7] There are conflicting reports of the political role of the Pythagorean society in Croton and of the "democratic" opposition to it, which resulted in violence against the Pythagoreans and in Pythagoras himself leaving Croton for Metapontum. The tradition is too partisan (both for and against the Pythagoreans) and too incomplete for us to reconstruct the political history with any confidence. But there is good reason to believe that in the early part of the fifth century members of the Pythagorean society attained positions of political power throughout southern Italy. For Polybius reports that when in the middle of that century the Pythagorean *synedria* or meeting places were burnt down in Magna Graecia, "the leading men from each city lost their lives."[8] This report implies that the organization founded by Pythagoras in Croton had extended its membership and influence into the neighboring cities. Pythagoras himself is said to have died as a refugee in Metapontum, after a popular revolt against Pythagorean control in Croton. In the late fifth century, after the catastrophe reported by Polybius, we find Pythagorean refugees in Greece proper, such as Philolaus in Thebes. But in the early fourth century, in the time of Plato, we again find Pythagoreans in a dominant position in Tarentum, where Plato's friend Archytas was repeatedly elected to high office. So Pythagorean influence in southern Italy is well attested for about 150 years.

Concerning the personal activity of Pythagoras we have a number of plausible but unverifiable stories. Thus Porphyry, on the authority of Dicaearchus, reports that at his arrival in Cro-

---

[7] The ancient references are cited in Burkert (1972), 116, nn. 44–5. For modern accounts, see T. J. Dunbabin, *The Western Greeks* (Oxford, 1948), 359–61 (followed by W. K. C. Guthrie, *A History of Greek Philosophy*, Vol. I: *The Earlier Presocratics and the Pythagoreans* [Cambridge, 1962], 174–6); L. Ferrero, *Storia del Pitagorismo* (Turin, 1955), 50–5. Cf. Burkert (1972), 115–20. Further discussion in K. von Fritz, *Pythagorean Politics in Southern Italy* (New York, 1950) and E. L. Minar, Jr., *Early Pythagorean Politics in Practice and Theory* (Baltimore, 1942).

[8] Polybius II.39.1–2.

ton, Pythagoras made such an impression upon the governing council of city elders by his presence, his wisdom, and his eloquence, that they invited him to address the young men of Croton, then the schoolboys, and finally an assembly of women.[9] As Burkert has suggested, this may reflect an archaic organization of society into specialized clubs or *hetairiai*.[10] There is independent evidence for the unusual role of women as active participants in the Pythagorean community: Pythagoras' wife and daughter were both renowned for their wisdom.[11] And we can of course infer a charismatic personality not only from the legendary accounts of his own life but from the historical fact of his extraordinary success in forming such a powerful and durable social organization.

The members of a Pythagorean community were bound together by common cult practices, including specific burial rites: Herodotus (II.81) reports that they could not be buried in woolen garments. (This restriction is presumably connected with respect for animal life.) Members were called *homakooi*, "those who come together to listen," and their assembly hall was a *homakoeion*, a place "for hearing together." What they heard was an *akousma*, a "hearing," or a *symbolon*, a "password." The content of what they heard was protected by a vow of silence: the teachings of Pythagoras were not to be revealed to nonmembers. Silence also seems to have played a part in the course of initiation. We are told of a five-year trial period during which initiates, who had put their property in common, were to listen in silence to the voice of Pythagoras. (*Koina ta philôn*, "friends have all things in common," was a Pythagorean saying that is often quoted by Plato.) During these "hearings" the speaker was shielded from their view by a linen curtain. Only after the successful completion of this test period were the initiates permitted inside: they then became "esoterics," members of Pythagoras' household or inner circle, and were allowed to see the master in person. If they failed the test, they received double their property back but were treated as dead

---

[9] Porphyry *VP* 18 = DK 14.8a.

[10] Burkert (1972), 115.

[11] D. L. VIII.42; Porphyry *VP* 4. Cf. Porphyry *VP* 19.

by their "fellow-hearers."[12] This report, which goes back to the historian Timaeus in the early Hellenistic period, may be exaggerated or even fictitious; but it is the best attested account of the procedure by which members were admitted into the Pythagorean society.

After the breakup of the original communities in Magna Graecia, the ban of silence seems to have lost its force. In any case, when Aristotle in the mid–fourth century set out to gather information on the Pythagoreans, he was able to collect a long list of *akousmata*, which includes the following items: Do not eat beans; do not pick up crumbs that fall from the table; do not eat white roosters; do not eat sacred fish. Do not break the bread, for bread brings friends together. Put salt on the table as a reminder of what is just.[13]

The most surprising fact about the dietary regulations reported by Aristotle is that they do not exclude the eating of meat. For Empedocles and later Pythagoreans, the belief in metempsychosis entails a rule of strict vegetarianism. But the most ancient form of the injunction seems to have been: eat only the flesh of animals that can be sacrificed. It has been plausibly suggested by Burkert that Pythagoras' original dietary restrictions were carefully designed not to conflict with the civic religion that was built around the ceremony of animal sacrifice.[14] Perhaps vegetarianism could become the rule only after the collapse of the Pythagorean sect as an organized political power, when smaller groups of individual Pythagoreans began to appear in a new kind of ascetic counterculture.

There are other commands preserved by late authors that seem to derive from the original community. One should have children, to leave behind someone to worship the gods. One should help a person to load but not to unload. One should not drive away (or

---

[12] D. L. VIII.10; Iamblichus *VP* 72f. For a fuller account of the Pythagorean community life, see W. Burkert, "Craft versus Sect: The Problem of Orphics and Pythagoreans" in *Jewish and Christian Self-Definition*, Vol. 3, B. F. Meyers and E. P. Sanders, eds. (Philadelphia, 1982), 14–9.

[13] D. L. VIII.34–5 = Aristotle fr. 195 (but the concluding reference to salt is omitted from the Aristotelian fragment as printed by Rose and Ross).

[14] Burkert (1972), 182, interpreting Iamblichus *VP* 85.

reject? *diôkein*) one's own wife, "for she is a suppliant."[15] The protected and even egalitarian position of women and the emphasis
on strictly conjugal sex and the begetting of children seem to reflect a family policy designed to enhance the prospects of the
community for physical survival.[16] Other *akousmata* contain mysterious sayings. What are the Isles of the Blest? Sun and moon. An
earthquake is a gathering of the dead. The thunder is to frighten
those in Tartarus. The rainbow is the bright ray of the sun. The sea
is the tears of Cronus. The Great Bear and the Little Bear are the
hands of Rhea. The most just thing is to sacrifice, the wisest is
number. The most beautiful figures are the circle and the sphere.[17]

Most of these sayings and prohibitions seem to have served
as observances and passwords to mark membership in the
Pythagorean community, to confirm the sense of group solidarity
by distinguishing members from nonmembers, and perhaps also
to reveal the degree of initiation. Very few of these *akousmata*
point in the direction of mathematics (as in the mention of numbers, the circle, and the sphere) or natural philosophy (like the
formula for the rainbow). What these archaic traditions reflect is a
communal way of life that seems to have persisted down to
Plato's own time. For in the only mention of Pythagoras by name
in all of Plato's work, he is referred to as someone "who was
beloved for his instruction (*synousia*) as a leader of culture and education (*paideia*), whose followers down to the present are
renowned for the way of life they call Pythagorean" (*Republic* X,
600a). The Pythagorean society may well have served as inspiration for the educational institution that Plato in turn was to organize in the Academy, and that was also destined to survive for
many generations (though of course Plato did not imitate the superstitious elements in the Pythagorean tradition).

If the existence of the Pythagorean community as a religious

---

[15] The sense of this enigmatic sentence is probably given by the late report that, when he had descended to Hades, Pythagoras saw there
among those being punished "those who were unwilling to sleep with
their wives." (D. L. VIII.21)

[16] As suggested by Burkert (1982), 18.

[17] Greek texts in DK 58C; full references in Burkert (1972), 170–3; cf.
166–9.

sect or cult society is well attested, it is more difficult to say what can have been the scientific or philosophical content of Pythagoras' teaching. The least unreliable report is given by Porphyry, who seems again to be following Dicaearchus:

> What he said to his followers no one can say with assurance, for it was no ordinary silence that they kept. But what has become best known to everyone is, first, that the soul is immortal and furthermore changes into other kinds of animals; in addition, that whatever happens will occur again according to certain cycles and nothing is absolutely new; and that one should consider all things born alive to belong to the same family (*homogenês*). Pythagoras seems to have been the first to introduce these teachings into Greece.[18]

The doctrine of eternal recurrence is also mentioned by Eudemus, who ascribes it simply to "the Pythagoreans."[19] But the first of these teachings, the belief in transmigration, is well attested for Pythagoras himself. We have an almost contemporary quotation from Xenophanes (fr. 7), in which Pythagoras is mocked for saying "Stop beating that dog! From his cries I recognize the ghost (*psychê*) of a friend." The special competence of Pythagoras in matters concerning the afterlife is reported, with occasional irony, by other fifth-century authors and in particular by Herodotus and Ion of Chios. Ion claims that the mysterious sixth-century figure Pherecydes will have "a pleasant life for his *psychê* after death, if Pythagoras is truly wise, he whose knowledge and understanding surpassed that of all humans" (Ion fr. 4 = DK 36B.4).[20] And a quotation from Empedocles which praises the vast extent of

---

[18] Porphyry *VP* 19 = DK 14.8a.

[19] DK 58B.34 = Eudemus fr. 88 Wehrli: "If one believes the Pythagoreans, things recur numerically the same; and I, with this staff in my hand, will be speaking to you seated in this manner, and everything else will be the same."

[20] These verses of Ion may be the source of the later legend (apparently due to Aristoxenus) that Pythagoras was responsible for burying Pherecydes, who had been his teacher (DK 7A.4). The two names are

Pythagoras' knowledge may also allude to his ability to recall earlier reincarnations: "He easily beheld all things, in ten and twenty lifetimes of men" (fr. 129). A more banal version of this kind of reputation is given by Isocrates, who is careful to make no reference to transmigration:

> Pythagoras of Samos, having traveled to Egypt and studied there, was the first to introduce high culture (*philosophia*) to the Greeks, and he became particularly distinguished for his practice of sacrificial ritual in the sanctuaries. He believed that, even if this practice brought him no advantage from the gods, it would succeed in making him famous among men. And that is what happened. So surpassing was his fame that all the youths wished to become his pupils, and the older men preferred to see their children associating with him rather than caring for their own affairs. And we must believe these stories. For to this day those who pretend to be his disciples are more admired for their silence than those who have the greatest reputation for speaking. (*Busiris* 28)

The professor of eloquence cannot refrain from a dig at Pythagorean silence, and we notice also Isocrates' suggestion that stories about Pythagoras tend to be incredible. The light tone of irony here ("we must believe these stories") recalls the more openly satirical spirit in which Pythagoras is invoked by Heraclitus and Xenophanes. The allusions to Pythagoras in Herodotus are similarly ambivalent. Herodotus tells the story of a Thracian named Salmoxis, said to have been a slave in Samos, who returned to his homeland and established there a cult of immortality on the basis of his own fraudulent return from the underworld. (He had, in fact, hidden himself in an underground chamber for three years.) Herodotus implies that such a trick was possible only because the Thracians have a rather backward

---

connected by Ion because Pherecydes too had a nonstandard view of the human soul after death. See the material collected in H. S. Schibli, *Pherekydes of Syros* (Oxford, 1990).

For Herodotus' references to Pythagoras, see the passages from II.23 and IV.95 cited in the text, below.

culture, whereas this Salmoxis was familiar with the Ionian way of life, "having lived with Greeks and with Pythagoras, not the feeblest intellectual (*sophistês*) among the Greeks" (Herodotus IV.95 = DK 14.2). And it is almost certainly Pythagoras, together with Empedocles, that Herodotus has in mind when, after attributing the doctrine of transmigration to the Egyptians, he concludes: "There are Greeks who presented this doctrine as their own, some earlier and some later. Although I know their names, I do not write them down."[21]

In these fifth- and early fourth-century echoes, the fame of Pythagoras is that of a fabulous sage and religious teacher, who was perhaps also a charlatan. The picture of Pythagoras changes radically with Plato and his school. Now it is no longer the religious leader and prophet of reincarnation who is admired, but the creator of mathematical philosophy. In the most explicit reference to Pythagoreans in Plato's dialogues, the mathematical sciences and specifically astronomy and harmonics are said to be "sister sciences, as the Pythagoreans assert and we agree" (*Rep.* VII.530d). This is, in effect, a quotation from Archytas, who describes astronomy, geometry, arithmetic, and music precisely in these terms, as "sister studies" (fr. 1).[22] (The medieval quadrivium is thus authentically Pythagorean, and it is entirely appropriate that, in the depiction of the liberal arts on the facade of the cathedral of Chartres, music is represented by the figure of Pythagoras. See the frontispiece.)

An even more important text for the Platonic interpretation of Pythagoras is found in the *Philebus*, where Socrates offers a description of dialectic based upon the principle that all things are derived "from one and from many, having Limit and Unlimited

---

[21] Herodotus II.23 = DK 14.1. Herodotus will not mention Empedocles' name because he is a contemporary and presumably still alive at the moment of writing. Pythagoras is long dead, and Herodotus' discretion here calls for a different explanation. A similar reluctance to name Pythagoras seems to be illustrated in Empedocles fr. 129. Compare Burkert (1972), 137.

[22] I accept the authenticity of Archytas fr. 1, as revised and defended by Huffman against Burkert's doubts. See C. Huffman, "The Authenticity of Archytas Fr. 1," *CQ* 35 (1985), 344–8, and below, p. 44, n. 16.

built into their nature" (16c). This principle is said to be "a gift of the gods to human beings, tossed down from the gods by some Prometheus together with the most brilliant fire. And the ancients, our superiors who dwelt nearer to the gods, have passed this word on to us." Limit and Unlimited are, as we shall see, fundamental principles in the Pythagorean cosmology of Philolaus. But Philolaus is scarcely the Promethean figure that Plato has in view. It is tempting to suppose that, when Plato speaks here of the ancients as "our superiors (*kreittones*) who dwelt nearer to the gods," he means us to think of Pythagoras as the Prometheus in question.[23] This passage in one of Plato's latest works may be seen as the first indication of that new image of Pythagoras as the semidivine source of philosophical wisdom grounded in mathematical principles. It is precisely this conception of Pythagoras as mathematical philosopher that Plato's disciples will develop and that the Platonic tradition will continue to elaborate until the end of antiquity.

We must now face the question whether or not this view of Pythagoras as a philosopher of mathematical ideas is essentially a fabrication of Plato's school, a projection onto the founder of a kind of Pythagorean philosophy that was first formulated by Philolaus in the later fifth century and then developed with more technical sophistication by Archytas and other mathematicians of Plato's own time. Such a view of Pythagoras is suggested by Walter Burkert's fundamental study of the Pythagoreans which we have already referred to. For Burkert, Pythagoras himself is the historical source for only one of the two clusters of ideas that we have identified as fundamental in the Pythagorean tradition. Pythagoras is indeed at the origin of the conception of the soul as immortal and as reborn in different animal forms. But he is not in any significant sense a mathematical thinker and the author of a view of the universe based upon number and proportion. As Carl

---

[23] The identification of Prometheus as Pythagoras has been generally accepted since antiquity. But the context is playful, and some readers would prefer to take the reference as less specific. For this view, see Carl Huffman, "Limite et Illimité chez les premiers philosophes grecs," in M. Dixsaut (ed.), *La Felure du Plaisir: Études sur le "Philèbe" de Platon*, Vol. II: *Contextes* (Paris, 1999).

Huffman has proposed in his development of Burkert's position, it is Philolaus, a century after Pythagoras, who became the first Pythagorean to enter the tradition of Presocratic cosmology, and he does so as an innovator with no philosophical debt to Pythagoras.[24] Pythagoras, according to Burkert, is a religious teacher and mystagogue who does not belong in the line of philosophical speculation that leads from Thales and Anaximander to Plato and Aristotle.

Now it is possible that this limited conception of Pythagoras is historically correct. But there is a good deal of evidence pointing in the other direction, towards a more positive evaluation of the tradition and a more philosophical interpretation of the figure of Pythagoras. In the first place, we must recognize that the idealizing conception of Pythagoras is not likely to be a new creation of Plato and his disciples. In a passage that can be traced back to Aristotle, Iamblichus reports the existence of two rival schools of Pythagoreans, the *akousmatikoi* and the *mathêmatikoi*, both of whom claimed to be the true followers of Pythagoras.[25] As their name indicates, the *akousmatikoi* must be those who faithfully preserve the tradition of ritual and taboo. They claim that the mathematical school derives not from Pythagoras but from a renegade Pythagorean named Hippasus. Hippasus is a little-known mathematician and natural philosopher who seems to have lived in the early fifth century.[26] He would thus antedate Philolaus, who appears then as the second name among the more "mathematical" Pythagoreans. Now the *mathêmatikoi* do not deny that the "acusmatic" school are also followers of Pythagoras; they claim only that they are *more* Pythagorean, more truly representative of Pythagoras' teaching.[27] Hence, when the Platonists credit Pythagoras with mathematical philosophy, they may be seen as following a genuine Pythagorean tradition of ascribing all

---

[24] This view of Philolaus' originality is expounded in Carl Huffman's valuable book *Philolaus of Croton* (Cambridge, 1993).

[25] Iamblichus *De communi mathematica scientia* 25. A deviant version is also given by Iamblichus in *VP* 81, cited in DK 18.2. Text and discussion in Burkert (1972), 193 n. 8.

[26] See DK 18, Guthrie (1962), 320–2.

[27] Iamblichus *VP* 87; Burkert (1972), 193–5.

discoveries to "that man," the semidivine founder whose name a scrupulous Pythagorean might even hesitate to pronounce.[28] It is natural to suppose that Philolaus and Archytas will have spoken of Pythagoras in similar terms, as the source of their own philosophy.[29] The historical question is: were they justified in doing so?

There is no unambiguous documentation that can settle this question. But two important early testimonies do lend support to a more positive conception of Pythagoras as a philosophical thinker in the tradition of Miletus. One testimony is that of Herodotus, who, as we have seen, refers to Pythagoras by understatement as "not the feeblest *sophistês* among the Greeks" (IV.95). Now the term *sophistês* here can mean many things. It was a term for the Seven Sages;[30] and it came to be applied to scientists and natural philosophers, but also to experts in any field, to poets for example, and even, with irony, to those who only claim to be experts. More unambiguous, however, is the terminology used in the even earlier testimony of Heraclitus (fr. 40), scarcely a generation later than Pythagoras himself, who attacks Pythagoras in the same breath with Hesiod, Xenophanes, and Hecataeus of Miletus, as three know-it-alls whose vast learning (*polymathiê*) did not teach them good sense. Another sentence of Heraclitus, already mentioned here, says that Pythagoras "pursued inquiry (*historiê*) further than anyone else" and created in his own name a wisdom that was really only a *kakotechniê*, a clever form of cheating and deception (fr. 129). Now Heraclitus' attack certainly construes Pythagoras as a religious imposter, but this attack is also based upon the assumption that Pythagoras is renowned for wide

---

[28] Iamblichus *VP* 88 and 255. We have noted the reluctance of some authors to refer to Pythagoras by name (above, n. 21). His name occurs only once in Plato's work and rarely in Aristotle, who prefers to speak of "those who are called Pythagorean." In some cases the avoidance of the name may be a sign of extraordinary respect, but perhaps it more often reflects some skepticism concerning a man about whom such marvelous stories are told.

[29] There may be a hint of this attitude in Archytas' fr. 1, which begins by acknowledging the wisdom of his predecessors in astronomy and mathematics. But (as Carl Huffman reminds me) not all of Archytas' predecessors were Pythagorean.

[30] Burkert (1972), 169.

knowledge (*polymathiê*) and special inquiry (*historiê*). Since the latter term is a standard designation for Milesian science, including geometry, astronomy, geography, and history, there is no reason to suppose that the great learning ascribed to Pythagoras is limited to theological genealogy in the style of Hesiod.[31] Pythagoras was, after all, both the neighbor and the contemporary of the two world-travelers, Xenophanes and Hecataeus, who are his fellow targets in Heraclitus' attack. The natural interpretation, then, of these two testimonies is that Pythagoras belongs with Xenophanes, Hecataeus, and Heraclitus in what we may call the earliest Greek Enlightenment, the first generation living in the intellectual world created by the new Milesian cosmology and the new view of nature.[32]

Indirect evidence for this more positive view of Pythagoras within the tradition of Ionian natural philosophy will emerge from the discussion of the system of Philolaus in the next chapter. For the moment, however, it is worth casting a glance at the parallel figure of Empedocles in the middle of the fifth century, two generations after Pythagoras. The documentation for Empedocles shows unmistakably how the same individual can figure as a religious prophet and *also* as a natural philosopher in the tradition that began in Miletus. In his role as an apostle of transmigration, Empedocles appears as an inspired but idiosyncratic follower of Pythagoras. Empedocles' abstinence from meat and from blood sacrifices is more rigorous than anything we know concerning Pythagoras; and his claim to be a god incarnate is

---

[31] As Burkert once suggested (1972), 210. For a more positive assessment of the testimony of Herodotus and Heraclitus, see L. Zhmud, *Wissenschaft, Philosophie und Religion im frühen Pythagoreismus* (Berlin, 1997), 30–9.

[32] The discrepancy between these two views of Pythagoras' intellectual position is reflected in two different conceptions of what kind of book Pythagoras might conceivably have composed, if—contrary to fact— he had consigned his world view to literary form. Walter Burkert, "Pythagoreische Retractationen: Von den Grenzen einer möglichen Editionen," in *Fragmentsammlungen philosophischer Texte der Antike* (Göttingen, 1998), 306, imagines "in the most favorable case, a book in the style of Pherecydes," if not an Orphic poem. I, on the other hand, would expect a work intermediate between that of Anaximander and that of Philolaus.

more categorical than the various hints of Pythagoras' Apollonian identity.[33] As a religious leader, Empedocles achieved no lasting results comparable to the formation of the Pythagorean community. Considered as a contribution to natural philosophy, on the other hand, Empedocles' system marks one of the decisive moments in Western intellectual history, since his doctrine of the four elements remained fundamental for the theory of matter for more than twenty centuries, until the rise of modern chemistry. For our purpose in understanding Pythagoras, the example of Empedocles shows how, in the mentality of archaic Greece, what strikes us as religious extremism is entirely compatible with important work in the new cosmology and philosophy of nature.

The parallel case of Empedocles shows that the dual role of religious prophet and mathematical philosopher which the tradition assigns to Pythagoras is historically possible, not that it is factually correct. We will return to the question of Pythagoras as philosopher and cosmologist at the end of the next chapter. What is not controversial, however, is his importance as the founder of a religious community and the evangelist of immortality based upon transmigration. This was a new doctrine in Greece in the sixth century B.C. It represents a radical break with the Homeric view of the *psychê* as the phantom of the dead man in Hades, doomed to a gloomy afterlife among the shades below.[34] Where did this new view of human destiny come from? There is no reason to suppose that it was invented by Pythagoras, although he probably gave it a new form and certainly made it widely known. Herodotus (IV.123) implies that Pythagoras borrowed it from the Egyptians but pretended that it was his own. Now the ancient Egyptians did believe in a meaningful afterlife for the dead; but they did not in fact have a doctrine of reincarnation. Some scholars suggest that Pythagoras learned of this doctrine from Pherecydes of Syros, with

---

[33] "I walk among you a deathless god, no longer mortal" (Empedocles fr. 112).

[34] See the classic account in E. Rohde, *Psyche*, English transl. W. B. Hillis (London, 1925); and for a more recent perspective, J. Bremmer, *The Early Greek Concept of the Soul* (Princeton, 1983).

whom he is traditionally associated. But the evidence that Pherecydes held such a view is late and inconclusive; and that would in any case only displace the question of origins by one generation. One important modern school (Meuli, Dodds, Burkert) connects the new Greek view of the soul with the influence of shamanistic practice and belief from the Black Sea area. Now it may in fact be useful to think of spirit-travelers like Aristeas of Proconessus and Abaris the Hyperborean in terms of the shamanistic traditions of central Asia. But there is no link, either logical or historical, between the shamanistic practice of religious trance and the systematic belief in a cycle of human and animal rebirth. The only religious tradition in which the doctrine of transmigration is at home from a very early period is that of India in pre-Buddhist times. The concept of *karma* (according to which one's destiny in the next reincarnation is a consequence of one's performance in this life) appears as a secret teaching in the earliest Upanishads.[35] After the conquests of Cyrus (who died c. 530 B.C.), the Persian empire stretched from Ionia to the Indus. From that time on, if not before, it was clearly possible for oriental doctrines to travel to the West. How exactly they reached Pythagoras we cannot even guess. But we can at least see that the later legend of Pythagoras' journey to India in search of the wisdom of the East may very well contain a grain of allegorical truth.[36]

An important question, which we cannot fully resolve, is the connection between Pythagorean teaching about the future destiny of the soul and the religious tradition associated with the name of Orpheus. It was once common scholarly practice to regard Orphism as the older, more widely diffused mystical tradition from which the Pythagoreans emerge as the more organized and more enlightened offshoot. But it is now recognized that the notion of Orphic cult and religion implies an essential reference to

---

[35] See S. Radhakrishnan, *The Principal Upaniṣads* (London, 1953), p. 217 (from the Brhad-aranyaka Upanishad): "What they said was karman, and what they praised was karman."

[36] Burkert now agrees that transmigration must have come from India: "After all Greeks and Indians had to meet regularly at the New Year festival at Persepolis" (private correspondence).

poetic texts attributed to Orpheus. Otherwise, it is difficult to know what is meant by the term "Orphic."[37]

This link to Orpheus has as a consequence that the history of Orphism is even more obscure than that of the Pythagoreans, since in this case the alleged origins of the movement go back not to a historical figure of the sixth century B.C. but to a legendary singer of the heroic age. Since there seems to be no good evidence for Orphic poetry before the time of Pythagoras, we should perhaps take seriously the judgment of those ancient critics who, in the fifth and fourth centuries B.C., claimed that the poems ascribed to Orpheus were in fact composed by Pythagoras and his followers.[38] A similar view is suggested by Herodotus' claim that the cults called Orphic are in fact Pythagorean:

> (The Egyptians do not allow woolen garments in their sanctuaries or in their burials.) And they agree in this with those who are called Orphic and Bacchic, but are really Egyptian and Pythagorean. For it is not allowed for participants in these rites (*orgia*) to be buried in woolen shrouds.[39]

The origin of Orphic cult and poetry is not an issue we can hope

---

[37] In his latest discussion in "Die neuen Orphischen Texte: Fragmente, Varianten, 'Sitz im Leben,'" in *Fragmentsammlungen philosophischer Texte der Antike* (Göttingen, 1998), 395–7, Burkert takes account of new evidence from fifth-century graffiti from Olbia (first published in 1978), which contain the word *Orphikoi* (or *Orphikon*) as well as "life death life," "peace war," "truth falsehood," *sôma psychê*, and an abbreviation for Dionysus. Burkert concludes that the term "Orphic" is thus associated with Bacchic-Dionysian mysteries attested in Olbia since the beginning of the fifth century. These are presumably the same kind of mystic initiations attacked by Heraclitus (fr. 14) and mentioned by Herodotus, who says that they "are called Orphic and Bacchic, but are really Egyptian and Pythagorean" (II.81, cited in the text).

[38] See M. L. West, *The Orphic Poems* (Oxford, 1983), 7–20. The ancient evidence for Pythagorean authorship of Orphic poems comes from Ion of Chios and a certain Epigenes (presumably the disciple of Socrates named at *Phaedo* 59b). Discussion in I. Linforth, *The Arts of Orpheus* (Berkeley and Los Angeles, 1941), 110–4.

[39] II.81, in the fuller text. For commentary, see Burkert (1972), 127f.

to resolve here. But it seems likely that the traits common to Orphic and Pythagorean teaching are older than either tradition: namely, the belief in immortality by way of transmigration, and hence the practice of certain dietary restrictions, burial rites, and ceremonies of ritual purification and initiation designed to guarantee a better fortune for the soul after death. Abstinence from meat, for example, is referred to indifferently in classical Greek literature as an Orphic or a Pythagorean way of life.[40] It is clear that we have here two parallel traditions, easily confused with one another but originally quite different in form. The early Pythagoreans relied upon oral teaching and committed nothing to writing; the Orphic cult is almost by definition based upon written texts, the poems of Orpheus. Orphic practice is associated with the ecstatic Bacchic cult of Dionysus; the Pythagorean tradition prefers the Pythian or Hyperborean Apollo and preaches an austere life. The cosmogony of the Orphic poems is filled with strange myths and weird divinities; there is no place in such "theologies" for Pythagorean mathematics or Ionian natural philosophy. Above all, there is no evidence of a lasting Orphic community of the type founded by Pythagoras. According to our literary texts, Orphic rites are typically organized by itinerant priests, like the ones described by Adeimantus in *Republic* II, who practice initiation and purification on the basis of a "mass of books," or like the *Orpheotelestês*, the "Orphic initiator" mentioned by Theophrastus, whom the superstitious character will visit every month for ritual purification.[41] Even where the ideology is similar, the expression of it seems to differ. Thus Plato distinguishes the doctrine of "the followers of Orpheus," who describe the body as the prison in which the soul is confined in punishment for wrongdoing, from the parallel view that the body (*sôma*) is the tomb (*sêma*) in which the soul is buried in this life, which is really its death (*Cratylus* 400C; cf. *Phaedo* 62B, 67D1). The latter view is

---

[40] Vegetarianism is Orphic in Euripides, *Hippolytus* 952–4, and in Plato, *Laws* VI, 782c. It is Pythagorean in Middle Comedy and Diodorus of Aspendus (early fourth century). See DK 58E and Burkert (1972), 199–202.

[41] Plato, *Rep.* II, 364e; Theophrastus, *Characters* xvi. See Linforth (1941), 77ff. and 101ff.

ascribed to "some Sicilian or Italian," that is, to Empedocles and the Pythagoreans (*Gorgias* 492E–93A). Eventually, of course, these two originally distinct traditions tend to merge, at least in their literary expression, and the lyre of Orpheus becomes the symbol for Pythagorean cosmic music. A syncretist tendency can be observed as early as the Derveni papyrus, which contains poetic quotations from an archaic Orphic theogony together with an allegorical prose commentary of about 400 B.C.[42] The aim of the Derveni commentator is to reinterpret the mythic figures of the old Orphic text in terms of Presocratic natural philosophy, and thus to prepare (indirectly) for the confluence of Orphic and Pythagorean traditions.

---

[42] See A. Laks and G. W. Most, eds. *Studies on the Derveni Papyrus* (Oxford, 1997).

III

PYTHAGOREAN PHILOSOPHY BEFORE PLATO

THE HISTORY OF PHILOSOPHY, LIKE OTHER HISTORY, REQUIRES WRITTEN documents. Since Pythagoras and his earliest disciples left behind no written record of their teaching, the history of Pythagorean philosophy must begin with the first known Pythagorean book. This is the work of Philolaus in the last half of the fifth century B.C. After more than a century of scholarly debate, Burkert's discussion has decisively established the authenticity of a substantial number of quotations from this book. Burkert's results have been confirmed and extended by Carl Huffman's careful analysis of the fragments and testimonia in the context of the development of cosmological theories in the fifth century.[1] These fragments reflect essentially the same world view that is attributed to the Pythagoreans by Aristotle and ascribed to Philolaus and the Pythagoreans in the later doxography deriving from Theophrastus. So it will be convenient to refer to this, the oldest attested version of Pythagorean theory, as the system of Philolaus, without prejudging the question of its originality. Once we have described this view and located it in the context of fifth-century natural philosophy, we can turn to the more controversial question, How far can the system of Philolaus be regarded as the continuation of an older Pythagorean tradition?

Our fullest information concerns the doctrine of first principles (*archai*), since we have this formulated in the verbatim fragments

---

[1] Huffman (1993).

of Philolaus. Diogenes Laertius tells us that Philolaus' book "On the Nature of Things" (*peri physeôs*) began with the following sentence: "Nature in the world-order (*kosmos*) was fitted together harmoniously (*harmochthê*) from unlimited things (*apeira*) and also from limiting ones (*perainonta*), both the world-order as a whole and all things within it" (fr. 1).

The terms in which this announcement is made are all familiar from Presocratic texts. The Unlimited (*apeiron*) is of course the starting point from which the world develops in Milesian cosmology. The contrasting notion of the limit (*peras*) is emphasized by Parmenides (fr. 8.30, 42) as a mark of the perfection of Being. Thus Philolaus' two principles combine Ionian natural philosophy with Eleatic ontology, and they are joined together here by means of the concept of *harmonia*, or consonance. *Harmonia* is known as a principle of cosmic union from the slightly earlier system of Empedocles (frs. 27 and 96) and earlier still from the fragments of Heraclitus (51 and 54); but in Philolaus' work this principle will receive an unprecedented, specifically Pythagorean development in terms of numerical ratios and musical scales.

First, however, Philolaus offers a logical argument in support of his opening thesis: the world cannot be derived from either unlimited origins or limiting principles alone, since it contains examples of both:

> It is necessary that the things-that-are (*ta eonta*) be either limiting or unlimited or both limiting and unlimited, but not always unlimited only. Since, then, they are manifestly neither from all limiting things nor from all unlimited ones, it is clear that the world-order (*kosmos*) and the things within it have been harmoniously fitted together from both limiting and unlimited. Things in their results (*erga*) also make this clear. Those of them that are from limiting things provide a limit, those from limiting and unlimited both limit and do not limit, while those from unlimited turn out to be unlimited. (fr. 2)

The rather clumsy form of this argument shows the influence of Eleatic reasoning, somewhat in the style of Melissus. Even more Parmenidean is Philolaus' further claim:

Concerning nature and harmony things are as follows: the Being (*estô*) of things, which is eternal, and Nature (*physis*) itself admit divine but not human knowledge (*gnôsis*); except that, of the things-that-are (*ta eonta*) and that are known by us, it was impossible for any of them to have come into being if there was not already the Being (*estô*) of those things from which the world-order is composed: both the limiting and the unlimited. (fr. 6, text and translation after Burkert)

Philolaus thus argues that all we can know of the reality of his two fundamental principles is that their eternal preexistence is a necessary condition for the coming-to-be of everything else. And the same text goes on to argue that since these principles are "unlike," that is, opposed to one another, they could be unified and bound together in a cosmos only by means of a *harmonia*, however that was produced. *Harmonia* thus serves here the same function as for Empedocles and also for Heraclitus: to produce unity out of multiplicity by bringing diverse and discordant elements into an agreement with one another.

In Empedocles' fragment 96 the bones of the body are blended together from the elements according to fixed ratios: two parts to four to eight. So likewise for Philolaus the *harmonia* is numerical in form: "all things which are known have number; for nothing can be known or understood without number" (fr. 4). But the distinctive feature of Philolaus' numbers is that they are arranged according to ratios that correspond to the three basic musical consonances. The first consonance, the scale one octave long, is called precisely by this name, *harmonia*; it corresponds to the ratio 2:1. The other two consonances, the fifth (3:2) and the fourth (4:3), are also specified by Philolaus in fragment 6a. Now if we add these four integers together, their sum is the number that (according to Aristotle, *Met.* A.5, 986a8) the Pythagoreans regard as perfect: $1 + 2 + 3 + 4 = 10$. More on this in a moment. First we need to complete the sketch of Philolaus' cosmology.

Since 10 is the perfect number, there must be 10 heavenly bodies. And since fire is the most precious thing, and since the center and circumference are the places of honor, there must be fire in the center of the cosmos (the so-called "hearth" of the universe, also called "the guardpost of Zeus") and also in the outermost sphere of the fixed stars.[2] Below the fixed stars come the 5 planets, then sun, moon, and earth, in that order. To make the number 10, says Aristotle, the Pythagoreans add a counter-earth, which is invisible to us, as is the central fire. Thus, the whole universe is "harmony and number," as Aristotle reports.[3] It is not expressly stated, but clearly assumed, that the periodic motions of these bodies around the central Hearth somehow instantiate the ratios of musical concord, so that their revolutions produce the cosmic music of the spheres.[4]

In this peculiar world system the earth is, as it were, a heavenly body, revolving around the central fire and producing night and day by its position relative to the sun (DK 58B.37). This permitted Copernicus to name "Philolaus the Pythagorean" as his predecessor; and in fact the Copernican system was originally known as *astronomia Pythagorica* or *Philolaica*.[5] The fact that Philolaus' scheme is not geocentric has led some scholars to admire the scientific genius of the early Pythagoreans and others to deny that such an advanced cosmic picture was possible at all in the fifth century B.C. The system does show a remarkable freedom of speculative imagination in departing from the usual assumption that the earth must occupy the center of the heavens. On the other hand, despite the presence of some genuine technical knowledge (notably the recognition of the five visible planets), the system of Philolaus taken as a whole seems less like scientific astronomy than like symbolical speculation, an imaginative expression of the view that the order of the universe is a function of musical

---

[2] DK 58B.37; cf. 44A.16.

[3] *Met.* A.5, 986a3 = DK 58B.4.

[4] Although the harmony of the spheres is not expressly attested for Philolaus, it seems to be implied as "a natural consequence of his broader philosophical outlook" (Huffman [1993], 283). For the doctrine of cosmic music, see Barker (1989), 33, citing Aristotle *De Caelo* II.9.

[5] Copernicus refers to Philolaus (as well as to Heraclides of Pontus and Ecphantus the Pythagorean) in his prefatory letter to *De Revolutionibus* (*Gesamtausgabe*, Vol. II, *De Revolutionibus. Kritischer Text*, eds. H. M. Nobis and B. Sticker [Hildesheim, 1984], 4), cited in T. S. Kuhn, *The Copernican Revolution: Planetary Astronomy in the Development of Western Thought* (Cambridge, Mass., 1957), 142.

harmony and meaningful numbers. But perhaps the contrast between scientific knowledge and speculative imagination is anachronistic here. I will return to this question later, but first we must deal with a problem in the interpretation of Philolaus' cosmology.

Aristotle reports that for the Pythagoreans "all things are numbers" or "imitate numbers," and Sextus Empiricus quotes a verse that says "all things resemble numbers."[6] What corresponds to this in the literal quotations from Philolaus is the claim that it is by means of number and proportion that the cosmos becomes organized and knowable for us: "all things which are known have number" (fr. 4). Hence the process by which the cosmos came into existence seems to have been conceived as analogous to a generation of the numbers. "The first thing harmoniously fitted together, the one in the center of the sphere, is called Hestia, the hearth" (fr. 7).

My account follows Aristotle in assuming that the Pythagoreans generate the heavens by the same process that generates the natural numbers, so that for Philolaus "the one in the center of the sphere" is both the central fire, or Hearth, and also the first integer. Thus Aristotle reports that the Pythagoreans "construct the whole heavens out of numbers, but not out of monads, for they assume that monads have magnitude" (*Met.* 1080b18). This interpretation has been challenged by Huffman, who claims that Philolaus did not confuse things with numbers but that it was Aristotle (in his rather uncharitable interpretation) who attributed this confusion to the Pythagoreans. On Huffman's reading of fragment 5, things "signify" or "point to" (*sêmainei*) the forms of number.[7] Hence the central fire points to the number one but is not identical with it. It is, Huffman claims, "impossible to imagine that he [Philolaus] confused the arithmetical unit with the central fire. For if he did, his arithmetical unit is more than a bare monad with position; it is also fiery and orbited by ten bodies."[8]

---

[6] ἀριθμῶι δέ τε πάντ᾽ ἐπίοικεν, Sextus Empiricus, *Adversus mathematicos* IV.2 and VII.94.

[7] Huffman (1993), 177–82.

[8] Huffman (1993), 205.

Is Aristotle mistaken when he reports that the Pythagoreans generate the physical universe out of numbers? The texts of Philolaus are too few and fragmentary for us to be sure. But fragment 7, which begins the cosmogony with "the one in the center of the sphere," is certainly compatible with Aristotle's report. And there is one other text that locates a number in the cosmos: "the sun, they say, is located there where [or "in reference to which" *kath'ho*] the number seven is; for it [the sun] has the seventh position of the bodies circling the central hearth."[9]

Although it is always risky to rely on Aristotle's report of his predecessors' views when we cannot confirm this report with original texts, in this case the texts seem to be compatible with what Aristotle tells us. Hence I am inclined to accept Aristotle's account of this numerical cosmology, despite Huffman's doubts.[10] But the fact that the number one comes into being as a central fire and that the number seven is correlated with the circle of the sun does not mean that these numbers are simply identical with specified portions of the physical universe. In the Pythagorean scheme, numbers seem to lead a double life: they are, as it were, both universals and privileged particulars. There are many ones in the cosmos; and the cosmos itself is *one* (fr. 17). But the *first* one is the central fire. The number two is both the higher limit of the octave (2:1) and the lower limit of the musical third (3:2). So we may imagine that for the Pythagoreans the *first* number two might have come into being as the celestial fire, the outer ("higher") limit of the cosmos, thus completing the celestial octave.

It would be a mistake to think of the Pythagoreans as offering a theory of what numbers are, or how they are related to the things we can count, such as physical bodies. The Pythagorean cosmology tells us only how the first numbers came into being or, more precisely, how the primordial instance of each of the first ten integers was constructed as a fundamental part of the cosmic order.

The One is prior to the numbers proper, which divide into even (unlimited) and odd (limiting); the One itself, however, is both,

---

[9] Aristotle fr. 203 = Huffman (1993), 234, text 2.

[10] I find myself here in partial agreement with H. S. Schibli's defense of the Aristotelian account; see "On 'The One' in Philolaus, Fragment 7," *CQ* 46 (1996), 124–7.

even-odd (fr. 5). Cosmogony begins as the numbers are generated, when the Unlimited is drawn in (or "breathed in") by the limiting principle.[11] Thus the cosmos arises from the One by breathing, like a newborn animal. The heavens take shape as breath (*pneuma*) and void are drawn in from the Unlimited, as a separation and differentiation of things within the sphere. "And this happens first in the numbers; for the void distinguishes their nature." As we have seen, the primitive One is not thought of as an abstract entity but as a fiery unit with a definite position in the center of the sphere. Thus no distinction seems to be made here between the generation of numbers, the emergence of geometric points, and the production of sensible magnitudes. Such conceptual refinements will be the work of Plato and his associates.

Scientific evaluations of the system of Philolaus have been very diverse. Since no explanation is provided for the retrograde motion of the planets, and since the theory posits a central fire and a counter-earth that have no observable consequences, Burkert judged that this was not scientific astronomy but rather "mythology in scientific clothing."[12] Huffman, on the other hand, describes the system of Philolaus as "the most impressive example of Presocratic speculative astronomy" and "a much more coherent model of the cosmos" than that of any other fifth-century thinker.[13] Although Huffman recognizes that Philolaus shows little interest in identifying physical causes or explaining celestial machinery, he insists that this system is "on a par with the rest of Presocratic astronomy in accounting for phenomena" and that Philolaus may even have been ahead of his contemporaries in as-

---

[11] Aristotle, *Physics* IV.6, 213b22 = DK 58B.30.

[12] Burkert (1972), 342. Similarly D. J. Furley, *The Greek Cosmologists*, Vol. I (Cambridge, 1987), 58: "the system as a whole makes very little astronomical sense, and it is hard to believe that it was intended to do so."

For the coherence of the theory there is a serious problem about the motion of the stellar sphere. See Burkert (1972), 340. For an attempt to deal with the problem, see Huffman (1993), 255–7.

For a new and very different attempt to interpret the system of Philolaus in terms of mythic symbolism, see P. Kingsley, *Ancient Philosophy, Mystery and Magic* (Oxford, 1995), 172ff.

[13] Huffman (1993), 241, 259f.

signing the correct relative positions to the planets. Above all, in attributing a single circular motion to each of the ten celestial bodies (perhaps with relative speeds inversely proportional to their distance from the center), Philolaus produces an elegant astronomical model, constructed according to mathematical principles of number and order.

Such praise may seem excessive for a system that is, after all, very strange. But we must remember that Philolaus and his Pythagorean colleagues were speculating in an age of breathtaking intellectual exploration, when the atomists were elaborating a world picture that would eventually serve as the starting point for modern physical theory, but which was created with scarcely a shred of empirical evidence, on the basis of a priori, metaphysical considerations alone. Just as the atomists, by their speculative imagination, anticipate the mechanistic world view, so do the Pythagoreans anticipate the mathematical interpretation of nature. Huffman is surely right to see that, by offering a cosmic model articulated according to the principles of symmetry and number, Philolaus was "the clear precursor of Plato."[14] In the *Timaeus* Plato has abandoned the central fire and the counter-earth (and presumably Archytas had done the same). But in constructing the world soul according to musical numbers and the world body out of elementary triangles, Plato's demiurge preserves the essentially mathematical spirit of the Pythagorean cosmos.

Aristotle's remark about the void distinguishing the numbers and defining their natures is best understood if we bear in mind the procedure of representing number by a grouping of points in geometric figures. Aristotle mentions a familiar practice of arranging pebbles to represent numbers as triangles or squares.[15] Later writers such as Nicomachus and Iamblichus give a fuller account. This practice reflects a very ancient method of representing the positive integers (the so-called natural numbers) by a grouping of units marked by dots or strokes, like the markings on dice

---

[14] Huffman (1993), 261.

[15] *Met.* N.5, 1092b12. Aristotle assumes as known this procedure, to which he compares the more elaborate pebble figures composed by Eurytus (ibid. with Theophrastus, *Metaphysics* 6a20, where the report of Eurytus' constructions is derived from Archytas).

and dominos. (A similar technique was used for indicating nu-
merals in cuneiform and in Linear B.) The Pythagoreans call attention to the fact that, if the construction begins with a unit-point
and adds markings for the odd numbers in a gnomon or carpen-
ter's angle, the result is always a square number. But if one begins
with two and adds even numbers, the result is a rectangle.

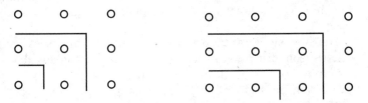

The geometric figures thus serve to classify groups of numbers,
of which the squares are obviously of special importance. Important also are triangular numbers, for at least two different reasons.
If we construct a triangle beginning with one by adding successive integers, the first four numbers give us the figure that the
Pythagoreans call *tetractus*, "fourness," since the number four is
represented by all three sides of an equilateral triangle.

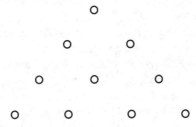

This is the figure by which the Pythagoreans are said to swear

By him who gave to our soul the *tetractus*,
The source and root of everflowing nature.[16]

---

[16] The earliest quotation of the oath is in a passage that Sextus has apparently taken from Posidonius (Burkert 1972: 54–6). For the possibility that the first verse is archaic, the second added later, see Burkert
(1972), 186f. The doctrine itself must be old, as we can see from the role
that the musical ratios and the number 10 play for Philolaus.

These hexameter verses reflect the unique significance of the *tetractus* pattern, which includes within itself—for the initiate who knows the secret doctrine—all three musical ratios: 2:1, 3:2, and 4:3, as successive pairs of lines beginning from any vertex. As we have already mentioned, the four integers represented in the *tetractus* have as their sum the number that the members of the order regard as perfect: $1 + 2 + 3 + 4 = 10$. For the Pythagoreans, then, the *tetractus* is a complete symbol for the musical-numerical order of the cosmos.

The other significant function of triangular numbers is of more strictly geometric interest. If one constructs a triangle with sides 3, 4, and 5 for any given unit, one can be sure that sides 3 and 4 form a right angle, in a right triangle whose hypotenuse is 5. This is an old procedure, known to the Babylonians (who constructed tables of such triplets of numbers) and still in use today by carpenters for making square corners. Now the triplet 3-4-5 is of course the simplest numerical exemplification of the Pythagorean theorem, that the square on the hypotenuse ($5 \times 5 = 25$) is equal to the sum of the squares on the other two sides ($3 \times 3 = 9$, $4 \times 4 = 16$, and $9 + 16 = 25$). Hence the practical content of the theorem, as a device for constructing right angles, was known long before Pythagoras. Although it is conceivable that Pythagoras was the person responsible for introducing the technique into Greece, we have not the slightest evidence for this. And there is certainly no reason to suppose that either Pythagoras himself or any early Pythagorean could have provided a deductive proof of the theorem, such as we find in Euclid I.47.

Why then did the theorem come to be so closely associated with the name of Pythagoras? We really do not know.[17] This may be simply a reflection of the mythical status of Pythagoras in the

---

[17] The earliest source is Plutarch. See T. L. Heath, *A History of Greek Mathematics*, Vol. 1 (Oxford, 1921) I, 144f. Proclus (in his *Commentary on Euclid* I.47 = DK 58B.19) reports the attribution to Pythagoras with some reservation ("if we listen to those who like to record antiquities"); the reliability of his sources is not strengthened by their claim that Pythagoras sacrificed a bull on the occasion of this discovery. Burkert suggests to me that the designation "theorem of Pythagoras" is the product of schoolteachers in the early modern period, when Euclid was a standard school text.

later tradition, where he is represented as the source of everything essential in philosophy and mathematics. On the other hand, it is conceivable that Pythagoras (or one of his followers) was the first to state the relationship between the sides and the squares as a general rule, without proof. Some historians of mathematics have even been willing to assign to Pythagoras various intuitive proofs of the theorem. The simplest case is that of the isosceles triangle formed by drawing the diagonal in a square. This is the construction illustrated by the geometry lesson in the *Meno*, where the square on the hypotenuse is shown to be twice the original square. It would be natural to assume some Pythagorean background for this geometric construction, since it is introduced in the *Meno* in support of the doctrines of transmigration and recollection. But this assumption can be no better than a guess, given our total ignorance of the history of geometric proof in this early period.

Another guess would be that Pythagoras or his followers simply seized upon the regularity of the right triangles generated by these basic integers (3, 4, and 5) as one more revelation of the secret order of nature encoded in the *tetractus*. There seems to be some indication of this in the Pythagorean designation of the number 5 as "marriage," which is explained as the union connecting the number 3 (which is odd, and therefore male) with the number 4 (which is even, and therefore female). In this way the simplest numerical formula for the right triangle ($3^2 + 4^2 = 5^2$) can be taken to signify the harmonious combination ("marriage") of the basic Limiting (odd) and Unlimited (even) principles of the cosmos.

In thus following the course of Pythagorean number speculation, we have moved away from the cosmological system connected with the name of Philolaus. But in this system, too, we can recognize an almost superstitious fixation on significant numbers such as 10 and 7. In the next generation Eurytus, a pupil of Philolaus, is said to have arranged pebbles in such a way that he could show how one number indicates the form of a man, another number the form of a horse, and so on.[18] This practice should probably be regarded as a decadent version of the more ancient use of num-

---

[18] See DK 45.2–3 and above, n. 15.

ber patterns as symbols of significant regularities and connections. It is this older, more expressive numerology that is exemplified in the musical ratios of the *tetractus* and in the identification of justice (understood as retaliation) with the number 4: the first square, the product of the first number taken an equal number of times.[19] (Two is the first number, since in Greek the concept of number, *arithmos*, implies plurality.) As we have remarked, the whole system of Philolaus is dominated by a bold, somewhat naive sense for symmetry and for the explanatory power of numbers.

If we ask, now, how much of this system is likely to be original with Philolaus, how much can be traced back to an earlier Pythagorean tradition, some parts of the answer are clear. On the one hand, Philolaus' rather awkward attempts to provide deductive arguments in the Eleatic manner ("Either A, B, or C; but not A and not B; therefore C") must be his own. These arguments resemble the reasoning of his two contemporaries, Melissus of Samos and Diogenes of Apollonia. In this respect, Philolaus' introductory section on first principles, preserved in fragments 1–6, bears clear marks of its time and place. We recognize here the attempt of a South Italian author to construct a prose cosmology, comparable to that of Anaxagoras or Diogenes, but in the heavy shadow of Eleatic logic and ontology. And certain features of the astronomy, such as the central fire and the explanation of the sun's light by derivation from ethereal fire, recall similar speculation in the cosmologies of Parmenides and Empedocles. In this case, it is possible, but not necessary, to posit an earlier Pythagorean tradition.

On the other hand, the importance of the number 10 in the cosmic scheme (as well as in the doubtfully authentic fragment 11),[20] suggests something essentially older than Philolaus. We cannot date the hexameter oath on the *tetractus*. But one of the *akousmata* asks, "What is the oracle in Delphi?" and answers, "*Tetractus*. This is the scale (*harmonia*) in which the Sirens sing."[21] Now in the myth of Er Plato has the Sirens sitting on eight celestial circles to produce the music of the spheres (*Rep.* X, 617B). But the *akousma*

---

[19] See the Aristotelian passages cited DK 58B.4.

[20] Huffman (1993), 347: "concerning the decad, both Archytas *On the Decad* and Philolaus *On Nature* have many things to say." (Philolaus fr. 11)

[21] Iamblichus *VP* 82 = DK 58C.4.

reported by Aristotle is certainly not derived from this passage in the *Republic*. As often, Plato is here making new use of an old theme. Since it is present among the *akousmata* as well as in the oath, the *tetractus* as a representation of cosmic music is likely to go back to the earliest stratum of Pythagorean tradition. The complex account of musical proportions given in Philolaus' fragment 6a is likely to be his own contribution.[22] (The place of Philolaus in the development of the Greek acoustical tradition will be discussed in the next chapter, in connection with the work of Archytas.) But there is no reason to suppose that the three ratios themselves, and the musical consonances they determine, are an invention of Philolaus. They must be at least as old as their mysterious symbol, the *tetractus*.

Besides Pythagoras, only one Pythagorean thinker older than Philolaus is known by name: the shadowy figure of Hippasus of Metapontum, who is mentioned by Aristotle, together with Heraclitus, as having taken fire as his first principle.[23] Hippasus seems to have lived in the first half of the fifth century and to have done work in mathematics and music theory, as well as in natural philosophy. (He is credited with an acoustic experiment and with a discovery of the harmonic mean.) The many stories about him and his punishment for revealing Pythagorean secrets, or for claiming them as his own, sound more like legend than history. What the evidence for Hippasus certainly shows, however, is that the Pythagorean interest in mathematics, music, and natural philosophy is older than Philolaus.

Contemporary scholars have rightly given up the attempt, pursued by Cornford and Raven, to reconstruct an early Pythagorean theory on the basis of what was assumed to be anti-

---

[22] Philolaus fr. 6a specifies, in archaic terminology, the ratios for the octave that are used by Plato for the construction of the world soul in the *Timaeus*. For the authenticity of the fragment and its interpretation see Huffman (1993), 145–65, with references there to Burkert, Barker, and the older literature. For a negative evaluation of Philolaus as a mathematician, see Mueller in Taylor (1997), 292f.

[23] *Met.* A.3, 984a7. For references to Hippasus, see p. 15, n. 26. Mueller counts him as "our only clear example of a Pythagorean mathematical scientist before Archytas," in Taylor, *Routledge History of Philosophy*, Vol. 1: *From the Beginnings to Plato* (London and New York, 1997), 292.

Pythagorean polemic in the fragments of Parmenides and Zeno. (These accounts of pre-Parmenidean Pythagorean philosophy were an exercise in circular reasoning, since the hypothesis itself of polemic between Eleatics and Pythagoreans generated the evidence on which it was supposed to be based, namely, the polemical reading of the Parmenidean fragments.) All we can do is note those features in the reliable pre-Platonic evidence, that is, in the system of Philolaus, that can reasonably be traced back to the earliest stage of the Pythagorean tradition. As I have argued, that is the case for the *tetractus*, and hence for the musical ratios and the conception of cosmic harmony. If we now review the Philolaic system with this question in mind, we can recognize several other features that may well go back to the earliest period.

The notion that cosmic order is built up out of opposing principles is familiar in Milesian philosophy from the time of Anaximander, as is the importance of numerical ratios. These are notions that we also find reflected in Heraclitus, and there is no reason why an inquisitive Samian of the sixth century B.C. would not have picked them up from Miletus. Speculation about the Unlimited as a cosmic starting point is, of course, also authentically Milesian.[24] A strikingly archaic feature of the cosmogony reported by Aristotle is the view that the heavens develop by breathing in void and air (*pneuma*).[25] There is actually some evidence that Xenophanes *denied* breathing for his cosmic god, and it seems plausible to construe this as a polemical response to a contemporary Pythagorean theory.[26] If so, it could only be the theory of

---

[24] On the other hand, as Carl Huffman reminds me, the contrast between Limiting and Unlimited may well reflect the Parmenidean insistence that Being must have a *peras*. I agree that the use of these two terms as principles is likely to be post-Eleatic and hence original with Philolaus.

[25] DK 58B.30.

[26] DK 21A.1,19 = D. L. IX.19: "(Xenophanes says that) the being of god is spherical, having nothing similar to a human being; it sees as a whole and hears as a whole, *but it does not breathe*; it is all mind (νοῦς) and intelligence (φρόνησις) and eternal." The close parallel to fragments 23–6 suggests that what we have here is a reliable excerpt from Theophrastus.

Pythagoras himself. Archaic also is the equivalence (or at least close parallel) between air and void; the corporeal nature of air was established by Anaxagoras and Empedocles, well before the time of Philolaus.

These considerations do not constitute proof. They are merely straws in the wind, suggestions that the tradition was not entirely mistaken in tracing the peculiarly Pythagorean blend of music, mathematics, and cosmology back to the founder himself. More significant, however, is the cosmic interpretation of *harmonia* in the thought of Heraclitus, for this definitely implies a musical conception of the world order, as represented in the tuning of the lyre (frs. 51 and 54; cf. frs. 8 and 10).[27] Heraclitus is by no means an admirer of Pythagoras, but his repeated attacks show that he took a peculiar interest in the Samian, as we have seen (Above, pp. 16f.). It seems reasonable to suppose that in his remarks about the soul (fr. 45) and about the equivalence of life and death, mortality and immortality (fr. 52), Heraclitus is deliberately exploiting a Pythagorean doctrine for his own purposes. So likewise in his remarks about *harmonia*, he is very likely developing a Pythagorean notion of cosmic harmony in his own way. For Heraclitus the order of nature is symbolized not only by the *harmonia* of the lyre but also by that of the bow, by the weapon as well as by the musical instrument of Apollo. The importance of strife for Heraclitus is a new and distinctive thought, but the role of *harmonia* looks like a development of Pythagorean ideas. Now Heraclitus lived just one generation later than Pythagoras, at the beginning of the fifth century. If Heraclitus is familiar with the connections between numerical proportion (*logos*), musical consonances, and cosmic order, this second great cluster of Pythagorean ideas must also go back to the master himself.

There is another, quite general consideration telling in favor of an authentic tradition attributing the mathematical conception of the cosmos to Pythagoras himself, even though we cannot recon-

---

[27] Burkert argues that ἁρμονίη in Heraclitus need not be musical, since the older usage refers to joints and carpentry (as in *Odyssey* 5.237–8). However, the root meaning is "fitting," and the application to musical tuning must be very early; it has already acquired a technical sense by the time of Pindar (Λυδία ἁρμονία in *Nemean* 4.45).

struct his view with any precision. The notion of cosmic harmony expressed in numerical ratios and conceived as astral music is one of those ideas of genius that have remained amazingly fruitful over the centuries. That Pythagoras was an intellectual figure of extraordinary stature is recognized in every reference to him, whether favorable or unfriendly, not only by admirers like Empedocles and Ion but also by Heraclitus, Herodotus, and Isocrates. There is no other early Pythagorean of whom this can be said. Philolaus may be a respectable thinker, but certainly no intellectual genius. And we know almost nothing of Hippasus. If we are right to assume that great ideas originate only in great minds, then we have only one candidate for this innovation: the Pythagorean conception of the cosmos must somehow be the work of Pythagoras himself. In the absence of reliable documentation, this can count only as an inference, or even a conjecture.[28] But such a conjecture seems to me infinitely more plausible than to suppose that one of the two great Pythagorean ideas was invented by Philolaus or by some nameless Pythagorean.[29]

---

[28] Zhmud (1997: 44) goes too far in claiming that "the philosophical and scientific activity of Pythagoras or his immediate followers is clearly and unambiguously attested in the early tradition."

[29] Recent scholarly opinion seems to be inclining to a more positive view of Pythagoras as mathematician and philosopher. See (in addition to Zhmud) Mueller and Hussey in Taylor (1997).

IV

PYTHAGOREAN PHILOSOPHY IN THE TIME OF ARCHYTAS AND PLATO

In the time of Plato we know of a rather wide variety of Pythagoreans. The most distinguished of them was Plato's friend Archytas of Tarentum. Archytas had an eminent career as statesman in his native city, but he was also an outstanding scientist and mathematician, a founder of the ancient tradition in mathematical harmonics and a pioneer in solid geometry and mathematical mechanics. He is also said to have been the teacher of the great mathematician Eudoxus.

The doxographical tradition reports that Archytas "was generally admired for excellence of every sort, and he was seven times elected to high office as general (*stratêgos*), whereas others were prevented by law from serving more than one year."[1] We know from Plato's Seventh Letter that, as leader of Tarentum, Archytas played an important role in the international affairs of South Italy and Sicily. Plato reports that he had personally arranged friendly political relations between Archytas and the Tarentines, on the one hand, and the tyrant Dionysius II of Syracuse, on the other. On Plato's third and final trip to Syracuse in 361 B.C. when his life was in danger, Archytas sent an ambassador with a ship from Tarentum, who persuaded Dionysius to allow Plato to leave for

---

[1] DK 47A.1 = D. L. VIII.79. More picturesque is the story from Aristoxenus cited by D. L. at VII.82: Archytas was never defeated as general; but on the one occasion when political hostility forced him to resign, his men were immediately captured by the enemy.

Athens in safety.[2] As a result, Archytas had the reputation of having saved Plato's life. It is pleasant to suppose that Plato has expressed his gratitude in the *Timaeus*, the most scientific of all his dialogues, where Plato's cosmological doctrine is placed in the mouth of an imaginary statesman-scientist from South Italy, Timaeus of Locri. Many of Plato's original readers would have recognized a resemblance to Archytas in the figure of Timaeus, as we today can surmise the influence of Archytas' natural philosophy in the Pythagorean mathematics of this dialogue.

Our knowledge of Archytas' work is so incomplete that it is difficult for us to form any very precise picture either of the magnitude of his achievements or of the extent of his influence on Plato.[3] However, there is every reason to suppose that Plato's general conception of mathematics was heavily indebted to Archytas. As we have seen, the mathematical curriculum of the *Republic* is directly based on the Pythagorean quadrivium (arithmetic, geometry, astronomy, and music), and it is in this connection that Plato actually cites the Pythagoreans by name, in a passage where he is apparently quoting from Archytas (*Rep.* VII, 530d). As one of the greatest scientists of the day, Archytas will have represented for Plato the Pythagorean contribution to mathematical knowledge. In particular, Plato's insistence on studying not only plane but also solid geometry, which he reports as just beginning in his own time (*Rep.* VII, 528b–d), must in part reflect Archytas' own work. For the latter's best-known mathematical achievement, solving the "Delian problem" by constructing two mean proportionals in order to double the cube, was "not a construction in a plane but a bold construction in three dimensions."[4] The duplication of the cube was one of the most famous problems

---

[2] *Ep.* VII, 350a–b; cf. 338c, 339d (= DK 47A.5).

[3] Our understanding of Archytas' work will be greatly improved by the publication of Carl Huffman's forthcoming study of the fragments and testimonia, *Archytas of Tarentum*. Huffman points out, however, that the cosmology of the *Timaeus* is not directly modeled on that of Archytas. For the world soul, for example, Plato uses the diatonic scale as defined by Philolaus, not by Archytas. And Archytas' universe is infinite, whereas the cosmos of the *Timaeus* is bounded.

[4] Heath (1921), 246f.

in Greek mathematics. Different solutions were proposed by a number of prominent mathematicians, and Archytas' solution is the earliest.[5] As Huffman has argued, Plato's comments on solid geometry in *Republic* VII reflect the exploratory stage of work in this area that is illustrated by the achievements of Archytas and Theaetetus (who defined the five regular solids), before the systematization of the field that is codified in Euclid.

In music theory or harmonics, on the other hand, Archytas' work sets the standard for the later mathematical tradition. His proof that an epimoric or superparticular ratio (i.e., a ratio of the form n + 1 : n) cannot be divided into two equal parts is almost identical with the proof ascribed to Euclid in the *Sectio Canonis*, although the Euclidean proof is slightly more advanced. Since Tannery, the dependence of the Euclidean proof on Archytas has been recognized. On the other hand, how much formal development in number theory is presupposed by Archytas' proof is a matter of scholarly dispute. The close parallel to the Euclidean proof suggests a mature deductive context, with definitions and preliminary theorems.[6] Furthermore, the point established is an important one for Greek music theorists, since they, in effect, define the tone by the ratio 9/8 (that is, as the difference between the fourth and the fifth). Both Archytas' and Euclid's proofs show that this ratio (or the corresponding interval) cannot be divided in half. On the other hand, Aristoxenus' musical theory makes abundant use

---

[5] DK 47A.14–15. Fuller documentation and discussion in Huffman (forthcoming).

[6] DK 47A.19. The Euclidean proof is Proposition 3 in A. Barker, *Greek Musical Writings, Vol. II: Harmonic and Acoustic Theory* (Cambridge, 1989), 195. For the relation between the two proofs, see Burkert (1972), 442–7. Huffman (forthcoming) argues that Burkert, reacting against van der Waerden's excessive claims, has understated the case, and that "a collection of theorems and definitions that dealt with central ideas which are later found in Book VII of Euclid's *Elements* is clearly presupposed by Archytas' proof." Mueller suggests more cautiously that what is presupposed is "a well-developed idea of mathematical reasoning and proof" (in Taylor [1997] 289). In general, Mueller takes a less favorable view of Archytas' achievements in harmonics; but that seems due to his attributing the nonsensical mathematics in A.17 to Archytas, whereas Archytas is cited only as reporting the work of his predecessors. Compare Barker (1989), 29.

of semitones.[7] So this theorem marks a fundamental difference separating the Pythagorean tradition in harmonics, based on the work of Archytas and committed to interpreting musical phenomena by numerical ratios, from the tradition deriving from Aristoxenus, which is more closely tied to musical practice and less concerned with mathematical rigor.[8]

Archytas' proof on the epimoric ratio provides a unique example of pre-Euclidean deductive rigor. We do, however, have other fragments from Archytas' harmonic theory that suggest a similar level of mathematical precision. These fragments show that his work was taken as fundamental in the later Pythagorean tradition in music theory, the tradition represented by the Euclidean *Sectio Canonis*, Nicomachus' *Enchiridion*, and Ptolemy's *Harmonica*, as well as by Porphyry's commentary on Ptolemy.

The importance of Archytas' harmonics for this later tradition is clear. What is less clear is how far his own work rests on the achievements of his predecessors, such as Philolaus. Archytas' fragment 1 (quoted below) begins by acknowledging the discoveries of earlier scientists, but there is no reason to suppose that these were only Pythagoreans. For example, Archytas' solution to doubling the cube obviously presupposes the work of Hippocrates of Chios, who had reduced the problem to the construction of two mean proportionals. But in music theory the most relevant predecessor is certainly Philolaus. In all likelihood, Archytas has taken over from Philolaus the recognition of the three musical means, and (as we have noted) it is Philolaus' construal of the diatonic scale, rather than Archytas' version, that is utilized by Plato in the *Timaeus*.[9] We may recognize the rigor and clarity of Archytas' harmonic theory as a work of original genius, but this was a genius working in the Pythagorean

---

[7] Aristoxenus *Elementa harmonica* I.21: "The tone is the difference in magnitude between the first two concords. It is to be divided in three ways, since the half, the third and the quarter of it should be considered melodic" (Barker [1989], 140).

[8] For the distinction between these two traditions in musical theory, see Barker (1989), 3–8.

[9] See Philolaus fr. 6a and Huffman (forthcoming) on Archytas fr. 2. Archytas' own analysis of the diatonic scale is given in A.16.

musical tradition that is represented for us by the earlier theory of Philolaus.

Besides this work in pure mathematics and music theory, Archytas was noted for having applied mathematical principles to problems in mechanics and optics and for having done fundamental work in physical acoustics, as will be seen in a moment.[10] He was also famous for inventing various toys and gadgets, including a wooden duck that could fly and a rattle for children.[11]

On his contributions to philosophy we are less well informed. The catalogue of Aristotle's works lists three books "On the Philosophy of Archytas." Unfortunately, the contents of these books are preserved only by a handful of scattered references. We may infer that Archytas discussed many problems in natural philosophy. We know that he was concerned with cosmology and the infinite expanse of the cosmos, since we have his famous argument against a limited universe: "If I come to the limit of the heavens, can I extend my arm or my staff outside, or not?"[12] In either case, I am not at the limit, since if I cannot go farther, there must be something outside that is stopping me.

Aristotle reports with approval several definitions proposed by Archytas that illustrate a genus-differentia structure, which is interpreted by Aristotle as a matter-form distinction: "What is still weather (νηνεμία)? Absence of motion in a large expanse of air. . . . What is a calm (γαλήνη)? Smoothness of the sea."[13] Each defini-

---

10 For mechanics, see D. L. VIII.83 (= DK 47A.1); for Archytas as "founder of theoretical mechanics," see F. Krafft, *Dynamische und statische Betrachtungsweise in der antiken Mechanik* (Wiesbaden, 1970), 3f., 144–54, and passim. For optics, see DK 47A.25, with Huffman's commentary (forthcoming).

11 DK 47A.10 and 10a.

12 DK 47.24 = Eudemus fr. 65 Wehrli. The doctrine that what lies outside the heavens (τὰ ἔξω τοῦ οὐρανοῦ) is infinite is attributed by Aristotle to "the Pythagoreans." Archytas' proof was apparently taken over by Epicurus, since it is developed in full by Lucretius at I.968–83.

13 DK 47A.22 = Aristotle *Met*. H.2, 1043a21. Perhaps we may connect with these definitions the reference in Aristotle's work on Archytas to a Pythagorean doctrine of matter as "flowing (ῥευστή) and always becoming different" (A.13). Eudemus in A.23 (fr. 60 Wehrli) expresses

tion proceeds by determining the specific case of a more general phenomenon: immobility or smoothness.[14] The *Problemata* handed down in the Aristotelian Corpus include the following citation from Archytas (presumably from Aristotle's lost work):

> Why are the parts of plants and animals (except for the organs) all round: of plants, the stem and branches; of animals, the legs, thighs, arms, thorax? Neither the whole animal nor any part is triangular or polygonal. Is this, as Archytas said, because there is a proportion of equality in natural motion, since all things move proportionately, and this is the only motion that returns back to itself, so that when it occurs, it produces circles and round curves?[15]

This text suggests a strongly geometric approach to the interpretation of natural phenomena, in the spirit of Plato's *Timaeus*. And that is what we would expect from this mathematician-philosopher.

Such an approach is explicitly advocated by Archytas in fragment 1, the most substantial quotation from his work. This comes from the beginning of a treatise cited both as *On Mathematical Science* (περὶ μαθηματικῆς) and as *The Theory of Harmony* (ὁ ἁρμονικός sc. λόγος).[16]

> The students of mathematics seem to me to have attained excellent knowledge, and it is not surprising that they have correctly understood how things stand in each matter. For since they have obtained knowledge of the nature of the

---

approval for Archytas' explanation of motion, which he does not describe. For a speculative reconstruction of Archytas' natural philosophy based on the *Timaeus*, see Frank (1923), 125ff.

[14] Huffman suggests that Archytas' definitions reflect Philolaus' distinction between Unlimiteds (air, sea) and Limiters (smoothness, rest).

[15] DK 47A.23a; discussion in Frank (1923), 379.

[16] Huffman (forthcoming) argues that the work dealt with musical theory and is properly entitled *Harmonics* or *Harmonic Theory* (ἁρμονικὸς λόγος). For the text of fragment 1, see Huffman's commentary and A. C. Cassio, "Nicomachus of Gerasa and the Dialect of Archytas, Fr. 1," in *CQ* 38 (1988), 135–9.

universe as a whole, they will have come to have a good view of how each thing stands in particular. Concerning the speed and risings and settings of the heavenly bodies they have handed down to us clear knowledge, concerning geometry and numbers, and not least concerning music. For these studies seem to be akin (or sisters, *adelphea*). (DK 47B.1)

This is the passage cited by Plato in *Republic* VII as the teaching of the Pythagoreans. The text goes on to explain that previous thinkers had understood that no sound can occur without a blow or impact (πλήγη). "But many of these sounds cannot be recognized by our nature, some because of the weakness of the blow, some because of the great distance from us, and some because their magnitude exceeds what can fit into our hearing, as when one pours too much into narrow-mouthed vessels and nothing goes in." The comparison must be due to Archytas himself, but the theory is presented by him as a doctrine handed down. The theory seems to form part of an explanation of why the music of the spheres is not audible to us. If so, Archytas appears to endorse this characteristically Pythagorean notion, which we find much later in a different form in Ptolemy.

Archytas then gives a series of examples and parallels designed to show that faster and stronger blows produce louder and higher sounds, whereas slower and weaker impacts produce lower sounds, because of the resistance of the air. Archytas' fragment 1 is the earliest statement of the theory that explains sound by impact (presumably, on the air), with sounds of higher pitch caused by stronger impacts: "sounds which arrive quickly and strongly from impacts appear high in pitch, those which arrive slowly and weakly seem to be low in pitch." The notion that pitch depends upon the speed at which a sound reaches us remained the standard view throughout antiquity.[17] Archytas' formulation fails, however, to distinguish between pitch and loudness; this is an error that is corrected in the modified versions of the theory retained by Plato and Aristotle.

---

[17] Barker (1989), 41, n.47.

A comparison with the discussion of sound in later authors shows that the views of Archytas represent a rather primitive stage in the development of ancient acoustic theory.[18] Perhaps the personal contribution of Archytas was to conceive the causal connection between impact and sound in strictly quantitative terms, "since all things move in accordance with proportion" (Archytas 23a). The optics of Archytas suggests a stage of development similar to that of his acoustics. The text that mentions his work in optics reports a theory of vision based on the assumption of a visual ray projected from the eye, a theory similar to but simpler than the view proposed by Plato in the *Timaeus*.[19]

This is all we know about Archytas' physical speculation. It is enough to suggest a major attempt to interpret the phenomena of nature and art in terms of geometry and number theory, an attempt that calls for comparison with Plato's similar enterprise in the *Timaeus*. What would Plato have thought of Archytas' achievement? He must have admired it, since he integrated much of it into his own synthesis. (Not everything would fit; we have noted that the diatonic scale of the *Timaeus* resembles that of Philolaus rather than Archytas.) But in the end, Plato seems to have judged Archytas' work in acoustics quite critically. Plato's own concern in *Republic* VII was for training in mathematics to turn the mind away from sensory experience to the study of abstract form, "the search for the beautiful and the good" (531c6), which were to be found only in noetic being. From this point of view, it was a failure of Archytas' mode of research "to seek the numbers in the heard consonances," just as it was a mistake in astronomy to be concerned ultimately with visual phenomena (531b8–c3). Plato seems to have thought that Archytas was an excellent mathematician but a bad philosopher, like those mathematicians in the *Euthydemus* who do not know that their results need to be turned over to dialecticians (290c).[20]

There is some anecdotal evidence to suggest that Archytas had a generous character and that he was particularly kind to children

---

[18] See Burkert (1972), 379ff.

[19] DK 47A.25, from Apuleius.

[20] I am following here Huffman's interpretation of Plato's criticism in *Republic* VII. There is a somewhat different view in Barker (1989), 52.

and slaves.[21] There is a hint of moral philosophy in an excerpt from the *Life* of Archytas by Aristoxenus (DK47A.9), which presents a dialogue between Archytas and a Sicilian hedonist named Polyarchus. Their debate on pleasure is vaguely reminiscent of the exchange between Socrates and Callicles in Plato's *Gorgias*. Polyarchus praises sensual pleasure as the goal of natural inclination, while Archytas attacks it as incompatible with intellectual activity. Now Aristoxenus is a highly imaginative writer, and this dialogue is probably his own invention.[22] The only reliable evidence for Archytas' thought in ethics and politics is fragment 3. This text begins with a praise of inquiry and discovery, and continues as follows:

> When calculation (or reasoning, *logismos*) is discovered, it puts an end to civil strife and reinforces concord. Where this is present, greed disappears and is replaced by equality (or fairness, *isotês*). It is by calculation that we are able to come to terms in dealings with one another. By this means do the poor receive from the affluent and the rich give to the needy, both parties believing that by this they will have what is fair (*ison*).

Fragment 3 continues in this rather rhetorical vein. The emphasis here on the social role of reason, understood as calculation (*logismos*), may represent a mathematician's reflection on fifth- and fourth-century theories of social contract as the rational basis for civil society and law.[23] But this text does not suggest that the author was a profound thinker in the moral domain. And there is some confirming evidence from the Seventh Epistle that Plato, despite his great regard for Archytas' character and his mastery of

---

[21] A.8; cf. A.7 and A.10.

[22] For a more generous interpretation of this dialogue, see Huffman (forthcoming). I accept Huffman's reconstruction of the material from Aristoxenus but am skeptical of its value for a historical account of Archytas.

[23] For an interpretation of fragment 3 in this sense, see Huffman (forthcoming).

mathematical science, did not regard him as a good judge in strictly philosophical matters.[24]

We know very little about the Pythagorean circle around Archytas in Tarentum, but there is a famous story about two Pythagoreans from the same period in Sicily.[25] Damon and Phintias were Pythagorean friends who proved to Dionysius II, tyrant of Syracuse, that they were willing to die for one another. Aristoxenus claims to have heard the story from the tyrant himself after he had lost power and was living in Corinth. The story is told to show how, for Pythagoreans, friends have "all things in common."

Some confidants of the young tyrant, when he was ruling in Syracuse, proposed to test the legendary moral strength of the Pythagoreans by accusing Phintias of treason and sentencing him to death. When he was suddenly summoned to court and condemned in the presence of the tyrant, Phintias was taken by surprise. He then requested a reprieve for the rest of the day, in order to settle his affairs and those of his younger friend Damon. (In Pythagorean fashion, the two shared a common life.) Phintias offered to send for Damon to remain as hostage in his place, until he could return. Dionysius and his companions were amazed when Damon answered the call to stand as personal surety for his friend. And they were even more amazed when Phintias returned at the end of the day to face his death. Full of admiration for the two men, Dionysius embraced them and begged to be admitted as a third in their friendship. But the tyrant's offer was refused.[26]

The *Phaedo* introduces us to a somewhat larger Pythagorean community in Phlius, in the northern Peloponnesus, whose spokesman in the dialogue is Echecrates. Echecrates and his friends are said to be disciples of Philolaus and Eurytus, and according to Aristoxenus they were among the last Pythagoreans.[27]

---

[24] See G. E. R. Lloyd, "Plato and Archytas in the Seventh Letter," *Phronesis* 35 (1990), 159–74.

[25] One little-known Pythagorean, perhaps a contemporary of Archytas, is Zopyrus of Tarentum, a specialist in mechanics. See the reconstruction in Kingsley (1995), 143–55, who dates him in the fifth century.

[26] Aristoxenus fr. 31 Wehrli.

[27] D. L. VIII.46 = Aristoxenus fr. 19 Wehrli.

From the *Phaedo* we can see that a certain amount of Pythagorean lore had also been brought to Thebes by Philolaus. Simmias and Cebes, the chief interlocutors of the *Phaedo*, are represented by Plato as a kind of link between the Pythagoreans and Socrates (*Phaedo* 61d). It was also in Thebes, at the beginning of the fourth century, that another refugee from South Italy, Lysis of Tarentum, became the teacher of the great Theban general Epaminondas.[28]

Besides these respectable Pythagorean communities of South Italy, Phlius and Thebes, whose members show an interest in science and philosophy, there is a quite different type represented by Diodorus from Aspendus in Asia Minor, a fourth-century ascetic sage living a vegetarian life, and described in terms that prefigure the Cynic sage: long hair, long beard, worn cloak, a beggar's wallet and staff.[29] For Athens we have fragments of a dialogue by Aeschines in which Socrates converses with a Pythagorean named Telauges, who is dressed like an eccentric hippie.[30] Also in fourth-century Athens we find unwashed, barefoot vegetarians mocked in Middle Comedy as "Pythagorists"(DK 58E). The pale, barefoot Pythagorist, who eats no meat, appears once again much later as a comic figure in Theocritus (14.5). But this seems to be a literary reminiscence. In real life, this type of mendicant philosopher was taken over by the Cynics. As a consequence, after the fourth century B.C. we hear no more of these counterculture Pythagoreans, whose contempt for the pleasures of this world is presumably motivated by a greater concern for the fate of their soul in the next life.

From the fourth century on, however, the future of the Pythagorean tradition is guaranteed by the absorption and transformation of Pythagorean ideas in the work of Plato and his immediate followers. We have already cited the *Phaedo* and the *Timaeus* as supreme expressions of the two central conceptions of Pythagorean thought: the immortal destiny of the human soul,

---

[28] DK 46.1.

[29] For Diodorus of Aspendus, see D. L. VI.13, Athenaeus IV.163c–f., and Burkert (1972), 202–5, who adds as a parallel Lycon of Iasus.

[30] Fragments of Aeschines' *Telauges* in H. Dittmar, *Aischines von Sphettos* (Berlin, 1912), 290–2; commentary there, 213–44. See also Gabriele Giannantoni, *Socratis et Socraticorum Reliquiae*,[2] Vol. II (Napoli, 1991), 622–4.

and the role of mathematics as the key for unlocking the secrets of the cosmos. These are the two great Pythagorean themes in Plato's work. Perhaps we should add a third: the role of music in moral education and moral psychology. But here Plato's originality is so great that it is difficult to know how much, if anything, he actually owes to the Pythagoreans. For the other two themes his debt is clear, and clearly recognized in the dialogues.

Plato's interest in Pythagorean ideas does not begin with the *Phaedo*. It is in the *Gorgias* that the Platonic Socrates indulges for the first time in mystic speculation concerning the fate of the soul after death—speculation that stands in stark contrast to the cautious skepticism in regard to the afterlife expressed by Socrates at the end of the *Apology*. In response to Callicles' praise of the unbridled pursuit of pleasure, Socrates abruptly cites Euripides: "Who knows if life is really death, and death is life?" (*Gorgias* 492e). He connects this with the notion that the body is a tomb (*sôma-sêma*) and with tales of the uninitiated in Hades carrying water in a sieve to fill a leaking *pithos*. As we have seen, Socrates suggests that this view of the soul is that of "some clever Sicilian or Italian" (493a–b), thus attributing it to the Pythagorean tradition, broadly understood to include Empedocles. The notion of punishment in the afterlife is developed further in the judgment myth at the end of the *Gorgias*. In this myth we can see Plato flirting with reincarnation and even with recollection, since *lêthê*, "forgetfulness," is noted as a defect of the soul (493c3). Reincarnation is certainly implied in the judgment myth, as Dodds and others have pointed out.[31] For if they were not destined to return to life in this world, how could the souls in the prison house of Hades benefit from the sight of incurable sinners enduring eternal punishment (525c)? But there is no explicit reference to transmigration in the *Gorgias*, and the myth of judgment in this dialogue remains as close as possible to traditional Greek views of the afterlife.

All this changes in the *Meno*. It is natural to connect the change with Plato's first voyage to the West and his personal contact with the Pythagoreans of Magna Graecia. It will be convenient to assume that the *Meno* is later than the *Gorgias*. But whatever the

---

[31] E. R. Dodds, *Plato: "Gorgias"* (Oxford, 1959), 303, 381.

biographical background may be, the attitude of the dialogues to Pythagorean teaching is now quite different. Whereas in the *Gorgias* reincarnation is alluded to but never asserted, in the *Meno* Socrates solemnly invokes the authority of "wise priests and priestesses who are concerned to be able to give an account" of their ritual practice, and who teach the immortality and transmigration of the soul (81a–b). According to their teaching, since the soul has seen and learned everything in its previous existence, our learning in this life is really recollection. This is a radically new conception presented in archaic dress. For the Pythagoreans recollection meant, first of all, remembering one's previous incarnations (as Pythagoras himself was reported to have done) and secondly, remembering the secret passwords and road markers communicated to the initiate for a safe passage in the realm of the dead.[32] Plato has transformed this magical, ritualistic notion of recollection into an epistemology of innate ideas and a priori knowledge. The *Meno* remains silent on the content of such knowledge, but the *Phaedo* makes clear that the basis of recollection is a prenatal acquaintance with eternal Forms. This experience of the disembodied soul, implied in the *Meno* and *Phaedo*, is fully portrayed only in the myth of the *Phaedrus*, which depicts a chariot journey of the soul beyond the visible heavens, in the company of the gods. The *Phaedrus* further develops the epistemic role of recollection in the acquisition of concepts (249b–c), and it adds a new explanation for the phenomena of love in terms of the recollection of Beauty itself (249d–251a). This philosophical theory of recollection, introduced in the *Meno* and completed in the *Phaedrus*, is entirely Plato's own creation. But he has built it upon a view of the eternal transmigrating soul that he inherited from the Pythagorean tradition. In this sense, in the *Meno* and *Phaedo* Plato has created a new Pythagorean philosophy.

The epistemology of recollection is only one aspect of Plato's philosophical use of the doctrine of transmigration. Of equal if not greater importance are the moral implications of the survival

---

[32] For Pythagoras' own recollections, see Burkert (1972), 138–41. The mystic passwords are recorded in the "Orphic" gold plates, DK 1.B 17–21; fuller text with commentary in G. Zuntz, *Persephone* (Oxford, 1971), 277–393; updating in Burkert (1998a).

of the soul. The *Meno* immediately makes this point, even before mentioning recollection: "therefore one should live one's life as piously as possible" (81b6). The great myths of the afterlife in the *Phaedo* and *Republic*, together with the myth of preexistence in the *Phaedrus*, present three complementary pictures of human destiny. In this Platonic-Pythagorean eschatology, the eternal rewards and punishments for the transmigrating soul provide both an incentive for the practice of virtue and a promise of just compensation in the long run. We know too little of early Pythagorean doctrine to be able to evaluate the extent and importance of traditional elements in these Platonic myths.[33] The cosmic scope of the vision and the richness of scientific and imaginative detail must be Plato's own.

For a Pythagorean as for any ancient mystic, the highest reward was for the soul to join in the life of the gods, in a partial or permanent escape from the cycle of rebirth. The most brilliant image of this prospect is the extracelestial cavalcade of gods and purified souls in the *Phaedrus*. But the Platonic formula for this conception is given in the *Theaetetus*, where the possibility of an escape from the evils of this world is described as *homoiôsis theôi*, the imitation of god as far as possible. But how does one assimilate oneself to the divine? The answer is clear: by "becoming just and pious with wisdom" (*Theaetetus* 176b). The Pythagorean way of "following god" thus becomes the life of philosophy, understood in Socratic-Platonic terms as the pursuit of the unity of virtue in wisdom.

What is called "becoming like god" in the *Theaetetus* was described in the *Phaedo* as the purification of the soul from bodily pleasures, pains, and fears, by the practice of the virtues under the guidance of wisdom (69b–c). As a discourse on immortality in the shadow of Socrates' impending death, the *Phaedo* is the most otherworldly and in this sense the most explicitly Pythagorean of all the dialogues. The dramatic setting is provided by the Pythagorean community of Phlius. There Phaedo, on his way home from Athens to Elis, meets Echecrates and his circle, and gives them an account of Socrates' last conversation.

---

[33] For a bold attempt, above all in reference to the *Phaedo* myth, see Kingsley (1995).

The doctrine of transmigration dominates the discussion of immortality as well as the final myth, and the myth itself is introduced by a cosmic picture that is, if not strictly Pythagorean, at least recognizably Italian rather than Ionian, with a spherical rather than a flat earth in the center of a spherical universe (108e–109a).[34] But Plato sees no incompatibility between the austere Pythagorean atmosphere of this dialogue, introduced by the reference to an Apollonian festival, and the allegorical interpretation of Dionysiac mysteries that seem to be more Orphic than Pythagorean. It must be an Orphic poem from which Socrates quotes when he invokes the claim that in Hades the uninitiated will lie in the mud, while the initiates will dwell with the gods: "For, as they say who deal in mystic initiations, 'Many are the narthex-bearers, but few are the Bacchoi.' These are, in my opinion, none other than those who have truly practiced philosophy" (69c–d). Thus in Plato's conception of philosophy the Orphic and Pythagorean streams merge, and both traditions find their *hyponoia*, their deeper meaning, in Plato's own theory of the soul and its transmundane destiny.

The second great theme of the Pythagorean tradition, the importance of mathematics as a key to knowledge, receives even more complex treatment in Plato's writing and teaching. We first consider what the dialogues have to say on this topic, and then discuss the problems concerning Plato's oral doctrine.

Here again the first tentative allusion to the Pythagorean theme appears in the *Gorgias*, followed by a major statement in the *Meno*. Probably the first mention of the importance of mathematics is in a passage of the *Gorgias* where Callicles' lust for power and luxury is attributed to his neglect of geometry: "You have not observed that geometrical equality is a mighty force both among gods and among men"; that is why "the experts call the world a *kosmos*, an ordered whole, not a disorder" (508a). In this passing reference to a mathematical conception of cosmic order, Plato probably has in mind a view that is specifically

---

[34] The spherical earth is a distinctive innovation of the Western (Pythagorean?) cosmological tradition (in Parmenides and Empedocles), whereas the Ionian tradition preserves the flat earth (in Anaxagoras and the atomists).

Pythagorean.[35] In the *Meno* the role of mathematics is much more conspicuous. Among several examples of definition, the geometrical definition of figure as "the limit of a solid" receives Socrates' preference (75e ff., 76e7). The doctrine of recollection is then illustrated by the famous geometry lesson with the slave boy, where a square is doubled by constructing the square on the diagonal that divides the unit square into two right triangles. This is of course a special case of the Pythagorean theorem. The construction is also equivalent to finding the square root of two, and it thus poses the problem of irrational magnitudes. Plato refers here neither to the general theorem nor to the problem of irrationality, but both must be in his mind when he selects this example. Finally, the *Meno* introduces the method of hypothesis as "the way geometers often pursue their inquiry"; and this method is illustrated by a complex mathematical example (86e–87b).

The method of hypothesis, as a method of mathematical proof, is not specifically Pythagorean. But Plato's philosophical development of this method, in the *Phaedo* and above all in books VI and VII of the *Republic*, serves to articulate a view of mathematics that makes use of Pythagorean elements. Plato presents the deductive structure of mathematical knowledge as essentially hypothetical and conditional. Hence the study of mathematics can serve only as a preliminary to dialectic, which is able to rise above the hypotheses to the nonhypothetical principle of all knowledge, the unconditional first principle of the universe (*Rep.* VI, 511b), which seems to be identical with the Form of the Good. The elaborate mathematical curriculum that will occupy the future guardians for ten years, between the ages of twenty and thirty, is thus designed to train the mind to turn its gaze away from the realm of visible change and Becoming to the un-

---

[35] Burkert suggests to me a possible reference here to Archytas. Compare Dodds (1959) on *Gorgias* 508a6, where "geometric equality" is connected with the Pythagorean interest in mean proportionals. But Dodds goes too far in regarding Plato's use of *kosmos* here (at 508a3) as distinctively Pythagorean. The sense "world" or "world order" is alluded to in Heraclitus and Parmenides and used literally by Anaxagoras, Empedocles, and in scientific prose generally. The usage may well go back to Miletus, as the conception of cosmic order certainly does.

changing Being of the Forms. Now this curriculum includes not only arithmetic and geometry but also astronomy and music—the four "sciences which the Pythagoreans call sisters of one another, and we agree," says Socrates. As we have noted, this is apparently a quotation from Archytas, fragment 1. Here again the Pythagorean contribution has been absorbed and transformed in the training program for the future rulers of the city. The study of Pythagorean mathematics is only a preparation for Platonic dialectic, which has an entirely new object: the invisible and incorporeal realm of Form. According to Aristotle's report, for the Pythagoreans before Plato there was no such distinction between the intelligible object of mathematics and the material world of nature.[36]

Thus we recognize an important Pythagorean coloring in many passages of the *Meno*, *Phaedo*, and *Republic*. And this Pythagorean connection acquires a fundamentally new significance in Plato's latest period, notably in the *Philebus*, the *Timaeus*, and the "unwritten doctrines" reported by Aristotle and elaborated by Plato's pupils. (Again, it is natural to connect this new Pythagoreanism with Plato's two later trips to Syracuse in 367 and 361, which afforded him the opportunity for more intimate contacts with Archytas and the Pythagoreans of Tarentum.) We have already quoted the extraordinary passage from the *Philebus*, where the Pythagorean principles of Limit and Unlimited are described as a gift from the gods, thrown down to us from heaven by some Prometheus and passed on to us by the ancients, our superiors (16c).[37] This passage announces a new conception of the Pythagorean tradition as a kind of channel connecting the school

---

[36] Aristotle *Met.* 987b28 (οἱ δ᾿ ἀριθμοὺς εἶναί φασιν αὐτὰ τὰ πράγματα) and passim.

[37] Many readers, both ancient and modern, have assumed that Plato's Prometheus is intended as a reference to Pythagoras. (See p. 14, n. 23.) It is also possible to read the text more generally, as recognizing a divine gift that happens to be best realized in the Pythagorean tradition. Whether intended by Plato or not, however, the identification of Pythagoras as the Prometheus in question was generally accepted in antiquity and certainly served to reinforce the idealization of Pythagoras as the source of superhuman wisdom.

of Plato with the wisdom of the gods. In this conception, the legendary semidivine status of Pythagoras is reinterpreted allegorically as primeval omniscience, and Pythagoras himself begins to assume the position of the *daimôn* in Parmenides' proem, the source of all philosophical knowledge.

This new importance of the Pythagorean tradition for Plato, announced in the Prometheus passage of the *Philebus*, is even more abundantly illustrated in the *Timaeus*. Timaeus himself must be fictitious, but he comes from Locri in Magna Graecia, the territory of the Pythagoreans. As I have suggested, the introductory description of Timaeus, as having occupied the highest offices and honors in his city and having attained the supreme level in every branch of philosophy, seems intended to remind the reader of Plato's scientist-friend Archytas, to whom the *Timaeus* is thus gracefully dedicated.

Probably no one now believes the theory of A. E. Taylor, according to which the doctrines of the *Timaeus* are not those of Plato himself but really the teachings of a fifth-century Pythagorean.[38] But it remains true that the *Timaeus* is particularly rich in Pythagorean numbers and cosmic geometry, inspired in part by Plato's contact with Archytas. The world soul, from which the human soul is eventually derived, is constructed by a series of odd and even integers beginning with 2 and 3, the first even and odd numbers, and proceeding through their squares (4 and 9) and cubes (8 and 27). (Recall that 1 does not count as a number, since in Greek the notion of number, *arithmos*, implies plurality.) This construction is completed by inserting intervals corresponding to the harmonic and arithmetical means between each two terms of the original series (*Timaeus* 35b–36b).[39] Finally, then, the world soul represents a section of the diatonic scale, but its basic structure is given by purely mathematical and physical (rather than acoustic) considerations. As Cornford points out, continuous geometric proportion, exemplified by the two series 2, 4, 8 and 3, 9, 27, "was chosen as the most perfect bond to connect the four solid

---

[38] A. E. Taylor, *A Commentary on Plato's Timaeus* (Oxford, 1928).

[39] These are two of the three musical means defined in Archytas fr. 2. But, as previously noted, the construction of the world soul follows the diatonic scale of Philolaus, not that of Archytas.

bodies forming the whole body of the world."[40] The even and odd series stop at 8 and 27, respectively, since these are the first cube numbers, and only three dimensions are required to accommodate solid bodies. Later in the *Timaeus*, when the Demiurge comes to organize the body of the cosmos, he constructs the four elementary bodies out of two right triangles that combine to form the five regular solids (53c–56c).

This mathematical construction of the cosmic soul and body in the *Timaeus* represents a genuinely Pythagorean blend of number theory, geometry, and musical harmony. Astronomy, the fourth member of the Pythagorean quadrivium, is also included, since the world soul is cut into two strips corresponding to the celestial equator and the ecliptic (*Timaeus* 36b). But Plato has reworked these Pythagorean elements (borrowed from Philolaus and Archytas) into a new world picture that is at once highly symbolic and mathematically precise. Numerical ratios, geometric progressions, and regular solids represent the cosmic order as a systematic structure of rational harmony. Furthermore, by portraying the mathematical order of nature as the work of a creator god, Plato becomes the precedent for modern mathematical theists like Kepler and Newton, who will claim that "God geometrizes," that geometry is the instrument by which God creates the world.[41]

The *Timaeus* is the single most important text for the future of the Pythagorean tradition. But it does not stand alone in Plato's later work. The *Statesman* distinguishes a kind of measurement of more and less based upon "due measure" (*to metrion*), as the necessary condition of all the arts and the source of all good results (283e–285b): this is normative mathematics. Plato's later dialectic, announced in the *Phaedrus* and practiced in the *Sophist* and *Statesman*, consists in the complementary operations of Collection into unities and Division into pluralities. It is the underlying principle of this dialectic that is referred to in the *Philebus* as the Promethean gift from heaven: "all things that are said to be are always derived from One and from Many, having Limit and Unlimitedness inher-

---

[40] F. M. Cornford, *Plato's Cosmology* (London, 1937; Indianapolis, 1997), 68.

[41] The phrase "god geometrizes" is cited by Plutarch as typically Platonic (*Quaest. conviv.* 718b–c).

ent in their nature" (16c). This is the eternal principle of reason and discourse (*logos*): that in rational analysis and discussion the same thing turns out to be both one and many (15d).

The One and the Many, then, are the fundamental principles that underlie all rational thought and discourse, corresponding to the principles of Limit and Unlimited that structure the cosmos. Something of this sort must be what Timaeus has in mind when he says of Fire and the like that it is a mistake to call them "elements" or "letters" (*stoicheia*), when they are not even syllables; and that the true principle (*archê*) or principles of all things are too difficult to be treated in his present mode of exposition (*Tim.* 48b–c). A little later, when he begins to construct the primary bodies out of elementary triangles, Timaeus declares: "This is the principle (*archê*) we posit for fire and the other bodies. . . . The principles yet higher than these are known to god and to him among men who is dear to the god" (53d). According to Aristotle and later authors, it was this deeper discussion of principles that Plato undertook in his famous lecture (or lecture course, *akroasis*) on the Good, where he identified the ultimate principles as the One and the Indefinite Dyad (*aoristos duas*): the principle of unity and the principle of indeterminate plurality.

This brings us to the question of Plato's oral teaching in the Academy, a question which is made hopelessly obscure by the fact that we are almost entirely dependent for our information on Aristotle's report. But Aristotle's account is unsympathetic, incomplete, and distorted for reasons of polemic and perhaps even of misunderstanding. Since Plato himself did not see fit to publish a written account of these teachings, and since the later reports in turn largely depend upon Aristotle, we cannot fully understand what Plato had in mind. It is nevertheless clear that certain features of this oral doctrine of first principles exerted a decisive influence on the philosophy of Plato's immediate students, Speusippus and Xenocrates, and through them on all later versions of Pythagorean cosmology. So we must attempt a sketch of the so-called unwritten doctrines, in order to understand their profound impact on the later tradition.[42]

---

[42] The term "unwritten doctrines" (*agrapha dogmata*) appears once in Aristotle (*Physics* 209b15), often in the commentators. The basis for modern scholarship on the oral teaching was laid by L. Robin, *La théorie platonicienne des idées et des nombres d'après Aristote* (Paris, 1908).

There is, first of all, the recognition of the One and the Indefinite Dyad as ultimate principles. The Dyad is also described as the Great and Small, an indication that the reference is not to numbers alone but to magnitude generally, and also (it will turn out) to diversity as represented by pairs of opposites. For Plato these two principles seem to be conceived as radically independent of one another, like the Forms and the Receptacle in the *Timaeus*, to which they are often compared. (In later theories, however, we will find a monistic tendency to derive the Dyad from the One.) Since the Dyad is defined as indefinitely great and small, we may think of it as a domain that is potentially quantitative but intrinsically indeterminate—stretching out indefinitely in opposite directions, like the different forms of "more and less" (hotter and colder, wetter and drier, etc.) that characterize the unlimited principle in *Philebus* 24a–e. (Speusippus will define this principle more narrowly as *plêthos*, plurality, the opposite of the One.) In its first set of determinations this principle takes on the forms of definite plurality, in the generation of the natural numbers from two to ten. The logical sequence of the numbers is thus conceived as a quasi-temporal process of generation.

First of all, the number Two is formed by the action of One on the Dyad, transforming indeterminate quantity or vague numerosity into a definite number. (As we have seen, One itself is not thought of as a number.) Modern interpreters have remarked that in this account the One acts just as Limit does in the *Philebus*, with the great-and-small corresponding here to the Unlimited. By limiting more of the Dyad, the One will then form the successor to Two as the definite number Three, and so on. The sequence could of course continue indefinitely, but Plato is said to have

---

Healthy but ultimately excessive skepticism was developed by H. Cherniss, *Aristotle's Criticisms of Plato and the Academy* (Baltimore, 1944) and *The Riddle of the Early Academy* (Berkeley and Los Angeles, 1945). For a sober survey, see W. D. Ross, *Plato's Theory of Ideas* (Oxford, 1951), 142–224. The relevant texts are printed with commentary as "Testimonia Platonica" in K. Gaiser, *Platons Ungeschriebene Lehre* (Stuttgart, 1963), 443–557. For a full statement of the Tübingen reconstruction, see H. J. Krämer, *Plato and the Foundations of Metaphysics*, Engl. ed. and transl. John R. Catan (Albany, 1990).

stopped at the number Ten, for reasons that a Pythagorean will understand.[43]

Simplicius quotes a passage from Porphyry that undertakes to explain how, in his lecture on the Good, Plato interpreted this generation of the numbers. Take a definite length, one cubit long, and divide it in half. Leave one-half undivided, but divide the other half again. If we continue dividing, Porphyry says, we see that "there is a certain infinite nature enclosed in the cubit, or rather several infinites, one proceeding to the great and one to the small."[44] The movement to the infinitely small is obviously the result of dividing and redividing. But where do we see the movement in the other direction, toward the indefinitely large? Porphyry does not tell us, but I think he must be counting the increasing number of segments. The first cut gives us the number Two, the second cut gives us Three (since one half-cubit remains undivided), and so on.[45] As Porphyry points out, both the double and the half are contained in Two, as the first even number. That is to say, every bisection produces both the more (in number of segments) and the less (in size of segments), and the process can continue indefinitely. Thus, says Porphyry, "the Indefinite Dyad is seen to be composed of the unit going to the Large and the unit going to the Small."[46]

Thus the Dyad, as principle of duality, is responsible for developing the plurality of the number series. On the other hand, the unity and uniqueness of each particular number is derived from the One, the source of limit and definiteness.[47] Once the natural numbers are formed, it is the numbers from Two to Four—the

---

[43] Aristotle *Physics* 206b32.

[44] Simplicius, in *Physicorum* 454, 6 = Gaiser (1963), 482.

[45] For a similar construction of the number Three by adding the unit to a pair, see Plato's *Parmenides* 143d, where this begins the series of odd and even numbers.

[46] For a discussion of this and related texts from Alexander on the generation of the numbers, see J. Annas, *Aristotle's "Metaphysics" Books M and N* (Oxford, 1976), 45ff. Alternative accounts in Robin (1908), 277–86; Ross (1951), 187–205; Gaiser (1963), 115–28.

[47] I avoid here the vexed problem of the relation of Plato's Ideal Numbers (from One or Two to Ten) to the full number series, on the one

numbers of the *tetractus*—that will then serve as structural principles to organize the Dyad into the forms of geometry. First of all, the number Two serves to determine the great-and-small conceived as the long-and-short (i.e., extension in one dimension): the result is a line, twoness in length. Three in turn will determine the great-and-small, conceived now as the broad-and-narrow (extension in two dimensions), to form a plane figure with three sides: the triangle. Finally, by determining the great-and-small conceived as the deep-and-shallow, the number Four adds the third dimension in the form of the simplest solid body, the tetrahedron or four-sided pyramid.[48]

At this point, the oral doctrine establishes contact with the cosmogony of the *Timaeus*, in which the tetrahedron constitutes fire, and the other primary bodies are built up as regular solids constructed from the elementary triangles. Now in the *Timaeus* these triangles and solids are introduced as determinations of the Receptacle, which must correspond in some way to the Indeterminate Dyad. But the fit between the reported oral teaching and the doctrine of the *Timaeus* is far from perfect, and many problems of interpretation remain unsolved. I am concerned here only to sketch some lines of continuity between the dialogues and the oral doctrine, as a basis for tracing the Platonic content in later accounts of Pythagorean philosophy.

How are Plato's Forms related to the One and the Dyad, and to the numbers generated from these principles? Our sources are inconsistent here. Aristotle often speaks as if the Forms were identified with numbers.[49] On the other hand, there is a text of

---

hand, and to the intermediate "mathematicals," on the other hand. See discussions in authors cited in preceding note.

[48] The basic text is *Met.* 1090b20–4. For a clear exposition, see Ross (1951), 208–12. A late reflection of this theory is ascribed to the Pythagoreans by Sextus; see Gaiser (1963), 501f. (= *Adv. mathem.* X.276–82).

[49] See *Met.* 987b18–25 and a dozen other passages cited by Annas (1976) 64, n. 78. Most commentators now regard Aristotle's statement as misleading. See Ross (1951) 216ff.; Annas (1976), 64–8, citing Cherniss (1945), 59. For the problematic text at *Met.* 987b21 (ἐξ ἐκείνων γὰρ κατὰ μέθεξιν τοῦ ἑνὸς τὰ εἴδη εἶναι τοὺς ἀριθμούς), see the defense of the full text by Cherniss (1944), 180–2, followed by Gaiser (1963), 477 n.

Theophrastus that locates the numbers *above* the Forms: "Plato, in the reduction (*anagein*) to principles, would seem to connect other things to the Ideas, to connect these to numbers, and from these to reach the principles."[50] This would put the numbers *between* Forms and principles.[51] It is perhaps impossible to determine just what Plato had in mind. What is clear is that Speusippus and Xenocrates each went his own way: Speusippus in replacing the Forms by numbers and mathematicals, Xenocrates by identifying Forms with numbers.

The geometrical solids constructed from the triangles of the *Timaeus* become physical bodies by being visible and tangible, that is to say, by their eventual contact with a percipient psyche. There is one cryptic sentence in the Tenth Book of the *Laws* that can only be understood as an allusion to this process. The context is a general discussion of change and coming-to-be:

> It is clear that when a first principle takes on increment [as a line] and passes into its second transition [to a plane figure] and from this to its neighbor [as a solid], having reached three transformations it provides perception to subjects that are percipient. (*Laws* 984a)

This is perhaps the only passage in Plato's written work that describes the mathematical generation of perceptible bodies from a first principle as in the unwritten doctrine, and it does so in such a way that no one unfamiliar with that doctrine could possibly understand what is said. But this single Platonic text is enough to show that the theory as reported by Aristotle and later writers is not entirely unfaithful to Plato's thought. And if we combine this text with the passage in the *Philebus* where the Forms are referred to as "monads" or "unities" (15a–b) and where all things are derived from One and Many, limit and limitlessness (16c), we see that the dialogues themselves point to a scheme of the general sort that we find in Aristotle, according to which all things come from, or are resolved into, the principles of unity and indefinite plurality.

---

[50] Theophrastus, *Metaphysics* 6b 11; translation according to A. Laks and G. W. Most, *Théophraste, Métaphysique* (Paris, 1993), 9.

[51] So Ross (1951), 218, following Robin.

V

THE NEW PYTHAGOREAN PHILOSOPHY IN THE EARLY ACADEMY

IN THE *PHILEBUS* PASSAGE DISCUSSED IN THE LAST CHAPTER, THE doctrine of One and Many, Limit and Unlimited is attributed to a Promethean figure that readers might naturally identify with Pythagoras. So it is not altogether surprising to discover that the later doxographical tradition credits Pythagoras and the Pythagoreans with a mathematical cosmology that derives all bodies from incorporeal principles, and derives the incorporeals in turn from our familiar first principles, the One and the Indefinite Dyad. This is the account of Pythagorean philosophy that we find in every Hellenistic source. However, as Burkert has demonstrated, this account is incompatible with Aristotle's report on Pythagorean ontology. The Pythagoreans studied by Aristotle have no notion of incorporeal principles; the heavens as a whole *are* numbers, and there are no numbers "distinct from sensible things" (*Met.* A.6, 987b27; cf. 986a21). In Aristotle's view, it was Plato who made the mistake of *separating* the incorporeals, and it was Plato who replaced the Pythagorean Unlimited by the Indeterminate Dyad. As we have seen, on these points Aristotle's report is fully confirmed by the Pythagorean doctrine represented in the fragments of Philolaus. The Platonizing elements in the Hellenistic doxography for Pythagoras and the Pythagoreans are entirely unhistorical.

But how did this doxography begin? Who was it that turned Pythagoras into a late Platonist? Perhaps it was Plato himself, by his allusion to Prometheus and to "the ancients, our superiors, who dwelt nearer to the gods, and who have passed this word on to us" (*Philebus* 16c). Even earlier, in the *Meno* and the *Phaedo*, Plato had set the fashion of presenting his newest theories as age-old wisdom. This archaizing, which is, in Plato's case, a kind of playful literary adornment, seems to have been taken quite literally by his closest pupils, Speusippus and Xenocrates.

As we have noted, Speusippus is said to have replaced Plato's Forms by numbers and mathematical objects. These played the role of the Forms in that they were intelligible entities (*noêta*), distinct both from soul and from sensible bodies.[1] For Speusippus the numbers in turn were derived from the two great principles, the One and Plurality (*plêthos*), which Speusippus substituted for the Indefinite Dyad. Thus, his system is a variant on Plato's oral teaching. But what is momentous for the history of Pythagoreanism is that Speusippus was willing, even eager, to attribute these principles to "the ancients," that is, to the Pythagoreans.[2] Furthermore, both Speusippus and Xenocrates apparently treated the cosmology of the *Timaeus* as the teaching of Pythagoras.[3] Speusippus composed a book *On Pythagorean Numbers*, half of which was devoted to the glories of the decad. The number Ten is said to be perfect for many reasons, including the fact that it contains One, Two, Three, and Four, corresponding respectively to point, line, plane, and solid.[4] The first half of this "Pythagorean" book included a discussion of the five Platonic solids, "assigned to the cosmic elements."[5] As far as we can tell from the preserved

---

[1] See Zeller II.i (1889), 1001–6; Cherniss (1945), 37–43. The account given by H. J. Krämer in H. Flashar, *Die Philosophie der Antike*, Vol. III: *Ältere Akademie, Aristoteles-Peripatos* (Basel and Stuttgart, 1983), 24ff., is distorted by his questionable attempt to reconstruct a late Platonic metaphysics.

[2] Burkert (1972), 63, citing the Speusippus fragment (no. 62 in Isnardi-Parente, *Speusippo: Frammenti* [Napoli, 1980]) from the Latin translation of Proclus, where "the ancients" are responsible for positing the One and the *interminabilis dualitas* as principles.

[3] Burkert (1972), 65: "the later tradition about Pythagoras is largely based on the exegesis of the *Timaeus* by Xenocrates, who understood the ideas contained in Plato's dialogue as the teaching of Pythagoras." For Xenocrates, too, there is evidence of Pythagorean writings, represented by the title Πυθαγόρεια in D. L. IV.13.

[4] Speusippus fr. 4,70 Lang = Isnardi-Parente fr. 122.

[5] Fr. 4,9 Lang = Isnardi-Parente fr. 122.

fragment of this book, Speusippus seems to have presented Platonic material in a form that anticipates neo-Pythagorean numerology. And the author (pseudo-Iamblichus) who quotes this text reports that Speusippus composed the book "from his extraordinary enthusiasm always for the Pythagorean teachings, and in particular for the treatises of Philolaus."

Thus in Plato's own Academy, and perhaps in Plato's own lifetime, the myth of Pythagoras as the archetypical Platonic philosopher was born. Aristotle stoutly resisted the myth in his careful study of Philolaus and the pre-Platonic Pythagorean tradition. But Aristotle was the last author to draw a clear distinction between the two schools. His pupil Theophrastus accepted the fusion created in the Academy, since he names "Plato and the Pythagoreans" as authors of the doctrine of the One and the Indefinite Dyad (*Met.* 11a27). From this time on, what Aristotle reports as Plato's oral doctrine will be uniformly identified with the teachings of the Pythagoreans.

This confusion between Pythagoreanism and late Platonism was probably facilitated by one doctrine that Aristotle himself attributes to the Pythagoreans: the table of ten opposites in *Metaphysics* A.5 (986a22). After his summary of the Pythagorean philosophy that we have identified as the system of Philolaus, Aristotle continues:

> Others from the same school say that the first principles are ten, arranged in double columns (*kata sustoichian*).

Limit	Unlimited
Odd	Even
One	Plurality
Right	Left
Male	Female
At rest	Moving
Straight	Crooked
Light	Darkness
Good	Bad
Square	Oblong.

We do not know who these other Pythagoreans were. The way in which abstract and concrete, mathematical and moral-aesthetic opposites are jumbled together here may indicate an archaic origin.

And the absence of the One-Dyad pair suggests that the list is independent of the main post-Speusippean tradition. On the other hand, the opposition of one-plurality (*hen-plêthos*) does remind us of Speusippus, and we know of similar *sustoichiai*, or tables of opposites, in the Academy.[6] If this particular table of ten opposites was actually the work of an earlier Pythagorean, it seems to have provided a model for other, more systematic schemes of derivation in the Academy, and it thus served as a genuine connecting link between Pythagorean and Platonic philosophy.

Pythagoras remained an object of intense interest for the philosophic circles around Plato and Aristotle. Besides Speusippus and Xenocrates, whose work tended to assimilate Pythagoras into the Platonic tradition, a member of the Academy who made even more imaginative use of Pythagorean ideas was Heraclides Ponticus. Heraclides was a prolific and successful author of dialogues, and in these he explored new versions of both the mystical psychology and the quasi-scientific cosmology of the Pythagorean tradition. On the mystic side, he represented Pythagoras as recounting one by one his previous incarnations, on the basis of a gift of memory from Hermes, his first father: Pythagoras had originally been Aithalides son of Hermes, then he became successively the Trojan hero Euphorbus killed by Menelaus, an archaic seer named Hermotimus whose soul went on travels away from his body, and finally Pyrrhus, a fisherman from Delos.[7] And in another work Heraclides described the vision of a certain Empedotimus, a name that seems to have been invented as a combination of the names of Empedocles and Hermotimus. In this work, Heraclides makes Empedotimus the recipient of a divine revelation concerning the nature of the heavens and the destiny of the soul. (Heraclides thus provides the model for the Dream of Scipio in Cicero's *De republica*.) In the vision of Empedotimus, the world below the sun is the realm of Hades (hence we are dead in this life, a genuinely Pythagorean thought), while the Milky Way is

---

[6] See Aristotle *Met.* Gamma.2, 1003b33–1004a2; 1004b27–1005a5; I.3, 1054a29–32.

[7] Fr. 89 Wehrli; see H. B. Gottschalk, *Heraclides of Pontus* (Oxford, 1980), 115–7. As Gottschalk points out, Heraclides seems to have invented this canonical series of incarnations. Cf. Burkert (1972), 138f.

the path that disembodied souls can follow on their journey to heaven. Their natural home is among the stars, since the souls themselves are composed of astral light.[8] Heraclides has clearly been inspired by Plato's myths to make a new literary use of Pythagorean doctrines on the wanderings of souls.

Above all, however, Heraclides is famous for developing the Philolaic conception of a moving earth in a way that prefigures various modern astronomical ideas. Heraclides abandoned the Philolaic hypothesis of the earth's rotation around an invisible central fire, but he offered instead the more fruitful hypothesis that the earth produces by its own rotation the apparent diurnal motion of the sun and stars (frs. 104–8). Hence Copernicus can refer to Heraclides as an ancient authority for his own hypothesis of a rotating earth.[9] Heraclides was apparently aware of the new astronomical insight into the distinction between the apparent and real position of the planets (first mentioned in Plato's *Laws* 821e ff.), and some scholars believe that he tried to account for the apparent movement of Venus by positing a real movement around the sun.[10]

In this connection Copernicus cites two Pythagoreans, Hicetas and Ecphantus of Syracuse, who, according to the ancient doxography, also taught the diurnal rotation of the earth. Of these two figures so little is known that it has been suggested that they were merely fictitious characters in one of Heraclides' dialogues. The doxographical report makes it more likely, however, that Hicetas and Ecphantus were historical persons of the fourth century B.C.

---

[8] Heraclides frs. 93–9 Wehrli; discussion in Burkert (1972), 366–8, Gottschalk (1980), 98–102.

[9] Copernicus (1984), 11.

[10] Fr. 109 with comments by Burkert (1972: 341) and Gottschalk (1980: 84f.). For the unending debate about whether Heraclides anticipated the system of Tycho Brahe, with Venus revolving not about the earth but about the sun, see the older literature in T. L. Heath, *Aristarchus of Samos* (Oxford, 1913), 255–83; more recent discussion in van der Waerden (*Die Astronomie der Pythagoreer* [Amsterdam, 1951], *Die Astronomie der Greichen* [Darmstadt, 1988]); Gottschalk (1980), 58–87; and Krämer in Flashar (1983), 95f., with full bibliography pp. 100f.

And if so, their existence tends to confirm our impression that Heraclides is exploiting a traditional line of Pythagorean speculation in his own brilliant suggestion that the observed phenomena of the heavens can be "saved" equally well by allowing the earth to rotate while the stars remain stationary.[11]

As a follower of Plato, Heraclides is happy to count Pythagoras as the first member of the Platonic school. Hence he introduces Pythagoras as the first person to call himself *philosophos*, a lover of wisdom, for the thoroughly Socratic-Platonic reason that only the god is wise (*sophos*).[12] Heraclides' two younger contemporaries, on the other hand, Dicaearchus of Messina and Aristoxenus of Tarentum, are members of Aristotle's school, and they paint a rather different picture of Pythagoras. As Greeks from the West, they both take a keen personal interest in things Pythagorean. But Dicaearchus denied any immortality or even any distinct existence for the soul; he said the psyche was only a name for the harmonious blending of elements in the body.[13] Hence Dicaearchus has no sympathy for transmigration or for any of the more religious aspects of the Pythagorean school. On the other hand, he shows considerable respect for Pythagoras as a moral guide and social reformer. As we have seen, Dicaearchus gives a sympathetic account of Pythagoras' arrival and political success in Croton and a plausible summary of his teaching concerning the soul

---

[11] The texts on Hicetas and Ecphantus are given in DK 50 and 51. For discussion, see Guthrie (1962) 323–9, Burkert (1972) 341, Krämer in Flashar (1983), 93f.

[12] Heraclides fr. 87 Wehrli = D. L. Prooimion 12. The explanation of the term *philosophia* was given by Pythagoras himself in the dialogue περὶ τῆς ἄπνου, "On the woman who had stopped breathing." I am following here the "pessimistic" explanation of the term as given by Diogenes. However, Gottschalk (1980: 23–31) provides strong arguments for attributing to Heraclides the more "optimistic" explanation for *philosophia* that Cicero gives in the famous parable of the three lives: those who come to the games to compete, to do business, and to watch. The philosopher's role is that of the spectator: his desire is not for honor or riches but for contemplating the universe and understanding the nature of things (Cicero, *Tusc. disp.* V.3.9).

[13] Dicaearchus frs. 5–12 Wehrli.

(above, pp. 7f. and 11). Dicaearchus thus becomes a probable source for the more sober historical elements in the tradition concerning Pythagoras.

Aristoxenus of Tarentum is a source of a very different stamp. He shared Dicaearchus' materialistic view of the soul as a mere blend or harmony of the bodily components (frs. 118–21 Wehrli), and is accordingly out of sympathy with the religious aspects of Pythagoreanism. He also deviated sharply from the Pythagorean tradition in music. In place of the quantitative, physical conception of harmony (where for Archytas the magnitude of a sound is correlated with the force of a collision), Aristoxenus developed a new science based not on physics or mathematics but on the perceived phenomena of sound as it appears to the ear, since "harmonic or musical properties attach only to what is heard."[14] His *Elementa Harmonica*, "The Elements of Harmonics," was the foundational work for the ancient tradition in musical theory most directly concerned with musical practice, in contrast to the more rigorous mathematical preoccupations of Pythagorean harmonics.[15]

Nevertheless, as a fellow-citizen of Archytas (whom he claims as a friend of his father) and a specialist in music theory, Aristoxenus undertakes to give an inspiring account of the Pythagorean tradition. He was apparently the first to write a *Life* of Pythagoras, and many of the more marvelous or moralistic features of the later biography (as preserved by Diogenes Laertius, Porphyry, and Iamblichus) must go back to this lost work of Aristoxenus. For example, Aristoxenus is quoted as a source for the report that Pythagoras piously buried Pherecydes in Delos, and that he left Samos for Italy because he deemed it ignoble for a free man to endure the tyranny of Polycrates (frs. 14 and 16 Wehrli). Aristox-

---

[14] A. D. Barker in *The Oxford Classical Dictionary*, 3rd ed. (New York, 1996), 170: "Harmonic theory became polarized into two main camps, 'Aristoxenian' and 'Pythagorean.'"

[15] On Aristoxenus: "So powerful was his novel conception of the subject, and so sophisticated and detailed were his studies, that his authority on matters of melodic analysis was accepted for centuries almost without criticism," A. Barker, *Greek Musical Writings, Vol. II. Harmonic and Acoustic Theory* (Cambridge, 1989), 120. Barker gives a full translation and discussion of Aristoxenus' work.

enus seems also to have begun the detailed account of Pythagoras' training period, reporting that he studied with Zoroaster (fr.
13) and also with a priestess at Delphi (fr. 15). In Aristoxenus' account, Pythagoras' success in South Italy was not limited to Croton and its immediate environment (as it was in Dicaearchus' version); Lucanians and Messapians and even Romans came to him
for guidance, the famous lawgivers Charondas and Zaleucus
were his pupils, and his influence produced peace and concord in
South Italy and Sicily for many generations.[16]

Aristoxenus' account is problematic in several respects. Not
only has Pythagoras become a mythical figure, but we have no
way of distinguishing in this mythology between an older oral
tradition and Aristoxenus' personal imagination. That imagination must have been quite active in enriching whatever reminis-
cences were available on the subject, since Aristoxenus dealt with
the Pythagoreans in at least three separate works. The biography
was entitled *On Pythagoras and his Friends (gnôrimoi)*, but there
was also a work *On the Pythagorean Life* and another entitled
Pythagorean Maxims (apophaseis). Aristoxenus' account of the
Pythagorean way of life was clearly an enlightened, revisionary
version designed to shield the name of Pythagoras from any
shadow of primitive superstition. So he reports that beans were
Pythagoras' favorite vegetable, and that the master was peculiarly fond of suckling pigs and tender kids (fr. 25). In the work on
moral maxims, many features of Plato's and Aristotle's ethical
teaching were assigned by Aristoxenus to the Pythagoreans. This
was perhaps justified by the claim that Plato had purchased the
writings of Philolaus for a huge sum and hence managed to appropriate the secret wisdom of Pythagoras.[17] We know that Aristoxenus' regard for historical fact is not too scrupulous, and he

---

[16] Fr. 17, from Porphyry. Some of the details may have been added by
later writers, but Porphyry cites Aristoxenus as his source for the
wider influence, and the connection with Charondas and Zaleucus is
confirmed by an Aristoxenus context in D. L. VIII.15 (fr. 43).

[17] Frs. 43 and 68, with Wehrli's commentary pp. 59, 67, and passim.
Wehrli, following others, holds Aristoxenus responsible for the story
that Plato purchased the unpublished works of Philolaus (D. L. 8.15).
But the textual basis for this attribution is extremely weak.

clearly enjoys saying unkind things about both Plato and Socrates. Thus Aristoxenus maintained that Socrates had two wives, was given to sexual indulgence, and had a particularly bad temper; in his *Life of Plato* he claimed that the contents of the *Republic* were almost entirely contained in the *Antilogika* of Protagoras (frs. 51–68). As a member of the rival school and a patriotic son of Magna Graecia, Aristoxenus could draw an unflattering inference from the Platonists' own adoption of Pythagoras as their ancestor: Pythagoras has now become the original philosopher, and Plato must simply play the role of his disciple or plagiarist.

The negative twist given to this relationship would be characteristic of Aristoxenus' sharp tongue. But the picture of Plato as a follower of Pythagoras, and of Platonic philosophy as fundamentally Pythagorean, will remain the standard view throughout antiquity. Such is the inevitable consequence of the new philosophical image of Pythagoras created in the early Academy.

VI

THE SURVIVAL OF PYTHAGOREANISM IN THE HELLENISTIC AGE

As WE HAVE SEEN, A LATE BUT CREDIBLE TRADITION REPORTS THAT the early Pythagoreans were divided into two schools, the *akousmatikoi*, characterized by their faithful adherence to the *akousmata* or ritual observances, and the *mathêmatikoi*, who were concerned with more scientific philosophy.[1] It would seem that both types had ceased to exist by the end of the fourth century B.C. Except for one sentence in Theocritus (14.5, cited above, p. 49), we hear no more of the mendicant Pythagoreans of Middle Comedy, the last recorded representatives of the *akousmatikoi*. And Aristoxenus, writing in the late fourth century, claims to have known the last scientific Pythagoreans, who belonged to the generation of Archytas and Plato.[2] The *akousmatikoi* are replaced as mendicant philosophers by the Cynics; the *mathêmatikoi* are absorbed into the Platonic school of Speusippus, Xenocrates, and Polemon. (Polemon, who was head of the Academy until about 267 B.C., maintains the Pythagorean link by including vegetarianism in his own conception of the good life as living "in accordance with nature.")[3] Other scientific types went their own way, as did Aristox-

---

[1] Texts and discussion in Burkert (1972), 192–208.

[2] Aristoxenus fr. 19 = D. L. VIII.46. One of them must have been the musician Xenophilus from Thracian Chalchis (DK 52), who is said to have been the teacher of Aristoxenus.

[3] *The Life according to Nature* was the title of Polemon's ethical work. For the reference to vegetarianism, see Krämer in Flashar (1983), 158.

enus, who, for all his Pythagorean sympathies, worked out an independent musical theory.

Writing many years later, in the last days of the Roman republic, Cicero begins his translation of Plato's *Timaeus* with a much-quoted reference to his own friend and contemporary, Publius Nigidius Figulus, who "arose to revive the teachings of the Pythagoreans which, after having flourished for several centuries in Italy and Sicily, had in some way been extinguished." It is only in the first century B.C., with Nigidius Figulus in Rome and with Eudorus and other Platonists in Alexandria, that we can detect the signs of a Pythagorean revival, leading to the birth of Neopythagorean philosophy with Moderatus of Gades and Nicomachus of Gerasa in the first and second centuries A.D.

Such is the traditional picture, as presented, for example, in the classic history by Eduard Zeller.[4] Upon closer inspection, however, the pattern of extinction and rebirth is not so simple. The Pythagorean silence of the two intervening centuries, from 300 to 100 B.C., is far from absolute. The name of Pythagoras remained in honor in Rome throughout this period, and an official statue of Pythagoras was erected there at the beginning of the third century, as we shall see. Many scholars have followed Zeller in supposing that Pythagorean influence survived at least among the Bacchic cults of Italy, which were powerful enough to produce a crisis in Rome in 186 B.C. (Livy gives a detailed account of Bacchanalian celebrations in Rome which had become so shocking that senatorial legislation was required to suppress them, and many initiates were put to death both in Rome and in the Greek south.)[5] But there is no mention of Pythagoreans in this connection. Other

---

4 Zeller III.ii (1881), 79ff. Zeller assumed, however, that Pythagorean cult was maintained throughout the Hellenistic period by the "Orphic-Dionysiac mysteries," whose importance in the region of Tarentum was demonstrated by the Bacchanalian affair (ibid., p. 81).

5 Livy 39.8–19; cf. 39.29.9 and 40.19.9–10. Livy reports that thousands were prosecuted for the "conspiracy" and many executed. Full details in F. Cumont, *Les religions orientales dans le paganisme romain* (Paris, 1929), 196–204; for recent discussion, see E. S. Gruen, "The Bacchanalian Affair," in *Studies in Greek Culture and Roman Policy* (Leiden, 1990), 34–78.

authors have argued that "Pythagoreanism continued to lead a more or less 'underground' existence in southern Italy under the Romans."[6] Some, like Zuntz, would recognize a Pythagorean community behind the "Orphic" gold tablets, which are found widely scattered over Italy and Greece for several centuries.[7] The Orphic and Pythagorean traditions were, after all, closely linked. But all this is historical speculation, without firm evidence. Even more controversial is the interpretation of archaeological finds, alleged as evidence for Pythagorean cult practice at Rome at a later date.[8] I know of only one specific text pointing to the continued existence of a distinctively Pythagorean cult community during the Hellenistic period. (This evidence will be discussed below, in connection with the *Pythagorean Notebooks* cited from Alexander Polyhistor.)

What is well attested, on the other hand, is the rise of a new kind of literature in this period, the creation of pseudonymous philosophical works attributed to Pythagoras and his followers. Many of these works are written in Doric prose, in imitation of the authentic treatises of Philolaus and Archytas, but their contents are heavily influenced by the new metaphysics elaborated in the Academy. Zeller thought this literature began only with the rise of Neopythagorean philosophy in the first century B.C., but recent studies have shown that the earliest examples must go back to the second or even the third century B.C.[9]

We know nothing about the authors of these works or the milieu within which they were produced. One of the most intriguing examples of this kind of literature is the so-called Pythagorean Notebooks (*Pythagorikai hypomnêmata*) preserved by Diogenes Laertius from an excerpt in Alexander Polyhistor. Alexander was writing in the first half of the first century B.C.

---

[6] Kingsley (1995), 322, citing Cumont and Nock.

[7] See Zuntz (1971), 337f., 383f.

[8] See, e.g., J. Carcopino, *La basilique pythagoricienne de la Porta Maggiore* (Paris, 1927).

[9] See Burkert (1961) and (1972a). H. Thesleff also concludes for an earlier dating; see his *Introduction to the Pythagorean Writings of the Hellenistic Period* (Åbo, 1961), 99. For evidence of Pythagorean numerology in the second century B.C., see below, p. 102, n. 16.

Hence the text that he is excerpting can scarcely be later than 100 B.C., and may be much earlier. Since what we have is an anonymous excerpt, we cannot tell whether the original text was in the Doric dialect and whether or not it was attributed to Pythagoras or to some other Pythagorean. So, despite its interest, this is not a typical pseudonymous text, and we will postpone our discussion of it until the new genre is described. I mention it here because of a possible connection with what may be one of the oldest extant pseudepigraphical texts, the Letter of Lysis to Hipparchus. Walter Burkert has offered an attractive suggestion that would identify the lost original of the Alexander *Notebooks* with a text mentioned in this letter.

As we noticed in Chapter IV, Lysis was a Pythagorean of the late fifth century who escaped from Italy and settled in Thebes, where he became the teacher of Epaminondas. The author of the letter, writing in Lysis' name, accuses a certain Hipparchus of "philosophizing in public, which Pythagoras condemned." The letter then tells the story of Pythagoras' daughter Damo, to whom he entrusted his notebooks (*hypomnêmata*), with the command "to hand them over to no one outside of the household. And although she could have sold the doctrines for a great deal of money, she refused to do so; she held poverty and her father's commands to be more precious than gold."[10]

Burkert has suggested that this famous letter—translated in modern times by Copernicus, among others—was forged precisely in order to authenticate the treatise or "notebooks" that someone was then publishing in the name of Pythagoras.[11] Burkert follows Festugière in dating the Alexander *Notebooks* in the third century;[12] as we have seen, they cannot be later than 100 B.C. If the letter was composed to introduce the *Notebooks*, it

---

[10] Greek text in H. Thesleff, *The Pythagorean Texts of the Hellenistic Period* (Åbo, 1965), 114; text and German translation in A. Städele, *Die Briefe des Pythagoras und der Pythagoreer* (Meisenheim am Glan, 1980), 158f.

[11] Burkert (1961), "Hellenistische Pseudopythagorica," *Philologus* 105, 17–28. Earlier scholars had suggested that the letter was forged to introduce some other work attributed to Pythagoras.

[12] Burkert (1961), 27.

must go back to the same period.[13] It seems clear from the letter
that, at the time of writing, such books could command a good
price. Assuming that it was written to introduce the extant *Notebooks*, the letter would probably date from the third century B.C.
when books circulating under Pythagoras' name first began to
appear.

Callimachus, in the middle of the third century, mentions an
astronomical poem attributed to Pythagoras, whose authenticity
he denied.[14] A more famous work is the "triple book" ascribed to
Pythagoras, with three separate sections devoted to Education,
Politics, and Physics. This was probably in circulation by about
200 B.C. Later, however, the tradition prevailed that Pythagoras
himself had left nothing in writing. Hence we then get Doric treatises attributed to Archytas and other followers of Pythagoras.
These may have begun earlier, but they seem to have become
common only in the first century B.C., about the time that Nigidius Figulus and others were reviving Pythagorean philosophy. To
this extent, Zeller's original dating of the pseudonymous literature to 100 B.C.–100 A.D. was not incorrect.[15] From then on, the
stream seems to flow unceasingly throughout antiquity into
Byzantine times. A late author attributes 80 works to Pythagoras
and 200 to his followers. This may be an exaggeration, but it gives
us some idea of the scope of this apocryphal literature. We may
guess that Rome and Alexandria were the chief sources for its

---

[13] The latest study of the Lysis letter dates it on linguistic grounds to the
first century A.D., which would make the link with these *Notebooks*
chronologically impossible. See Städele (1980), 212 and 352. However,
I do not find Städele's argument convincing; and he himself admits
the possibility that substantial portions of the letter are older (p. 206
with n. 8).

[14] D. L. IX.23. Burkert (1961), 28–42, argues for the existence of another
quasi-astronomical work attributed to Pythagoras, which would have
been composed around 200–168 B.C.

[15] For confirmation of this dating, see Burkert in (1972a), 27–47: he suggests 150 B.C. as the upper limit for the appearance of the Doric treatises. Similarly, B. Centrone, *Pseudopythagorica Ethica* (Rome, 1990),
41–4. (The earlier works attributed to Pythagoras would have been in
Ionic prose or epic verse.)

production, since these are the two cities where Pythagorean (or neo-Pythagorean) activity is attested for the first century B.C.

The most popular suppositious author for these pseudonymous books was Archytas. The works attributed to Archytas cover a wide range of topics. For some of these we have the titles only: "On Flutes," "On Agriculture," "On the Decad."[16] In other cases we have substantial excerpts and even mini-treatises, running from 3 to 11 pages of Greek text. One of the most interesting works ascribed to Archytas is a short cosmological text "On First Principles" (*peri archôn*), which contains a highly eclectic but largely Aristotelian version of the two principles of Philolaus, the Limiting and Unlimited, identified here as Form and Matter, the former beneficent, the latter a cause of evil. What is new and significant is that a third principle is required to bring the two together: "this principle is first in power and superior to the others; it is appropriate to name this 'god' (*theos*)." This divine Mover or Artificer (*technitês*) "is not only Mind (*nous*) but greater than Mind."[17] In introducing this superior third power, the text reflects a monistic tendency to subvert the fundamental dualism of the two unwritten Platonic "principles"—a tendency associated with Eudorus in the first century B.C.[18] (We will meet a similar tendency in the *Notebooks*.) But Eudorus' formulation of the monistic principle is quite different, and there is no evidence of direct influence in either direction.

Under Archytas' name we also find an epistemological text containing a summary of the Divided Line from Plato, *Republic VI* (*Peri nou kai aisthasios*, "On Intellect and Perception," in Thesleff [1965], 36–9), and two or three short ethical discussions representing the kind of eclectic-Aristotelian moral philosophy known

---

16 Thesleff (1965), 20f.

17 Thesleff (1965), 19f.

18 On Eudorus' monism, see below, pp. 97f., and J. Dillon, *The Middle Platonists* (Ithaca, N.Y., 1977), 126f. As evidence for this tendency Dillon (120f.) cites this text from pseudo-Archytas with other parallels from the pseudonymous literature. From the *Notebooks* we can see that the tendency is older than Eudorus, and Dillon conjectures that the latter had some pseudonymous work as his precedent.

from Arius Didymus in the late first century B.C.[19] A number of logical works are also attributed to Archytas, including two treatises on the ten Aristotelian Categories. The older of these two treatises is the most frequently quoted work under Archytas' name; it is a standard source for Neoplatonic commentators such as Simplicius.[20] Their familiarity with the doctrine of Categories may indicate that these treatises were both composed after Andronicus' edition of the Aristotelian corpus, that is, not earlier than the first century B.C. (One of them is, in fact, much later, as we shall see.)

It might at first sight seem surprising that a Pythagorean like Archytas should be assumed to be familiar with Aristotelian philosophy, and even with such a technical work. But that is understandable enough, if we bear in mind the Hellenistic or post-Speusippean view that Pythagoras taught Platonic doctrines. After all, if Plato's philosophy derives from Pythagoras, then a fortiori, Aristotle's philosophy must do so. And the Categories provide a natural theme for this kind of literature, since ten is such an honorable Pythagorean number. What is more surprising than the concern with Categories is that one of these two works turns out to be an extract from a Byzantine school manual, in which the name "Aristotle" for the author of the doctrine has been eliminated and the vocabulary slightly changed, in order to let the work appear under the name of Archytas.[21]

Thus the fashion of producing pseudo-Pythagorean literature lasted for more than a millennium and covered every branch of

---

[19] Pseudo-Archytas, *On the good and happy man* and *On moral education*, in Thesleff (1965), 8–15 and 40–3. Text and Italian translation with two other pseudepigraphical treatises in Centrone (1990).

[20] This information was supplied by Carl Huffman from his forthcoming work on Archytas.

[21] Both of these texts are published, with translation and commentary, by T. A. Szlezák, *Pseudo-Archytas über die Kategorien* (Berlin, 1972). The very late date of the second treatise was confirmed by Szlezák in his *Nachtrag*, 184–8, after he discovered the origin of the text in a Byzantine treatise on Aristotelian logic from the early eleventh century. See also Burkert (1972a), 27f., who would date this Archytas forgery to the Renaissance.

philosophy. The doctrines were mostly banal, drawn from Plato or Aristotle with some Stoic contamination and, later, with Neoplatonic overlay. The best-known Platonic example is the treatise "On the nature of the cosmos and the soul" attributed to Timaeus of Locri, the fictitious speaker in Plato's dialogue. Because of its supposed authority as the Pythagorean original from which Plato's cosmology was derived, this text in Doric dialect was faithfully recopied into the medieval period, and hence it has come down to us intact.[22] Its Aristotelian counterpart is a short work "On the nature of the universe" ascribed to Occelus of Lucania.[23] This work denies any doctrine of creation or world formation and argues for the eternity of the cosmic order. In the early first century A.D. this was already an established Pythagorean text, and, as a result, a learned man like Philo of Alexandria was perplexed. Philo reports that some say it was not Aristotle who invented the view that the world is eternal but some Pythagoreans; and he cites Occelus in support of this claim.[24]

The existence and continued success of this forged literature testifies to the enduring prestige of the Pythagorean name. But most of this literature tells us little or nothing about an authentic Pythagorean tradition. For that we turn instead to two Hellenistic texts that give us a better indication of how the conception of Pythagorean philosophy was transmitted and transformed during this period. The first text is one we have already encountered, the excerpt from *Pythagorean Notebooks* preserved by Diogenes Laertius from Alexander Polyhistor. The second is an account of Pythagorean doctrine apparently derived from Posidonius and preserved in Sextus Empiricus.

The *Pythagorean Notebooks* known to Alexander Polyhistor cannot be later than 100 B.C. and must be later than 350 B.C., since their content clearly depends both on Plato's *Timaeus* and on his unwritten doctrines. There are no definite clues for a date in between. Festugière and Burkert have argued for a date in the

---

[22] Thesleff (1965), 205–25. Also, *Timaeus Locrus*, text and transl. by W. Marg (Leiden, 1972).

[23] Thesleff (1965), 125–38. Also *Ocellus Lucanus de rerum natura*, ed. R. Harder (Berlin, 1926).

[24] Quoted by Dillon (1977), 156n.

middle or late third century; but the matter seems to me quite uncertain.[25] The text is unlike the pseudonymous literature in exhibiting some archaic or pre-Platonic features that apparently reflect an older tradition. The influence of Stoic doctrine and terminology, which is unmistakable, may be due in part to the double excerpting, first by Alexander and again by Diogenes.

The document begins with a cosmology of the late Platonic form, but with the tendency to monism that we have mentioned. In this case, however, the monism consists not in introducing a third, superior principle (as in the doctrine of pseudo-Archytas and Eudorus) but rather in privileging the principle of Unity.

> The first principle of all things is the monad. Out of the monad arises the indefinite dyad as matter for the monad which is cause. Out of the monad and indefinite dyad come the numbers, out of the numbers come the points, out of these the lines, from which (are formed) the plane figures; from the plane figures (are formed) the solid figures, from these the sensible bodies, whose elements are four: fire, water, earth, air. . . . Out of the transformation of the elements comes to be an animate cosmos, intelligent, spherical, surrounding the earth as its center. The earth in turn is spherical and inhabited all around. There are people living at the antipodes (literally "with their feet opposite ours") and what is down for us is up for them. (D. L. VIII.25 = DK 58B.1a)

The author thus gives us a simplified version of the *Timaeus* cosmology, introduced by this deviant account of the doctrine of principles. The mathematical derivation, in which points, geometric figures, and sensible bodies are successively generated from the numbers, is obviously Academic rather than properly Pythagorean. This is not the old, pre-Platonic cosmogony that begins with a centrally situated monad breathing in the void. What we have here comes directly from late Plato and the early Acad-

---

[25] See A.-J. Festugière, "Les 'Mémoires Pythagoriques' cités par Alexandre Polyhistor," *REG* 58 (1945), 1–65; Burkert (1972), 53.

emy.[26] Perhaps only the monistic turn points in the direction of the Neopythagoreans.[27]

The rest of the cosmology from the *Notebooks* combines archaic elements (the cosmic role of the opposites: "light and darkness, hot and cold, dry and moist have equal shares in the cosmos") with a division between the mortal, sluggish region of the cosmos around the earth and the purer, divine region of eternal motion in the upper heavens, a division that vaguely parallels or recalls the Aristotelian division between the sublunary world of change and the purer spheres above. Neither Platonic nor Aristotelian, however, is the explanation why the heavenly bodies are divine: "because the hot predominates in them, and this is cause of life"; the kinship between gods and human beings is due to the fact that "a human being shares in the hot" (VIII.27). "All things live which share in the hot . . . but not all have a psyche. The psyche is a fragment (*apospasma*) of celestial aether . . . and it is immortal, because what it comes from is immortal." "The human soul is divided in three, into *nous* and *phrenes* and *thumos*; *nous* and *thumos* are present in the animals, *phrenes* only in human beings" (VIII.30).

The role of heat as a mark of divinity recalls the dominant position of fire in Stoic thought. But this physical conception of the psyche as the basis for immortality is not necessarily Hellenistic.[28] This view can be paralleled in the astral psychology of Heraclides Ponticus and in even older beliefs, as reflected in the famous Potidaea inscription of 432 B.C.: "the aether received their *psychai*,

---

[26] The replacement of the Ideas by numbers suggests the predominant influence of Speusippus. The monism might also come from Speusippus.

[27] For a parallel but more complex derivation of the Dyad from the Monad, continued by a derivation first of Platonic categories (including absolute and relative) and then of the numbers, see the text of Sextus *Adv. phys.* II.248–84, discussed by Dillon (1977), 342–4. As Dillon suggests, the entire doctrine attributed by Sextus to Pythagoras and his followers may go back ultimately to a "Pythagorean" text of Speusippus or Xenocrates.

[28] Huffman reminds me of the importance of heat in Philolaus' biology. See DK 44A.27, Huffman (1993), 289ff.

the earth received their bodies." In this respect, the psychology of the *Notebooks* belongs to a tradition of what we may call mystical materialism—a tradition that begins with the Presocratics and continues throughout antiquity. What is unparalleled, however, is the distinction between *nous* and *phrenes*. This use of the term *phrenes* for the intellectual part of the soul (as in Homer) is probably the most archaic feature of our text.[29]

The doxography of the *Notebooks* is structured in a traditional way, beginning with principles, then elements and heavenly phenomena, and then living things. Thus the cosmology is completed by an account of sensation, embryology, and a smattering of physiology, all of which resemble the physical speculations of various treatises in the Hippocratic Corpus. We come then to an account of the souls when they leave the body at death. Hermes leads the pure souls to the highest region, the region of the fixed stars. "But unpurified souls can consort neither with the pure nor with one another, but they are bound in unbreakable chains by the Furies" (VIII.31). (This strikes a note quite unlike the dull rationalism of the pseudonymous treatises.) There are also souls in the air around us, worshipped as daimons and heroes, a source of dreams and prophecy and the powers to which rites of purification are directed. Happiness depends upon the goodness of one's soul.

There is little in our text so far that can be identified as specifically Pythagorean.[30] But the final section on morality and religion suggests that the connection of this very eclectic treatise with the name of Pythagoras is not altogether arbitrary:

> Virtue is harmony, and so is health and everything good, and the deity. Hence the universe is constructed in accordance with harmony. Friendship is harmonic equality.

---

[29] This archaic use of *phrenes* seems, however, to have been preserved in medical usage, as the term *phreneitis* for brain-fever shows. Festugière (1945), 44f., cites the *Anonymus Londinensis* iv.13–7, where *phrenes* refers to the brain.

[30] We might, however, recognize as genuinely Pythagorean the repeated reference to ratios of harmony (οἱ τῆς ἁρμονίης λόγοι) in the formation of the human embryo (VIII.29).

Honors paid to gods and heroes should not be equal, but gods should always be worshipped with pious silence, in white garments in a state of holiness (*hagneuontas*); sacrifices to heroes should be performed after noon. Holiness (*hagneia*) is achieved through purifications and baths and ablutions and keeping oneself pure from funeral rites and childbirth and all pollution, and by abstaining from meat and carcasses and red mullet and blacktail fish and eggs and egg-laying animals and from beans and from other things forbidden by those who perform ritual initiations (*teletai*) in the sanctuaries. (VIII.33)

This curious text thus claims to reflect a living cult that maintains a number of ritual observances characteristic of the Pythagorean tradition from the earliest times. On the face of it, this text represents the updated doctrines or doxography of a Pythagorean community from the third or second century B.C., which has preserved features from both the theoretical tradition of the *mathēmatikoi* and the ritual tradition of the *akousmatikoi*, all of this blended in a strange medley of Presocratic, Platonic, and Stoic elements. If this impression is correct, this text is the only unmistakable trace of a Pythagorean (or Neopythagorean) ritual community from the Hellenistic centuries before 100 B.C.[31]

Our second text can be more firmly dated, if, as seems likely, Sextus Empiricus is following here an account of Pythagorean doctrine given by Posidonius, the Stoic philosopher with Platonizing tendencies, at the beginning of the first century B.C.[32] Sextus is explaining why, for the Pythagoreans, the criterion of truth is reason (*logos*) in the mathematical sense of rational proportion or, more generally, number. Since number is the principle

---

[31] Alternatively (but in my opinion much less probably) these *Notebooks* might represent a purely literary phenomenon, the creation of a learned Hellenistic scholar who is more interested in older traditions and more successful in avoiding glaring anachronism than the usual authors of pseudo-Pythagorica.

[32] *Adv. math.* VII.94–108. Burkert previously (1972: 54–6) argued in detail for the dependence of this text on Posidonius. He now expresses doubts.

of the structure of the universe, it is by number and *logos* that we can grasp this structure. "And this is what the Pythagoreans mean when, in the first place, they are in the habit of saying 'all things resemble number,' and, in the second place, they swear this most naturalistic (*phusikôtaton*) oath." Sextus then cites the oath on the *tetractus* which we have discussed in Chapter III. He goes on to give a detailed explication of the *tetractus* in terms of the ratios between successive pairs of the numbers 1, 2, 3, and 4: "since the whole cosmos is organized by means of *harmonia* (harmony, scale), and *harmonia* is a complex of three concordances." Furthermore, says Sextus,

> both body and what is incorporeal are conceptualized (*noeitai*) according to the ratios of these four numbers. For by a point in flux we form the image of a line, which is length without breadth. But by a line that flows we produce breadth, which is a surface without depth. And by a surface in flux a solid body is produced. In the case of the point we have a monad that is indivisible, just as the point is; but in the case of the line we have the number two. And in the case of the plane surface, the number three.[33] The line stretches from here to there, that is, from point to point, and then on to another point. In the case of the solid body we have the number four. For if over three points we place a fourth point, a pyramid is produced, which is the first form of a solid body. (VII.100)

All this is familiar. Sextus goes on to give exemplifications of numbers and ratios both in bodily substances and in incorporeal things like time. He then cites examples of measures used in daily life and in the arts and crafts, ending with the story of the architect Chares who began the construction of the Colossus of Rhodes. After his first estimate of the expense, the Rhodians asked him how much it would cost to make the statue twice as big. He asked for twice the sum of money, and the Rhodians agreed. But Chares used up all the money on the preliminary

---

[33] I follow the text of Mutschmann. There is some difficulty in interpreting the next sentence.

work and then committed suicide. The experts understood that it was his own mistake for asking only twice the original sum. He should, of course, have asked for eight times as much, "since he was obliged to increase not only the height but all the dimensions of the work" (VII.108).

This dramatic Rhodian example of how cube numbers represent a three-dimensional solid may be taken as Posidonius' signature to his account of Pythagorean number theory, as we find it reported in Sextus. This account combines reliable information about the original interpretation of the *tetractus* in terms of the musical ratios with a version of the generation of line, triangle, and pyramid from a point-monad by "flowing" that parallels the passage quoted earlier from Plato's *Laws* (p. 62), with no explicit reference to the Indeterminate Dyad. So old and new Pythagorean material is mixed together here, with the addition of further examples that must be Posidonius' own contribution.

These two texts may serve to illustrate the continuing concern with, and the rather free reshaping of, the Pythagorean philosophical tradition in Hellenistic times. But Posidonius brings us down to the early first century B.C. and to the threshold of a new age. With the revival of Pythagorean teaching later in that century by Nigidius Figulus in Rome and Eudorus in Alexandria, the history of Pythagoreanism enters a new phase.

VII

THE PYTHAGOREAN TRADITION IN ROME

IT WAS APPROPRIATE THAT ROME BECOME ONE OF THE CENTERS IN THE renewed interest in Pythagoras and his teachings. The Pythagorean order was, after all, created in the Italian peninsula, in Magna Graecia. Aristotle and later authors regularly refer to its teaching as "the Italian philosophy." This geographical proximity meant that Pythagorean influence could be felt, or imagined, at Rome from an early period, and that Romans would be among the most enthusiastic in following, or at least admiring, a tradition that was native to their own region. So the name of Pythagoras was held in high esteem, and it was almost an act of patriotism for a Roman to invoke the wisdom of this local sage.

The earliest indication of this Pythagorean prestige occurred at the beginning of the third century, during the Samnite War (298–290 B.C.), when, according to Pliny's report, a statue of Pythagoras was erected in the Roman forum in response to a Delphic oracle, presumably solicited because the war was going badly for the Romans.[1] When the oracle commanded them to honor the wisest and the bravest of the Greeks, the Romans chose Pythagoras and Alcibiades! The Romans won that war, of course, and thereafter a statue of Pythagoras stood in the Roman forum for two centuries, until Sulla built the new Senate house on that spot.[2]

A century later, Ennius, the father of Latin poetry and himself a

---

[1] References in Burkert (1961), 237 n. 2. Cf. Ferrero (1955), 138f.

[2] Pliny, *Natural History* 34.26.

Hellenized South Italian, introduced Pythagorean reincarnation into the proem of his great historical epic, the *Annales*. The poem opened with an invocation of the Muses, followed by a dream in which Homer appeared to the poet on Parnassus, the mountain of the Muses, and informed Ennius that his own soul had passed into Ennius' body. A more satirical work of Ennius, named after the Sicilian comic poet Epicharmus, expounded another dream, in which Ennius received a cosmic vision after his death (a vision apparently inspired either by Plato's myth of Er or by the vision of Heraclides' Empedotimus). The few surviving fragments of this work suggest a Stoic theory of elemental change with a vaguely Pythagorean flavor, as in the *Notebooks* of Alexander Polyhistor. (Epicharmus himself was later counted among the Pythagoreans.) Thus Pythagorean influence enters Latin literature in its earliest phase, with Ennius.

It was about the same time (in 181 B.C.) that some suspicious books of Numa were discovered on the Janiculum, and officially burnt as a danger to traditional piety. These books claimed to display the wisdom that Numa had acquired as a pupil of Pythagoras. The legendary date of Numa is some two hundred years before Pythagoras' arrival in Italy, so the connection is historically impossible, as Cicero and other Romans knew. But as folklore, this story testifies to the continuing prestige of Pythagoras at Rome.[3] It also provides the background for a famous passage in Ovid's *Metamorphoses*, which we will consider in our last chapter.

M. Fulvius Nobilior, the patron of Ennius and consul in 189 B.C., brought back from his conquests in Greece both artistic treasures and Hellenistic learning. With his plunder he dedicated a temple to Hercules and the Muses. From his learning he composed a work, *De fastis*, on the Roman religious calendar. It is probably from this work that we have a late quotation claiming to give "what Fulvius reports from Numa." The quoted passage reflects an astral theology in the tradition of the *Timaeus*, includ-

---

[3] References in Burkert (1961), 237 nn. 3–4. For the discovery of the books and their reception, see A. Willi, "Numa's Dangerous Books: The Exegetical History of a Roman Forgery," *Museum Helveticum* 55 (1998), 139–72.

ing a reference to "the ineffable father of all things," in other words, the Platonic demiurge. As Burkert points out, Numa ranks as an authority on these matters because he is reputed to have studied with Pythagoras. Pythagorean (or pseudo-Pythagorean) literature must be the pipeline by which this Platonic cosmology is transmitted to Rome, and Numa is designated as the legendary point of connection.[4]

Another trace of Pythagorean influence in Rome in the early second century B.C. is a reference in Cato's *De agricultura* 157 to a species of cabbage as *brassica Pythagorea*. As the corresponding passages in Pliny's *Natural History* make clear, Cato is relying on a pseudonymous treatise known as "Pythagoras on the Power of Plants," which described the medicinal and magical virtues of different plants.[5] (The Greek precedent for this kind of supernatural botany is probably the work of an Egyptian, Bolus of Mendes, to whom we will return in due course.)

We see from these indications from the third and second centuries that, to some extent, Pythagoreanism was always in vogue in Rome, and the impossible connection with Numa shows how popular this tradition had become. The vogue continues in the first century B.C. when we find both Varro and Cicero showing a special interest in things Pythagorean. A different aspect of the same interest is expressed in Horace's famous Ode (1.28) addressed to Archytas, "the measurer of earth and sea and sands without number."[6]

Varro, who died in 27 B.C., is reported to have been buried "in the Pythagorean manner," in a clay coffin with leaves of myrtle, olive and black poplar.[7] Varro's book entitled *Hebdomades*, or *On Portraits*, began with an elaborate praise of the number seven in the Pythagorean style, and with an astronomical quotation from Nigidius Figulus.[8] If Varro was not formally a Pythagorean, he

---

[4] Burkert (1961), 241f., following Boyancé.

[5] Ibid., 239, following Wellman. Burkert notes the parallel to Bolus. For "Pythagoras" on the cabbage, see Pliny, *Nat. Hist.* 24.158.

[6] Huffman points out to me that Archytas is mentioned also by Propertius (4.1) and twice by Cicero.

[7] Pliny, *Nat. Hist.* 35.160.

[8] Aulus Gellius III.10.1–2.

was at least a fellow traveler. And Cicero displayed his own Pythagorean sympathies not only by selecting the *Timaeus* as the Platonic dialogue he undertook to translate but by, in effect, dedicating his translation to Nigidius. Beyond that, Cicero reports his emotion on visiting Metapontum and seeking out the house where Pythagoras died (*De finibus* V.2). One has, however, the impression that Cicero's veneration for Pythagoras reflects his admiration for a great man of the remote past rather than his indebtedness to a philosophical teacher. If we set aside the symbolic content of the *Dream of Scipio*, it is difficult to find Pythagorean influence in Cicero's philosophical work. Even in the *Dream* the principal model is Plato's myth of Er; the *Dream of Scipio* was, after all, composed as conclusion to Cicero's own *De republica*. Nevertheless, a Pythagorean background for the *Dream* is indicated by the form taken here by the music of the spheres, and probably also by the identification of the Milky Way as the home of disembodied souls.[9] Cicero's Pythagorean sympathies are conspicuous again in the proem to Book IV of the *Tusculan Disputations*, where, in discussing the literary and cultural debt of early Rome to Greece, Cicero begins by mentioning that the Romans of the early Republic "had before their eyes Pythagoras flourishing in wisdom and celebrity."

> As the doctrine of Pythagoras flowed far and wide, it appears to me to have diffused itself into this city. . . . For who can think, when Greece called the Great [i.e., Magna Graecia] flourished in Italy, with most powerful and populous cities, and when in these the name, first of Pythagoras himself, and then of the Pythagoreans afterwards, sounded so high, that the ears of our countrymen were closed to the most eloquent voice of wisdom? Indeed, I think it was through their admiration for Pythagoras, that Numa the king was reputed a Pythagorean by posterity; for, knowing the system and institutions of Pythagoras, and having

---

[9] *Somnium Scipionis* III.16. Cf. P. Boyancé, *Études sur le Songe de Scipion* (Bordeaux, 1936), 136f. For Cicero's "Pythagorean" deviation from Plato on the music of the spheres, ibid., 104–15. Further literature in J. G. F. Powell, *Cicero: On Friendship and The Dream of Scipio* (Warminster, 1990).

> received from their ancestors the renown of that king for
> wisdom and integrity, but ignorant, through distance, of
> ages and times, they inferred that, because he excelled in
> wisdom, he was the disciple of Pythagoras. (*Tusc. disput.*
> IV.1.2–3., transl. G. A. Otis)

After giving this avowedly conjectural account of early contacts
between Rome and Pythagoras, Cicero goes on to identify what
he takes to be vestiges of Pythagorean influence in archaic Roman
musical practice and poetry (ibid., IV.2).

It was probably in the first century B.C., in the age of Varro and
Cicero, that Rome became a center for the book-selling and book-
collecting of Pythagorean pseudepigrapha. King Juba II of Nu-
midia, educated in Rome in the latter half of that century, was an
enthusiastic collector who was known to be particularly fond of
Pythagorean books.[10] The charm of Pythagorean authorship for
the Roman literary public, and hence for the book market, is obviously linked to the fact that Pythagorean philosophy is, as Aristotle said, "Italian." In the period in which Rome is digesting its
conquest of the Greek-speaking East, and Roman authors are beginning to match or copy Greek achievements in rhetoric, poetry,
history, and philosophy, it is a considerable advantage for a newly
discovered text to bear the name of an ancient philosopher from
Croton, Tarentum, Locri, or Lucania.

The proem to Cicero's translation of the *Timaeus* reminds us
that, by the middle of the first century, Nigidius Figulus had
brought back to life the teaching of the Pythagoreans. If
Pythagorean philosophy was reborn in Alexandria (as we shall
see in the next chapter), it is in the Rome of Nigidius, Varro, and
Cicero that we encounter the first definite trace of a Pythagorean
ritual community (aside from the indirect evidence provided by
the *Notebooks*, as discussed above). The existence of such a community, or at least of rules to govern one, is attested by the report
that Varro's burial conformed to the "Pythagorean style"
(*Pythagoreus modus*). The details of Nigidius' activity are not
recorded, but he is remembered as *Pythagoricus et magus*, the center of a circle of initiates, devoted to esoteric teaching and cult.[11]

---

[10] Zeller III.ii (1881), 97.

[11] For Nigidius, see W. Kroll in *RE* XVII.1 (1936), 200–12. There is a

Cicero describes him as "a man distinguished in all the liberal arts, but a particularly acute investigator of those matters which nature has made obscure."[12] Nigidius was not only a master of arcane knowledge; he was reputed to have occult powers, including second sight. He was also extremely learned, the author of many books—on grammar, on natural philosophy, on dreams, and above all on theology. His theological work was designed to connect the Roman religious tradition not only with Greek myth, cult, and philosophy but also with Etruscan ritual and with ideas from the Orient, including astrology. In astrology Nigidius was an expert; he composed one or more books on the planets and the zodiac, including predictions of political events. (This is probably what Cicero had in mind as "those matters which nature has made obscure.") Nigidius is said to have predicted the glorious future of Augustus from his horoscope at birth. He was familiar with Egyptian and Babylonian lore, both of which he probably studied in Greek sources. The Roman conquest of the eastern Mediterranean coincided with a general interest in old cultures as depositories of ancient wisdom. And in the case of Nigidius, the revival of Pythagoreanism meant not only contact with Hellenism and the Orient but also the blurring of any clear demarcation between magic and science, as in the example of the pseudo-Pythagorean treatise on plants mentioned above.

There were surely other avowed Pythagoreans in the circle around Nigidius, and presumably some form of ritual initiation. We happen to know of one contemporary, a supporter of Caesar named Vatinius, who boasted of his Pythagorean affiliation. We have the speech in which Cicero attacks the credibility of Vatinius as a witness and accuses him of all sorts of impiety, despite the fact that he "calls himself a Pythagorean and tries to shield his monstrous and barbarous behavior with the name of this most learned man (*homo doctissimus*)."[13] The point of Cicero's charge is

---

detailed account of Nigidius' known writings in Elizabeth Rawson, *Intellectual Life in the Late Roman Republic* (Baltimore, 1985), 309–12. According to Rawson (p. 310), Pythagoreanism "for Nigidius and his friends meant primarily a belief in magic."

[12] Cicero, *Timaeus* 1.

[13] *In Vatinium* 6: *tu qui te Pythagoreum soles dicere, et hominis doctissimi*

that a true Pythagorean should be outstanding in piety and distinguished by a sober lifestyle. As we have seen, Cicero likes to
compare Pythagorean moral decorum with the austere manners
of the early Romans.[14]

The Pythagorean influence in Rome was prolonged into the
first century A.D. by many literary echoes (the most memorable of
which, the appearance of Pythagoras himself in Ovid's *Metamorphoses*, will be discussed later) and by a philosophical movement
initiated by Quintus Sextius, whose followers were known as Sextians.[15] One of these was Sotion, the teacher of Seneca, and it is by
Seneca's writings that the memory of this school has been preserved. The movement was characterized by the strong moral
personality of its spokesmen, including both Sextius and his son.
But the school did not last beyond the second generation, presumably because its teaching was not sufficiently distinct from
that of the Stoics.[16] The only difference lay in a more exclusive,
typically Roman focus on the moral and practical aspects of philosophy, and in two points of contact with the Pythagorean tradition: (1) the rejection of animal food and (2) the practice, at the
end of each day, of taking stock of one's own moral improvement
or failing during the day.[17]

The earliest reference to this interesting practice is in Cicero,
who calls it a Pythagorean custom (*Pythagoriorum mos*) and treats
it as an exercise in memory (*De senectute* 38). The fullest account is
given by Seneca, who describes Sextius as interrogating himself
each night before going to sleep: "What bad habit have you cured
today? What fault have you resisted? In what respects are you
better?"[18] Precisely the same practice is prescribed in Greek hexa-

---

nomen tuis immanibus et barbaris moribus praetendere. Cf. Ferrero (1955),
308f.

[14] *Tusculanae* IV.2.4: *multa etiam sunt in nostris institutis ducta ab illis* (sc.
Pythagoreis).

[15] For a full account of Sextius and his school, see Zeller III.i (1880),
675–82.

[16] Ibid., following Seneca.

[17] Ibid., 681 n. 5, comparing Seneca *De ira* III.36.1 with the Pythagorean
Golden Verses, 40ff.

[18] Seneca (loc. cit.), Loeb transl., cited by J. C. Thom, *The Pythagorean*

meter verse in the late collection known as the Pythagorean *Golden Verses* 40–44, where the three questions are, "Where did I go wrong today? What did I accomplish? What obligation did I not perform?" The hexameter version is very frequently quoted in antiquity (beginning with Plutarch), and the reference in Cicero *De senectute* shows that the practice was recognized as Pythagorean as early as the first century B.C. Once again we have evidence for an established Pythagorean way of life in the time of Nigidius Figulus, a way of life whose Hellenistic origins we can only guess at. If the practice of self-interrogation formed part of the archaic Pythagorean tradition, it would most likely have originally referred to the observance and violation of the rules formulated in the *akousmata*. (See above, pp. 8–10.) If so, the change in application is extraordinary, for the reference now is to an ideal of moral perfection represented by the Stoic sage. The convergence of Pythagorean ritualism with the Socratic tradition in ethics has produced a new moment in the history of moral consciousness, a new degree of inwardness and self-criticism. An almost modern moral sensitivity has thus penetrated and transformed the classical ideal of directing one's life in "the footsteps of divine Virtue (*theia aretê*)," to quote the Pythagorean *Golden Verses* (verse 46).

In describing his experience with the Sextians, Seneca tells the story of how he, as a young man, was persuaded by Sotion to give up meat, which he did for more than a year. He abandoned this meatless habit when, under Tiberius, it seemed dangerous to be seen practicing a foreign cult. Under these circumstances Seneca's father, who disapproved of a vegetarian diet because (says Seneca) of his hatred for philosophy, had no difficulty in convincing his son to return to a fuller lifestyle. What is striking here are the strongly symbolic connotations of a meatless diet: the elder Seneca sees it as a commitment to (Pythagorean) philosophy; the suspicious emperor will perhaps see it as the practice of an alien cult and hence as conspiratorial behavior. In any case, after Seneca we hear no more of the Sextians. But vegetarianism has a future, of course, as does the practice of nightly self-interrogation.

Golden Verses (Leiden, New York and Köln, 1995), who gives full if uncritical references.

VIII

THE NEOPYTHAGOREAN PHILOSOPHERS

THE TERM "NEOPYTHAGOREAN" HAS BEEN WIDELY AND DIVERSELY used. As a recent historian rightly points out, "Neopythagore-anism comprises both number mysticism, theosophy, belief in miracles . . . , and philosophy; but the name is a loose catch-all—what holds it together is a semi-religious belief in Pythagoras' wisdom."[1] In this chapter the term will be used more narrowly, and it will apply only to philosophers. By the Neopythagoreans I mean those thinkers in the Platonic tradition who derived Plato's philosophy from Pythagoras. We will consider six of these thinkers, beginning with Eudorus.

1. Posidonius, in the early first century B.C., may be regarded as a precursor of the Neopythagorean movement since, although himself a member of the Stoic school, he showed a special interest in the *Timaeus* and cited Pythagoras as a source for the Platonic view of the emotions, which he incorporated into his own

---

[1] K. F. Johansen, *A History of Ancient Philosophy: From the Beginnings to Augustine*, transl. H. Rosenmeier (London and New York, 1998), 514. Hence several recent authors have protested against the use of the term "Neopythagorean." For discussion see M. Bonazzi, "Plotino e la tradizione pitagorica," *ΣΥΝΟΥΣΙΑΙ. Seminario di filosofica antica*, Annali della Facultà di Lettere e Filosofia dell'Università de Milano LIII (2000) 38–73. Bonazzi (46, n. 19) cites a forthcoming study by B. Centrone of "What it means to be a Pythagorean in the period of the Empire."

system.[2] (Posidonius is also apparently responsible for the account of Pythagorean philosophy that we have cited from Sextus in chapter VI.) But the first Hellenistic philosopher known to have expounded a version of Platonic philosophy that is explicitly attributed to the Pythagoreans is Eudorus of Alexandria. Eudorus lived in the second half of the first century B.C., shortly after the renewal of Pythagorean philosophy by Nigidius Figulus in Rome. Apparently, after the decline of skepticism in the Academy under Philo of Larissa, times were ripe for this new movement, which was to change profoundly the Platonic tradition and prepare the way for Neoplatonism.[3]

Eudorus' writings are lost, but we have fragmentary quotations, a summary of his ethical doctrines in Stobaeus (via Arius Didymus), and abundant echoes of his astronomical and logical works in later authors. His work covered every field of philosophy, including a commentary on the *Timaeus* and an attack on Aristotle's *Categories*.[4] Plutarch's essay *On the Generation of the Soul in the Timaeus* repeatedly cites Eudorus' commentary and

---

[2] Posidonius fr. 165, line 168 (Edelstein-Kidd): "Not only Aristotle or Plato held this view [of the emotions as distinct from reason] but others even earlier, including Pythagoras, as Posidonius says, who claims that the view was originally his [viz., Pythagoras'] but Plato developed it and made it more perfect." (Similarly fr. 151.) This is the standard Neopythagorean view of the relation between Pythagoras and Plato. Could it be Posidonius who formulated it for the first time? But see the next note.

[3] The tendency to derive Plato's philosophy from Pythagoras may be older than Posidonius and Eudorus. Michael Frede has suggested that it was probably in the second century B.C., when the Platonic Academy was dominated by skepticism, that philosophers who sought to revive a more dogmatic version of Platonism found it convenient to ascribe the origin of these doctrines to Pythagoras, since there was no place for them in the skeptical Academy. See Frede, "Numenius," *ANRW* II.36.2 (1987), 1043.

[4] For a full discussion, see Dillon (1977), 115–35; recent literature in P. T. Keyser, "Orreries, the Date of [Plato] *Letter* ii, and Eudorus of Alexandria," *Archiv für Geschichte der Philosophie* 80 (1998), 262, n. 104. Keyser refers to a collection of Eudorus' fragments by C. Mazzarelli in *Revista di Filosofia Neoscolastica* 77 (1985), 197–209, 535–55.

seems to be following it closely. He reports that "Eudorus gave a simple and clear explication" of the complex numerology in Plato's construction of the world soul in *Timaeus* 35b–36b.[5] Eudorus' exegesis of the cosmology of the *Timaeus* nicely parallels Cicero's contemporary translation from that same dialogue, the most "Pythagorean" of Plato's works. (And we recall that Cicero actually dedicates his translation to the Roman renewer of the Pythagorean tradition, Nigidius Fibulus.) Both in cosmology and in ethics, Eudorus develops his Platonism in the direction of a transcendental world view conceived as Pythagorean. Eudorus' definition of the *telos*, or supreme good, sets the tone for his conception of Pythagorean philosophy:

> Socrates and Plato agree with Pythagoras that the *telos* is becoming like god (*homoiôsis theôi*). But Plato articulated it more clearly by adding "as far as possible" [*Theaetetus* 176b]; it is possible only by means of wisdom: this is the life according to virtue.[6]

Eudorus presents this Platonic formula as an explication of the traditional Pythagorean command "Follow god," and he makes clear that, for Pythagoras, god is to be understood as an intelligible rather than a visible being "and as source of harmony for the cosmic order." The *Timaeus*, *Republic* and *Theaetetus* are all cited as elaborations of this Pythagorean conception of the *telos* as the divine aim of human life.

In both respects—in his concern with specific Platonic texts and in his developing Platonic doctrine in a theological or otherwordly direction—Eudorus announces the new form of Platon-

---

5 *De animae procr.* 1019e. As Cherniss points out, Plutarch seems to be relying on Eudorus for the views of Xenocrates and Crantor; see Cherniss' note *e* on p. 163 and note *c* on 164f. of the Loeb ed. (Plutarch *Moralia* XII Part I).

6 Stobaeus ii.7.3, p. 49 Wachsmuth. I follow Dillon (1977: 122f.) in assuming that Arius Didymus is here still quoting or paraphrasing Eudorus, whom he began to cite a few pages earlier (p. 42 W.). Note that the assumed relation of Plato to Pythagoras is the same as that in the quotation from Posidonius cited above (p. 95, n. 2).

ism that calls itself Pythagorean. This tendency marks the sharpest possible break with the skepticism of the New Academy, and its doctrinal claims will have an important influence on Middle Platonism as represented in the later *Didaskalikos* or *Handbook* of Alcinous. So, in defining the *telos*, that scholastic manual will repeat the quotation of "becoming like god" from the *Theaetetus*.[7] But the otherwordly tendency that is characteristic of Eudorus will be most conspicuous in that line of Middle Platonic thinkers known as Neopythagorean. Thus in the Roman period the name "Pythagoras" becomes again the code word for a tradition of transcendental Platonism, the very same tradition that was initiated two centuries earlier by Speusippus and Xenocrates. In this respect, and also in the central role assigned to numbers, the Neopythagorean movement can be seen as a return to the doctrines of the late-fourth-century Academy.[8]

The most decisive innovation of Eudorus is his conception of a supreme One, located above the dualism of Monad and Dyad. In this case we have Eudorus' own words in a text preserved by Simplicius:

> One must say that the Pythagoreans teach that on the highest account (*logos*) the One is principle of all things, but on the second account there are two principles of what is produced, the One and the nature opposite to this. And ranked below these are all those things that are conceived in terms of opposition: good things under the One, bad things under the nature opposed to it. Hence these two are not really first principles (*archai*) for this school. For if each is principle of a different set, they are not universal principles of all things, as the One is. . . . Hence in another way the One is first principle of all things, since matter and all Beings (*onta*, presumably Forms) have come into being from it. And this is the supreme god.

---

[7] *Alcinous: The Handbook of Platonism*, transl. J. Dillon (Oxford, 1993), 37.

[8] This is an old observation that bears repeating. A hundred years ago Richard Heinze could write that "it is not yet generally enough appreciated, how closely certain directions in Neopythagoreanism were connected with the Old Academy" (*Xenokrates* [Leipzig, 1892], 38).

Thus, says Simplicius, when Eudorus speaks more precisely, he calls only the highest One a principle (*archê*); the second One, or Monad, and its opposite, the Indefinite Dyad, are named "elements" (*stoicheia*).

> The followers of Pythagoras . . . call these two elements by many appellations: the first is named ordered, definite, known, male, odd, right, light; its opposite is disordered, indefinite, unknown, female, left, even, darkness. So there is the One as first principle, and there is the One and the indefinite Dyad as elements, both of which are in turn one. And it is clear that the One that is principle of all things is distinct from the One opposed to the Dyad, which they also call Monad.[9]

Thus the Old Academy doctrine of the One and the Dyad has been developed by Eudorus as a systematic dualism, articulated in two sets of Pythagorean-sounding opposites; but the One of this pair is not the primeval One. Above these two "principles" is something more primary and universal, the true One or supreme god that is the source of everything else.

We saw that, in the *Pythagorean Notebooks* excerpted by Alexander, there was a monistic tendency to derive the Dyad from the One. In Eudorus this monism becomes more explicit: there is only one genuine *archê*, a first principle from which everything else is derived, including matter; and this first principle is called "the supreme god." Below this comes a secondary One or Monad that has the Dyad as its opposite. But this traditional pair of Platonic or "Pythagorean" opposites are not properly called principles (*archai*) at all but only elements (*stoicheia*), since neither one is universal and both are derived from the primary One.

Because we do not possess a full report, we cannot evaluate Eudorus' originality or recognize to what extent he is returning to an early Academic system like that of Speusippus or Xenocrates. What we can say is that Eudorus is the first known proponent of the kind of transcendental monism that leads to the system of Plotinus, in which a divine One occupies the highest position in a

---

[9] Simplicius, *In Phys.* 181, 10–30.

stratified scheme of levels of reality, all strata of which are in some sense generated from the One.[10]

2. It is a Platonism of just this sort, with heavy Pythagorean overtones, that we find reflected a generation or two later in the Biblical allegories of Philo of Alexandria. Philo is not in the usual sense a Platonic philosopher, and there is no obvious trace of his influence in the later Platonic tradition before the Christian Church Fathers (in particular the Alexandrians, Clement and Origen), who took over his allegorical interpretation of the Old Testament. This great importance for the Christian tradition explains, of course, why Philo's writings have been so well preserved. But it is a further (and much disputed) question how far the new perspective introduced by Philo from Jewish monotheism contributed significantly to the increasingly transcendental conception of deity in Neopythagorean and Neoplatonic philosophy.

Philo's great achievement was to make use of Greek philosophy, and the Greek allegorical technique of finding moral and cosmological doctrine in Homer, in order to provide a systematically philosophical reading of the Hebrew Bible, and thus to give the Bible a secure home in the Greek intellectual world. Philo's importance for us, on the other hand, is that, since he had mastered the philosophy of his day, and since most of his work has reached us intact, his writings present us with a full-scale example of Alexandrian Platonism in the first half of the first century A.D. They thus serve to put flesh and bones on the bare skeleton provided by the fragments and testimonia for Eudorus.[11]

Like Eudorus, Philo is a Platonist who has absorbed many terms and concepts from other philosophical traditions: from Aristotle, for example, and above all from Stoicism as the major

---

[10] The closest parallel to Eudorus' monism in the pseudopythagorean literature is pseudo-Archytas *Peri archôn*, cited above, p. 77. The date of this treatise is unknown, but the echoes of technical Aristotelian terminology (*to tode ti* and *to hypokeimenon* in Thesleff [1965], 19) suggest to me a post-Hellenistic date.

[11] For a full discussion, see Dillon (1977), 139–83, who points out that Philo does not follow Eudorus slavishly but represents the same general position. See also D. T. Runia, "Why does Clement of Alexandria call Philo 'The Pythagorean'?" *Vigiliae Christianae* 49 (1995), 1–22.

creative force in Hellenistic philosophy. Like Eudorus again, his Platonism emphasizes the transcendental tendency in Plato's world view. And Philo, like Eudorus, thinks of this view as inherited by Plato from Pythagoras.

In his account of creation, Philo anticipates Augustine and the Neoplatonists by finding in the first verses of Genesis the creation of an intelligible world, which serves as paradigm for the creation of the natural world that follows.[12] Whereas for Plato the Forms are independent of the demiurge and provide him with a model for the creation of the natural world, for Philo (as later for Augustine) the intelligible model is itself an object created by God. Thus, as a pious Jew, Philo conceives the ontological distance between God and the world as even greater than in the hierarchical system of Eudorus.

Philo is perhaps the first Platonist to describe God as "unnameable," "unspeakable," and "incomprehensible."[13] What we know of God is his *logos* and his other Powers. This divine *logos* corresponds to the noetic model for creation in the *Timaeus* and thus to the realm of Platonic Forms. In Philo's exposition, the Forms are sometimes conceived as ideas or thoughts in the mind of God (as in the Middle Platonism of Alcinous), but more properly as the rationally accessible aspect of God Himself and the instrument by which He creates the world. Apparently the Ideas are also interpreted as numbers, in the tradition going back to Xenocrates. In recounting the six days of creation, Philo pauses to explain the special virtues of the number four (the day on which God completed the creation of the heavens) and the number six (when the whole creation was complete). The number four is celebrated for containing the musical ratios (2:1, 3:2, 4:3), which are displayed in

---

[12] *De opific.* 16, cited by Dillon (1977), 159. Philo also anticipates Augustine by denying the creation of the world in time· "There was no time before the world, but it came to be either with the world or after it" (*De opific.* 26).

[13] Dillon (1977), 155, citing *Somn.* I.67: ἀκατανόμαστος καὶ ἄρρητος καὶ κατὰ πάσας ἰδέας ἀκατάληπτος. Dillon finds here a reflection of the negative theology that describes the highest deity only by denying attributes, as later in Alcinous 10.4–5. However, the negative theology is in fact not attested before Philo, as Dillon recognizes.

the heavens. But it also contains the number three, for the three dimensions of the physical body that is created (length, breadth, height), while four denotes the four stages in the generation of such a body: point, line, plane surface, solid (*De opificio mundi*, 48–9). These are all familiar Platonic-Pythagorean notions. Like Platonic Forms, the incorporeal essences of number thus make possible both the creation of the physical world and our understanding of it. (This recalls Speusippus' view, in which the numbers replace Platonic Forms.) But it is above all the number seven, for the day of the Sabbath, that receives Philo's most elaborate praise. "I do not know if anyone can adequately sing the virtues of the number seven, for they are greater than any rational account (*logos*). . . . But even if we cannot describe all or the most important, we must dare to make clear what is accessible to our thought" (*De opificio mundi* 90). Included in Philo's praise of seven, which goes on for a dozen pages, is the following comment:

> As I have said, seven is the only number whose nature is neither to generate [another number within the decad] nor be generated. Hence some philosophers compare this number to the motherless Victory and Maiden [i.e., Athena] . . . , but the Pythagoreans compare it to the ruler of the universe. . . . My statement is confirmed by the testimony of Philolaus, who says "One god, who is forever, is prince and ruler of all things, stable, unmoved, himself similar to himself, different from others." (ibid., 100)[14]

Thus Philo's numerology is deliberately Pythagorean. It has its roots not only in genuine Old Pythagorean tradition but also in Plato's construction of the world soul in the *Timaeus*, and in Speusippus' reinterpretation of Platonic Forms as the first ten natural numbers.[15] Philo is apparently making use of some standard

---

[14] This quotation from "Philolaus" (fr. 20 DK) is assigned by another author to Onatas of Tarentum; see Thesleff (1965), 140, 151. For discussion, see Huffman (1993), 334–9. Huffman points out that Aristotle fr. 203 (from Alexander) attributes this view of seven as the "motherless Athena" to the early Pythagoreans.

[15] Cf. Dillon (1977), 159: "Philo is fully acquainted with Pythagorean

expositions of Pythagorean number-symbolism, the source for which seems to go back to the second century B.C.[16]

Many texts in Philo suggest a hierarchical system like the one we have described for Eudorus. The following is a striking example:

> In the first place there is He who is elder than the One and the Monad and the Beginning (*archê*). Then comes the Logos of the Existent (*to on*, or *ho ôn*), the seminal substance of existing things. And from the divine Logos, as from a spring, there divide two Powers. One is the creative power, through which the Artificer (*technitês*) established and ordered all things; this is named "God." And the other is the royal power, since through it the Creator (*demiourgos*) rules over created things; this is named "Lord." And from these two Powers have grown the others. . . . And below these and beside them is the Ark; and the Ark is a symbol of the intelligible world.[17]

In this text the Platonic demiurge, the creator of our visible world, stands as it were at third remove from Philo's ineffable God, with the divine Logos or realm of Platonic Ideas in between. As a monotheist, Philo will of course not conceive this hierarchy as a descending series of gods, but only as powers or emanations from the unique, unnameable God. Yet we see how easily such a scheme in pagan hands will generate a hierarchy of gods. The effect in either case is to increase the distance between the highest

---

numerology in the form in which we find it in Plutarch, Theon of Smyrna or Nicomachus of Gerasa." See the next note.

[16] See F. E. Robbins, "The Tradition of Greek Arithmology," *CP* 16 (1921), 97–123, who shows by elaborate parallels between many authors that the enormous literature on Pythagorean numerology must go back to an influential source known to Varro and apparently to Posidonius as well (fr. 291 Edelstein-Kidd) and hence no later than the second century B.C. This source may be roughly contemporary with (although entirely independent of) the *Pythagorean Notebooks* excerpted by Alexander Polyhistor. See above, pp. 79f.

[17] *Questions and Answers on "Exodus"* II. 68, translation after Marcus in Loeb ed. of Philo, Supplement II, pp. 116f.

deity (or the one God) and the natural world. That is why for Philo the true God is not only "unspeakable" (*arrêtos*) but Unknowable (*agnôstos*). Philo does not actually use this epithet, made familiar by Paul's reference to an Unknown God in his sermon on the Areopagus (Acts 17:23), but Philo's doctrine would support it.[18] Like the Stoics (and like Aquinas much later), Philo believes that reason can establish the existence of God but cannot know His nature.

> For reason (*logos*) cannot ascend to God, who is in every way untouchable and unattainable; . . . it cannot find the proper words to use as a basis for revealing, I do not say Him Who Is (*ho ôn*), for if the whole heaven should become an articulate voice, it would lack the apt and appropriate terms required for this, but [reason cannot describe] even God's attendant powers (*doruphoroi dunameis*).[19]

Even Moses, who was privileged to converse with God, was not able to see His face but only what comes behind God. Philo comments:

> Everything that is after God is comprehensible to the good person, but He only is incomprehensible (*akatalêptos*) . . . but comprehensible from the powers that attend on him; for they manifest not his essence (*ousia*) but his existence (*hyparxis*) from the things that he accomplishes."[20]

---

[18] On the subject of the Unknown God, the classic work is Eduard Norden, *Agnostos Theos* (Berlin, 1913). Norden's penetrating study employs a crude distinction between the "purely Hellenic" and the Oriental-Semitic. (See especially pp. 83f., 97f.; the alleged change begins with Posidonius, who comes from Syria.) See the response of A.-J. Festugière, *La révélation d'Hermes Trismégiste*, Vol. IV: *Le dieu inconnu et la gnose* (Paris, 1954), 2–5, and the comments of E. R. Dodds, *Proclus: The Elements of Theology* (2nd ed., Oxford, 1963), 310–3.

[19] *Legatio ad Gaium* 6, translation after Dillon (1977), 156.

[20] *De posteritate Caini* 169, cited by B. A. Pearson, "Philo and Gnosticism," *ANRW* 21.1 (1984), 305.

For Gnostics, access to the highest god is made possible by a special, transrational mode of cognition, or *gnôsis*. Philo occasionally refers to an experience of this kind, which he compares to the prophetic knowledge of God and contrasts with the intellectual attempt to comprehend the Creator by reasoning from his creation. The latter procedure is guesswork, like trying to understand the monad from the dyad, whereas one must begin with the monad, as the first principle (*archê*). Access to God is from Himself alone, a free gift to the suppliant: "They seek truth who apprehend God through God, light through light."[21]

When Philo attempts to describe this transrational experience, he combines the Platonic notion of divine madness with more popular concepts of inspiration and possession:

> When the divine light shines, the human light sets . . . and this is what happens to the race of prophets. For our reason (*nous*) leaves home at the arrival of the divine Spirit (*pneuma*), and at its departure the former returns. For it is not lawful for the mortal and immortal to dwell together. Hence the setting of reason (*logismos*) and the darkness around it beget ecstasy (*ekstasis*) and god-given madness.[22]

This appeal to transrational experience is, however, not typical of Philo's theological stance. He normally relies on revelation in a more prosaic sense. In a religion with a divinely inspired Bible, the alternative to rational knowledge is not so much mystical vision as simply the Word of God revealed in His Book. That is what Philo sets out to explicate, with the help of Platonic philosophy. When Philo calls God "unnameable" and "unspeakable" (*arrhêtos*), he is not only echoing Plato's Seventh Epistle[23] but also reflecting the Jewish ban on pronouncing the proper name of God. In this respect Philo's Judaism, with its ceremonial awe before the Name of God, gives its own form to the development of transcendental theology in the Platonic-Pythagorean tradition.

---

[21] *De praemiis* 43–6, cited by Pearson (1984), 305f.

[22] *Heres*, 264–5, cited by Pearson (1984), 306f.

[23] *Ep.* VII, 341c5: ῥῆτον οὐδαμῶς.

3. It is against this background of Alexandrian Platonism, as represented by Eudorus and Philo in the period from approximately 50 B.C. to 50 A.D., that we can comprehend the emergence of doctrinaire Neopythagoreanism in the works of three obscure but influential figures: Moderatus of Gades in the latter half of the first century A.D., Nicomachus of Gerasa and Numenius of Apamea in the second century. Unlike Eudorus, these three philosophers do not simply report the views of Pythagoras with sympathy; they adopt his teachings as their own. Their activity spans two centuries and the whole breadth of the Roman empire: Moderatus is from western Spain (Gades is the modern Cadíz); the other two are from the Middle East (Gerasa today is Jerash in Jordan; Apamea lies in Syria).

The first of these, Moderatus, is the most outspoken. For him Plato and his school are not simply followers of Pythagoras; they are actually plagiarists. "Plato and Aristotle, Speusippus, Aristoxenus, and Xenocrates have taken for themselves the fairest fruit of Pythagorean thought, only arranging it a little; they collected and assigned as proper to the school only what is superficial and trivial and what is serviceable for the rejection and mockery of this school by those who later slander it maliciously."[24] (The slanderous collections in question must include Aristotle's work in recording Pythagorean taboos and *akousmata*; these Neopythagoreans have no use for the more primitive features of the Pythagorean tradition.) Moderatus' hostile view of Plato and his school as ungrateful heirs to Pythagorean wisdom may owe something to Aristoxenus' account, which it resembles (above, pp. 70f.). But it must above all reflect Moderatus' acceptance of Pythagorean pseudepigrapha (which largely consist of Platonic and Aristotelian material) as genuine writings of the early Pythagorean school, and hence as older than Plato. If the works ascribed to them are authentic, Philolaus, Archytas, and Timaeus of Locri were in possession of Platonic and Aristotelian philosophy well before Plato and Aristotle.

The authentic Pythagorean doctrine, according to Moderatus, is much more subtle than the traditional account of this teaching. Because of the difficulty in explaining primary Forms and prin-

---

[24] Porphyry *VP* 53.

ciples, these philosophers could not describe them directly but had recourse to numbers for the sake of pedagogical clarity. The numbers represent the Forms, just as written letters represent the spoken sounds of the language, and as a geometric diagram illustrates the triangle in a mathematical theorem.

> Unable to give a clear account in language (*logos*) of the primary Forms and first principles because of the difficulty in conceiving and expressing them, the Pythagoreans resorted to numbers for the sake of a lucid exposition (εὔσημος διδασκαλία), imitating the geometers and grammarians. For the latter, when they want to teach the elements of language (*stoicheia*) and their powers, resort to written characters [i.e., the letters of the alphabet] for the first instruction and say that these are the elements (*stoicheia*). Later, however, they teach that these characters are not the elements but through them one acquires a conception of the true elements [viz., the sounds]. And the geometers, who are unable to present incorporeal things in language (*logos*), resort to figures in diagrams and say that this is a triangle; they do not mean that the triangle is this visible thing but that it is of this sort (*to toiouto*), and they present the concept of triangle by means of this diagram. The Pythagoreans did the same in the case of primary reasons (*logoi*) and Forms. Since they are unable to communicate in language (*logôi paradidonai*) the incorporeal Forms and first principles, they resorted to an explanation by means of numbers.[25]

Thus Moderatus reinterprets in semiotic terms the epistemic and pedagogical function of mathematics as a prelude to dialectic, as described by Plato in the *Republic*. All the mysteries of Pythagorean numerology are to be understood as so many symbols, hints, or tokens for a deeper comprehension of the immaterial Forms, the principles of cosmic order. The Pythagorean One, on this account, is not a numerical unit at all, but a unifying principle:

---

[25] Porphyry *VP*, 48–9, citing Moderatus' collection of Pythagorean doctrine of numbers in eleven books.

> In this way they called "one" the *logos* of unity and sameness and equality and the cause of affinity (*sympnoia*) and sympathy in the universe and (the cause) of preservation for stability and invariance. . . . They called Dyad and duality the principle of otherness and inequality and everything divisible and changing and variable.[26]

Similarly, the number three signifies a nature that has beginning, middle, and end, and is accordingly ordered so as to be complete. And so on for the other numbers up to ten.

What Moderatus offers, then, is a sophisticated reinterpretation of Pythagorean number theory in the light of the kind of conceptual analysis exemplified in Plato's discussion of the One and the Others in the second part of the *Parmenides*. We shall see that, for other reasons as well, that dialogue turns out to be of fundamental importance for the Neopythagorean and Neoplatonic traditions.

A passage in Simplicius cites Moderatus in connection with a more systematic scheme, in which there are three distinct levels of unity:

> He declares that, according to the Pythagoreans, the first One is above Being (*to einai*) and all essence (*ousia*); the second One, which is true and intelligible Being (*to ontôs on kai noêton*), he says is the Forms; the third or psychic One participates in the (first) One and in the Forms. After this, the last nature is that of sensible things; it no longer participates [in the higher levels] but is ordered by their reflection or manifestation (*emphasis*). Matter in sensible things is a shadow of Not-Being, whose primary form is Quantity (*to poson*), but matter has descended still further even from that [i.e., from Quantity as a formal expression of Not-Being].[27]

Simplicius goes on to quote from Porphyry ("in his second book

---

[26] Ibid., 49–50.

[27] Simplicius, *In Phys.* 230f. The last clause is obscure, but it seems that Not-Being as a Form and Quantity as a category connected with number both belong to the higher, intelligible level, so that sensible matter can only manifest their shadow.

On Matter, where he is presenting the views of Moderatus") the
following account of matter:

> As Plato says somewhere, since the unitary principle (*ho he-
> niaios logos*) decided to construct the becoming of beings
> from itself, it made room for Quantity (*posotês*) by depriving
> itself of all its own *logoi* and Forms. . . .[28] [This account of
> quantity by privation is then presented as an interpretation
> of the passage on the Receptacle in the *Timaeus*.] . . . This
> Form, intelligibly conceived (*nooumenon*) by privation of the
> unitary principle . . . is model (*paradeigma*) for the matter of
> bodies, which is also called quantity (*poson*) by the
> Pythagoreans and Plato, not quantity as a Form but quantity
> by privation and weakening and extension and scattering
> and deviation from Being (*to on*). Hence matter seems evil,
> since it flees from the Good. But it is contained by the latter
> and is not permitted to pass beyond the boundaries (*hoi
> horoi*), since extension admits the *logos* of formal magnitude
> and is determined by this, and scattering is structured by
> numerical distinction. (Ibid.)

Here we have the typical Neopythagorean reading of the *Timaeus*,
in which the physical universe is conceived as matter (Aristotle's
term now applied to Plato's Receptacle) structured by principles
or *logoi*, like the spermatic *logoi* of the Stoics except that these *logoi*
are interpreted Platonically, in numerical or mathematical terms.
And these quantitative *logoi* of the physical world are sharply distinguished from the intelligible Quantity that is a Form or category, the subject of pure mathematics. Furthermore, since matter
is here conceived not only as a privation of Being but as a scatter-
ing or dismemberment (*diaspasmos*) and a flight from Being, with
Moderatus we begin to have, perhaps for the first time, a morally
loaded conception of matter as the source of evil in the universe.
This radically negative view of matter is often thought of as typically "Gnostic." But such a conception was perhaps implicit from

---

[28] Or (reading ἐχώρισε for ἐχώρησε in 231, 9 with Zeller and Festugière):
"separated quantity from itself by privation." See Festugière (1954)
IV, 38.

the beginning in the Pythagorean table of opposites, for instance in the view formulated by Eudorus, where "good things (*to asteion*) are ranked under the One, and inferior things (*to phaulon*) under the nature opposite to this" (above, p. 97). One can perhaps find the seed of such a view in the *Timaeus*, where the Receptacle as material principle is associated with *anankê*, "Necessity," as the force resisting the rational activity of the demiurge. But the Receptacle, as mother of becoming, is certainly not represented by Plato as a source of evil, and there is no trace of such a conception in the chapter on matter in Alcinous, the handbook of Middle Platonism. It is this negative view of matter, implicit in Eudorus, that becomes explicit in Moderatus. Perhaps we should regard this view not as distinctively Gnostic but as genuinely Neopythagorean. At the same time, the monistic tendency in both Eudorus and Moderatus (and even earlier in the *Pythagorean Notebooks*), which derives all things including matter from the One as universal *archê*, sets limits to the dualism that will ultimately recognize matter as a radically independent principle. In the latter case, matter tends to be conceived not in terms of privation, as the absence of structure and form, but as a positive power, an aggressive source of evil. It is perhaps only this extreme dualism that is distinctively Gnostic—and we shall find such dualism in Numenius. Moderatus, on the other hand, insists upon the principle of monism by deriving the Dyad from the Monad.

As Simplicius is not quoting Moderatus directly but citing him from a paraphrase in Porphyry, we cannot be certain of the accuracy of these texts. In the first passage quoted above, the three levels of the incorporeal world resemble so closely the system of Plotinus that Zeller argued that the similarity must result from Porphyry's retroactive reshaping of Moderatus' view according to the Plotinian model.[29] However, in an epoch-making article in 1928 on the origins of the Neoplatonic One, E. R. Dodds showed that two of the three unities in Moderatus' scheme correspond to the Ones of the first two deductions in the second part of Plato's *Parmenides*.[30] The One beyond Being corresponds to the absolute

---

[29] Zeller III.ii (1881), 126, n. 2.

[30] "The *Parmenides* of Plato and the Origin of the Neoplatonic 'One,'" *CQ* 22 (1928), 129–42.

One of the first deduction, in which all attributes are denied (*Parm.* 137c–42a); the One of *nous* and the Forms corresponds to the inclusive One of the second deduction, the One for which all attributes are affirmed (142b ff.). Dodds argued convincingly that this Neoplatonic interpretation of the *Parmenides* (and the negative theology that goes with it) was older than Plotinus, and must originate either with Moderatus or with some unknown earlier Neopythagorean. Dodds also suggested that the basic idea here, of a series of ontological levels descending from the One, may well go back to Speusippus as founding father of the Neopythagorean tradition.[31]

Since our information concerning Moderatus is so scanty, and our knowledge of Speusippus hardly better, we cannot well judge the originality of Moderatus' scheme. In any case, what is subject to dispute here among scholars is largely a matter of degree. The Neopythagorean One above the Forms in Moderatus, like the supreme One of Eudorus that lies above the Monad-Dyad opposition, clearly points the way to a hierarchical system for the intelligible cosmos that resembles what we find later in Plotinus. Or, looking at the same sequence from the later point of view, we can say that Plotinus incorporates fundamental concepts from the Neopythagorean tradition into his own great Neoplatonic synthesis.

4. With Nicomachus in the second century A.D., we encounter a less significant Pythagorean philosopher but a highly influential writer on arithmetic, music, and theological numerology.[32] His treatises on arithmetic and harmonics have come down to us intact, as well as large excerpts from his work on numerology. I will first survey his writings and then summarize his philosophical views.

Nicomachus' *Introduction to Arithmetic* became one of the great

---

[31] Ibid., 140. For recent discussion see C. Turnau, "Die Prinzipienlehre des Moderatus von Gades," *Rheinisches Museum für Philologie* 143 (2000), 197–220.

[32] Nicomachus must have lived in the early second century if it is true that Apuleius (born c. 125 A.D.) translated his *Introduction to Arithmetic* into Latin.

textbook successes both in late antiquity and in the middle ages. Of the many Greek commentaries, those by Iamblichus, Asclepius of Tralles, and Philoponus have survived.[33] Apuleius is said to have made the first translation into Latin, but the classic Latin version was composed by Boethius. Boethius' *De institutione arithmetica* (which "has so little claim to originality that it may be called a translation")[34] became for many centuries the standard text for arithmetic in the West, paralleling Euclid's treatise in geometry.

Nicomachus' book is essentially a school manual, not the work of a major mathematician. As Heath has observed, the *Introduction* must be judged not as a contribution to mathematics but as "a popular treatment of the subject calculated to awaken in the beginner an interest in the theory of numbers. . . . It was the mystic rather than the mathematical side of the theory of numbers that interested Nicomachus."[35]

Much the same can be said for Nicomachus' *Enchiridion* or *Handbook of Harmonics*. Its popularity in antiquity is attested by the fact that it "has the honor of being the only work on the subject to survive complete from the period between Euclid and Ptolemy," that is, between 300 B.C. and 150 A.D.[36] Although it does not rank as a significant contribution to the subject considered as

---

[33] See F. E. Robbins, chapter IX, pp. 124–37 in M. L. D'Ooge, transl., *Nicomachus of Gerasa: Introduction to Arithmetic* (New York, 1926); and, more recently L. Tarán, "Asclepius of Tralles' commentary to Nicomachus' Introduction to Arithmetic," *Transactions of the American Philosophical Society* n.s. 59.8 (1969). Tarán (p. 10) argues that the commentaries of Asclepius and Philoponus both go back to a course on Nicomachus' *Introduction* given by their teacher Ammonius.

[34] F. E. Robbins in D'Ooge (1926), 132. For the importance of the Nicomachus-Boethius school tradition in establishing Pythagoras as the creator of Greek mathematics, see Burkert (1972), 406.

[35] Heath (1921), 98. Compare the similar judgment of Robbins (1926), 65.

[36] A. Barker (1989), 245, who offers a translation of the *Enchiridion*. There is reason to believe that Nicomachus also composed a more substantial *Introduction to Music*, preserved in Books 1–3 of Boethius' Latin version. See C. M. Bower, *Boethius, Fundamentals of Music* (New Haven, 1989), xxvii.

a branch of mathematics, it does expound the theory of music from a Pythagorean point of view, including an attempt to connect the ratios of musical harmony with regularities governing the movement of the heavenly bodies.[37] Nicomachus' version of harmonics thus preserves the traditional aspiration of Pythagorean cosmology to interpret the celestial motions in terms of the musical numbers, the aspiration that will be continued by Ptolemy and eventually find its greatest achievement in the work of Kepler.

Nicomachus also wrote an *Introduction to Geometry* and a *Life of Pythagoras*, both of which are lost. Important sections of the book on Pythagoras' life can, however, be reconstructed from parallel passages in the two extant *Lives* of Pythagoras by Porphyry and Iamblichus. From these parallels, we see that Nicomachus' lost work gave a full account of Pythagoras' more miraculous achievements, and that it thus played an important role in transmitting and reshaping the hagiographical version of the Master's life.[38]

Nicomachus does not present a clear and coherent metaphysical scheme. However, since his works are preserved, while those of Moderatus and Numenius are almost entirely lost, it will be useful to survey his views as a standard account of Neopythagorean philosophy in the second century A.D.

Nicomachus begins like an orthodox Platonist by quoting the *Timaeus* for the distinction between unchanging, noetic Being and corporeal, sensible Becoming; the former are truly Beings (*onta*); the changing participants are beings only homonymously, "called by the same name." Like Moderatus, Nicomachus interprets Plato's Receptacle in terms of matter: "Bodily, material things are forever involved in continuous flow and change, imitating the nature of that eternal matter and substance (*hupostasis*) which has been from the beginning, changeable and variable throughout."[39] In an even greater deviation from the *Timaeus*, Nicomachus

---

[37] Barker (1989), pp. 250–3.

[38] For the reconstruction of Nicomachus' *Life of Pythagoras*, see Burkert (1972), 98, nn. 5–6. For the miraculous elements, see Burkert's notes to pp. 141f.

[39] *Introductio arithmeticae* I.1.3, translation after D'Ooge.

recognizes a class of incorporeal attributes modeled on Aristotle's categories:

> the incorporeals which we conceive in connection with or together with matter, such as qualities, quantities, configurations, magnitude, smallness, equality, relations, actualities, dispositions, places, times, in a word all those things which comprise the properties in each body—these are in themselves unmoved and unchanging, but accidentally they share in and partake of the affections of the body which is their subject (*hupokeimenon*).[40]

It is these immaterial forms or categories that are studied by the four "sister sciences" recognized by the Pythagoreans; and here Nicomachus cites Archytas (fr. 1) for a description of the sister sciences: arithmetic, geometry, astronomy, and music (*Introduction* I.3.4). In contrast with the order in Euclid, which begins with geometry, Nicomachus argues that arithmetic is the first and most fundamental science, since arithmetic can exist without geometry but not conversely. Furthermore, in studying numbers arithmetic studies the highest Beings in the intelligible realm. For Nicomachus, number theory can almost take the place of metaphysics, since arithmetic is itself the primary science in the mind of the demiurge, a plan and pattern for the creation of the material universe.

> Arithmetic itself pre-exists in the thought of the artisan god before everything else, as a paradigmatic ordering plan (*logos*), on which the craftsman (*demiourgos*) of the universe relies as on a design and archetype for ordering the things produced from matter and making them achieve their proper end (*telos*).[41]

---

[40] Ibid. This can scarcely count as a systematic list of categories, since (as Robbins points out, in D'Ooge [1926], 95, n. 1) for Nicomachus, quantity belongs under magnitude (I.2.5), and equality is a relation (II.6.3). Nicomachus is relying on a familiar doctrine of Middle Platonism which holds (against the Stoics) that the qualities that determine bodies are themselves incorporeal. Compare Alcinous, *Handbook*, ch. 11.

[41] *Introductio arithmeticae* I.4.2.

Two chapters later the craftsman of the universe is called *nous*, and it is number rather than arithmetic that is said to preexist in the thought of the cosmic god:

> All things in the world that have been arranged by nature in an artistic process . . . appear to have been distinguished and ordered according to number, by providence and the Intellect (*nous*) that creates the universe. For the pattern was fixed, like a preliminary sketch, by the controlling role of number, pre-existent in the thought of the world-making god, number intelligible only and altogether immaterial, and yet the true and eternal Being (*ousia*), so that by reference to this as to an artistic plan (*logos technikos*), all these things should be produced: time, motion, heaven, stars, revolutions of all sorts (*Introduction to Arithmetic* I.6.1, transl. after D'Ooge).

Mathematics in general and the theory of numbers in particular have thus taken over the role assigned to paradigmatic Forms in the *Timaeus*, as the model for the construction of the circular motions of the heavens. The Forms had already been absorbed as Ideas in the mind of god in Philo and in Middle Platonism; they are now reinterpreted in Pythagorean (i.e., Speusippean) style as the numbers.[42] Or, speaking more precisely, we might say that Nicomachus has replaced Plato's Forms in two or three different ways. First of all, there are the categories or properties that inform matter and thus structure the physical world, as illustrated by the list given above (qualities, quantities, places, times, etc.). Not sharply distinguished from these is what Nicomachus calls "scientific number," and which he studies in the *Introduction to Arithmetic*. Scientific number consists of two opposing species, the odd and the even, which contain the essence (*ousia*) of quantity and are harmoniously fitted together in all the ways that the science of

---

[42] Close links between the metaphysics of Nicomachus and the doctrines of the Old Academy are also noted by H. J. Krämer, *Der Ursprung der Geistmetaphysik* (Amsterdam, 1967), 23–7, who, however, detects the influence of Xenocrates rather than Speusippus.

arithmetic will unfold (I.6.4).[43] But above all these formal principles, at the highest noetic level, stand the ten numbers of the
Pythagorean decad. As purely noetic entities, they will be the object of the highest science of all, which turns out to be theological
numerology.

Nicomachus' *Introduction to Arithmetic* had as its sequel a
Greater Arithmetic or *Arithmetical Theology*, which is partially preserved in a text entitled "Theology of Arithmetic" (*Theologoumena
arithmeticae*) attributed to Iamblichus. From the point of view of
intellectual history, this was Nicomachus' most epoch-making
work. In standard examples of Pythagorean numerology such as
we find in Philo and Varro, the significance of numbers is illustrated by applications to cosmology and natural philosophy, including the medical and magical properties of plants, or to moral
concepts like justice and friendship.[44] But there is another line in
the Pythagorean tradition where the numbers are associated with
the pagan gods, sometimes identified astrologically as the heavenly bodies. This tradition is certainly older than Philo, and in
some respects probably older than the Stoic practice of allegorical
interpretation for the traditional gods. The origins may go back to
the Platonic Academy, where Xenocrates is reported to have identified the Monad and Dyad as gods: "the former as male holds the
position of father and rules as king in heaven; he [Xenocrates] calls
it Zeus and odd and *nous*, who is for him the first god; the dyad as
feminine, in the fashion of mother of the gods, governs the realm
under the heavens; she is for Xenocrates the world soul."[45]

Our evidence is incomplete, but it suggests that Xenocrates de-
ified only the Monad and the Dyad as supreme principles, not all

---

[43] For a full discussion of Nicomachus' philosophy of mathematics, see
F. E. Robbins in chs. VII and VIII of D'Ooge (1926).

[44] See Robbins (1921). Compare the earlier discussion in A. Delatte,
Études sur la littérature pythagoricienne (Paris, 1915), especially 139–64,
206–8. Recent literature on Nicomachus and Anatolius is cited by D. J.
O'Meara *Pythagoras Revived: Mathematics and Philosophy in Late Antiquity*, (Oxford, 1989), 14–25.

[45] Xenocrates fr. 15 Heinze = Aetius I.7.30. Instead of "in the fashion of

the numbers up to ten, which is what we find in Nicomachus. As the title "Theology of Arithmetic" implies, in Nicomachus' work the theological interpretation of the numbers becomes the most significant aspect of the subject, and it remains decisive for Iamblichus and Proclus in the following centuries. Nicomachus thus serves as the major authority for the most irrational tendency in later Neopythagorean and Neoplatonic traditions.[46] Plato's dialectic, as the highest philosophical study, is in effect replaced by theosophical numerology.

A few examples will serve to illustrate this aspect of Nicomachus' work. His exposition follows in order the ten numbers of the decad, as in Speusippus' *On Pythagorean Numbers*, in Anatolius' *On the Decad*, and no doubt in many lost Pythagorean treatises. Concerning the first unit or monad, Nicomachus has the following to say:

> It is fitting to match god with the monad, since god is in a seminal way (*spermatikôs*) all beings in nature, as the monad is [potentially all things] in number; for things which appear in actuality to be extreme opposites, in absolutely every mode of opposition, are potentially contained within it, just as we saw, throughout the *Introduction to Arithmetic*, that the monad took on every form by a certain ineffable nature. . . . The monad is absolutely the most authoritative of all things, like a pure light, sunlike and governing (*hêgemonikos*), so that it may resemble god in each of these respects, and above all in being a source of friendship and union for things mul-

---

mother of the gods" (μητρὸς θεῶν δίκην), some scholars would read "Justice (Δίκη), mother of the gods." See Krämer (1967), 36, n. 50.

There may be an even earlier Pythagorean tradition of numerical theology, if we can trust the report in Aristotle fr. 203, that the (pre-Platonic) Pythagoreans identified the number seven as the "motherless Athena." See above, p. 101, n. 14.

[46] Hence we can understand why Iamblichus wrote commentaries on Nicomachus' works and Proclus claimed to be a reincarnation of Nicomachus (Marinus, *Life of Proclus*, 28).

tifarious and most diverse, as god has harmonized and unified this universe from things similarly opposed.[47]

Nicomachus goes on to show that the monad is resembled or represented not only by god but also by mind (*nous*), as being "what is most governing in god, not only in world-making but in every art and rational structure (*logos*)," as well as by the fate Atropos as being unchanging, by Prometheus as "not running forward" (an etymological pun on the name: *prosô mê thein*), by *chaos* as being the primordial entity in Hesiod's cosmogony, and by other divine principles as well. Thus the monad is both male and female, as universal father and mother. And it produces the dyad by dispersion (*diaphorêtheisa*).[48]

For the dyad we may quote Robbins's summary:

> The dyad naturally derives most of its titles from its character as "otherness," the opposite of the monad [which is characterized as "sameness"]. Hence comes the title "matter," and thence in turn "unequal," "excess," "deficiency"; but on the other hand "equality" was seen in it because $2 \times 2 = 2 + 2$. It is the root of all relativity, because 2:1 is the first ratio; and a very old epithet, repeated by Nicomachus, is "daring," derived from the idea that 2 first "dares" to separate itself from the original unity. . . . Among deities, Erato, Phanes, Zeus, Isis, Rhea-Demeter, Artemis, and Aphrodite were associated with the dyad.[49]

The gods of pagan polytheism thus reappear as aspects or symbolical equivalents of the Pythagorean numbers. Looking ahead, we

---

[47] Excerpt from Nicomachus in Iamblichus (?) *Theologoumena arithmeticae*, p. 3 De Falco = pp. 4–5 Ast.

[48] Ibid., pp. 3–5 De Falco = pp. 5–6 Ast. Photius' paraphrase reports that the monad was also identified as Styx, Atlas, the Tower of Zeus, the spermatic *logos*, and Apollo. Parallels show that here again Nicomachus is reflecting a very old, cumulative tradition, that may go back even to Xenocrates, who identified Atropos with the unchangeable noetic region beyond the heavens (fr. 5 Heinze).

[49] Robbins in D'Ooge (1926), 104f. For a fuller summary of Nicomachus' divine numerology, see Dillon (1977), 355–9.

can note how important this numerical theology became in late Neoplatonic philosophy. For example, in the scheme of Iamblichus at the end of the third century, above the intelligible Being of ideal numbers or Forms there was a higher level transcending all: the gods conceived as divine numbers.[50] Despite its absence from Plotinus' own thought, this arithmetical theology becomes codified in the final Neoplatonic synthesis by Proclus in the fifth century A.D. Proposition 114 in Proclus' *Elements of Theology* states that "every god is a self-complete henad or unit, and every self-complete henad is a god." The gods in question are in fact the gods of traditional Greek mythology, such as Zeus and Hera. Proclus' scheme of henads was, of course, a great deal more complex than the old *tetractus*. But it was Nicomachus' systematic correlation between the first ten numbers and the Olympian gods that provided Iamblichus and Proclus with this peculiar device, in their desperate effort to "maintain the united front of Hellenic philosophy and Hellenic religion against the inroads of Christianity."[51]

5. The last important Neopythagorean philosopher was Numenius, who is perhaps the most original thinker and certainly the most colorful writer in the ancient Pythagorean tradition. Even more than in the case of Moderatus, in Numenius we can recognize an anticipation of many lines of thought that were later taken up in the work of Plotinus. Numenius' writings were read and discussed in Plotinus' seminar; one of Plotinus' closest associates, Amelius, was an enthusiastic collector of Numenius' works; and when Plotinus was accused of plagiarizing Numenius, Amelius felt obliged to compose a book entitled "On the Difference between the Doctrines of Plotinus and Numenius."[52] So we will not be surprised to find in the thought of Numenius features that strikingly recall Plotinus.

A native of Apamea in Syria, the homeland of Posidonius,

---

[50] For henads in Iamblichus, see J. Dillon, "Iamblichus of Chalcis," in *ANRW* 36.2 (1987), 883f. Cf. O'Meara (1989), 79.

[51] Dodds (1963), 259. Dodds describes this as "a singular example of the survival of an obsolete creed in mummy form—a mode of preservation which becomes possible only when the creed is already dead."

[52] Porphyry, *Life of Plotinus* 3, 14, 17f., 21.

Numenius is notable for two apparently contrary tendencies: an insistence on returning to the pure teaching of the Old Academy and, on the other hand, a willingness to find the original version of Platonic wisdom not only in Pythagoras but in the spiritual conception of god that Pythagoras is thought to derive from more ancient theologies, in particular from those of the Orient. In agreement with the most generous account of Pythagoras' legendary travels and discipleship, Numenius finds Platonic philosophy preexisting among the Brahmans, the Magi, the Egyptian priests, and above all in the Hebrew scriptures, which he is fond of quoting as a particularly ancient documentary authority. It was Numenius who asked the famous question, "Who is Plato but Moses speaking Greek?"[53] Like a modern romantic, Numenius combines his belief in the profound wisdom of the earliest ages with a concept of historical decadence, a decadence that he traces in a brilliant study of "the secession (*diastasis*) of the Academics from Plato." In this work Numenius pursues a systematic deconstruction of the Platonic tradition, in order to present his own thought (in which Plato is equated with Pythagoras) as a return to the primal sources. His Plato is defined by the Pythagorean tradition that takes its beginning from the Unwritten Doctrines concerning the Monad and the Dyad.[54] Numenius may be alluding to this link with Plato's oral teaching by choosing for his own major work the title of Plato's lecture *On the Good*.

---

[53] Fr. 8, from Eusebius. (Fragments are cited from E. Des Places, *Numénius: Fragments* [Paris, 1973].) Origen reports that Numenius frequently quotes "Moses and the prophets" (fr. 1c) and that he tells the story of Moses and the Egyptian magicians, as well as a story concerning Jesus, whom he does not name (fr. 10a; for the Egyptian story in Numenius' own words, see fr. 9, which reports that the Egyptian magi were able to avert the plagues invoked by Moses). The only Biblical quotation in the preserved fragments is from the first chapter of Genesis (fr. 30, cited by Porphyry): "The prophet said that the spirit of God was borne upon the waters."

[54] As Michael Frede reminds me, the same tradition is reflected in the quotation from Longinus in Porphyry's *Life of Plotinus* 20, 72: "Plotinus, it would seem, has expounded the principles of Pythagorean and Platonic philosophy more clearly than anyone before him" (transl. Armstrong), where Numenius and Moderatus are named among his

We have fragmentary quotations from a number of Numenius' writings, including an elaborate allegorical commentary on the myth of Er and the cave of the Nymphs,[55] and one interesting quotation from a work entitled *On Things Unsaid in Plato* (*Peri tôn para Platôni aporrêtôn*). In this passage (fr. 23 Des Places), Numenius explains how Plato presented Socrates' refutation of Euthyphro in such a way as to express his own repugnance for the traditional accounts of divine misbehavior (quarrels, incest, sons taking vengeance on fathers), without running the risk of being put to death for impiety like Socrates.

A literary sensitivity of this kind, combined with a powerful gift for satire, is characteristic of the lengthy excerpts that Eusebius has preserved from the tract *On the Secession of the Academics from Plato* (frs. 24–28 Des Places). We have here a polemical history of the Platonic school from Speusippus to Philo of Larissa (probably the last official scholarch of the Academy, 110–88 B.C.) and his eclectic student, Antiochus of Ascalon.[56] Numenius also refers briefly to the Epicureans (whom he admires for their fidelity to the doctrines of their Master) and to the Stoics, whom he compares to the followers of Socrates for their lack of doctrinal unity. His chief enemies are the skeptical Platonists of the New Academy, above all Arcesilaus, Lacydes, and Carneades. Numenius' account of them is lively reading. At one point, Arcesilaus is compared to the cuttlefish: as the cuttlefish protects itself by squirting ink, so Arcesilaus protected himself from refutation by "uttering no clear doctrine and projecting in front of himself the screen of *epochê*," that is, the suspension of belief (fr. 25). For Plato, on the other hand, Numenius is full of admiration: "he was not

---

predecessors. Plotinus' interest in expounding the "doctrines of the Pythagoreans" is mentioned again by Porphyry in the next chapter (21, 6).

[55] The citations do not make clear how much of this is due to Numenius himself, how much to "his associate Kronios" (fr. 30); cf. οἱ περὶ Νουμήνιον in fr. 33.

[56] Why does Numenius' account end with Philo and Antiochus? Probably because he saw the *diastasis* from Plato as coming to an end in the first century B.C., with the return to Platonic-Pythagorean verities beginning with Eudorus. (So Frede, 1987: 1050.)

superior to the great Pythagoras, but perhaps not inferior either." Socrates himself was a Pythagorean, and hence he "posited three gods and philosophized in the form appropriate to each."[57] Plato constitutes the mean between Pythagoras and Socrates: "He reduced the solemnity of the former to human friendliness, and raised the refinement and playfulness of the latter from irony to dignity and gravity, thus combining Pythagoras with Socrates; Plato was seen as more accessible than the one and more serious than the other" (fr. 24).

Numenius' work *On the Good* was a treatise in at least six books in diatribe form, that is to say, in a continuous exposition occasionally interrupted by exchanges with an imaginary auditor. The first book opens with a survey of the primeval wisdom that Numenius discovers in various non-Greek traditions, including the Hebrew Bible. He then proceeds to offer systematic proofs that Being (*ousia, to on*) cannot be corporeal or material, since matter is indefinite and subject to continual change (frs. 3–8).[58] But how is

---

[57] Fr. 24. The reference to three gods clearly implies that the doctrine was recognizably Pythagorean, but its origin is a matter of dispute. Some commentators take the context here to be an echo of the riddling reference to three kings in the pseudo-Platonic Letter II. (See E. Des Places, 1973, p. 10.) But the forger of this letter is more likely to be alluding to some traditional view. Thus P. T. Keyser (1998: 263) has recently proposed Eudorus as source for the mysterious trinity in the Second Letter. Compare the three Ones in the passage quoted above from Moderatus (pp. 109f.).

Proclus identifies three gods in Numenius (fr. 21); and three gods are also recognized in the *Chaldean Oracles*, which show close parallels to Numenius. (See the comparison of parallel texts in Festugière [1953] III, 54.) Scholarly opinion is divided as to who is the initiator here, but the *Chaldean Oracles* seem to me clearly derivative and hence more likely to be influenced by Numenius. For a contrary argument, on stylistic grounds, see Dodds, "Numenius and Ammonius," in *Les Sources de Plotin*, Entretiens Hardt V (Vandoeuvres-Genève, 1960), 11.

[58] For a fuller analysis of these arguments, see Frede (1987), 1051. We can ignore fr. 4b (from Nemesius), which presents a parallel argument to show that the psyche is incorporeal. This thesis does not fit into the context of Books I–II, where the subject is Being, not the soul. Fr. 4b is not a verbatim citation, and the argument is in any case attributed to "Ammonius and Numenius."

one to apprehend this incorporeal reality? There is nothing present to us, no sensible object to serve as a basis for knowledge of the Good.

> But, like someone seated in a lookout post, who, straining his eyes, manages to catch a glimpse of one of those little fishing vessels, a one-man skiff all alone, isolated, engulfed in the waves, even so must one remove oneself far from the things of sense, and consort alone with the Good alone, where there is neither human being nor any other living thing, nor any body great or small, but some unspeakable and truly indescribable wondrous solitude—there where are the accustomed places, the haunts and celebrations of the Good, and it itself in peace, in benevolence, the tranquil one, the sovereign, mounted graciously upon Being (*ousia*). (fr. 2, transl. after Dillon)

No reader of Plotinus can fail to be reminded here of passages in the *Enneads* where Plotinus is describing a mystical contact with the One. (And the phrase "alone with the Good alone" is in fact echoed by Plotinus' closing words in *Ennead* VI.9, "escape of the alone to the alone.") For Numenius, however, the highest principle is initially designated not as the One but as the Good and the First God. And the access to this principle is described in terms both Platonic and Pythagorean: "The mode of approach (*methodos*) to the Good is not easy but divine. The best way is to disregard sensibles, devote oneself enthusiastically to learning the sciences and studying the numbers, and thus to attain the knowledge of what is Being (*ti esti to on*)."

Numenius' own concern is less with number theory than with cosmic theology, and above all with the doctrine of three gods. The origin of this doctrine is obscure; there is no trace of it in the Platonic *Handbook* of Alcinous, which may be roughly contemporary with Numenius. Since Numenius refers to this doctrine elsewhere as typically Pythagorean (above, note 57), it probably derives from an interpretation of the first three Ones in Plato's *Parmenides*, the interpretation that we (following Dodds and others) have recognized in the views of Moderatus reported by Simplicius (above, pp. 109f.). Someone else, or Moderatus himself, had represented these three Ones as three gods. But the background for Numenius' view is provided not only by this Pythagorean trinity but also by several problems raised by Plato's account of creation in the *Timaeus*. In fact Numenius' entire system can be regarded as a creative interpretation of the *Timaeus*, an interpretation conditioned by the Neopythagorean doctrine of three gods. We recall that in the tradition of Platonic commentary, beginning perhaps with Xenocrates, the transcendental Forms which serve in the *Timaeus* as the demiurge's model for creation have regularly been reinterpreted as Ideas in the mind of the highest god. This god is usually identified with the demiurge or world-maker, but he (or it) can also be conceived on the model of Aristotle's Prime Mover, as an Intellect that takes itself as object. (This is the view given in Alcinous, chapter 10.) There is a tension, then, between a view of the highest god as self-focused and self-contained and a view of the demiurge as responsible for ordering the cosmos. Numenius will find a place for both these principles within his own conception of the three gods. His way of formulating this view is, however, rather cryptic:

> The first god is simple and remains in himself; since he holds converse entirely with himself, he is in no way divisible. The god who is second and third, however, is one. In associating with matter which is a dyad,[59] it provides unity to matter while being at the same time separated (or split, *schizetai*) by matter, since the latter is in flux and has an appetitive character (*epithumêtikon êthos*). Because it looks towards matter it is not in touch with the intelligible (*to noêton*), for it would be in touch with itself; in its regard for matter it becomes careless of itself. And it grasps the sensible (*to aisthêton*) and takes care of it and raises it up to its own character, having directed its desire towards matter (*eporêxamenos tês hulês*). (fr. 11, transl. after Des Places)

Is Numenius referring to three gods here, or only to two? His statement ("the second and third gods are one") is deliberately paradoxical. Numenius seems to be accepting as given the

---

[59] Matter as dyad is a reading of the "Pythagorean" One-Dyad principles taken over from late Platonism.

doctrine of three gods (like the three Ones of Moderatus), in which the second god is a demiurge and the third god may be either the cosmos itself or its animating principle, the world soul. In our text, the second god is an Intellect or Nous that serves as world-maker, and Numenius' first innovation is to insist that it is the *same* god who also animates the cosmos. As he tells us in a later passage, "the first god is concerned with the intelligibles, the second is concerned with the intelligibles and sensibles" (fr. 15). It is second in its relation to the first god, in its concern for intelligibles only; but it splits and becomes third by turning its attention to matter.

This is Numenius' metaphysical version of cosmogony: "the first god and king remains idle and exempt from all work; the demiurgic god governs by its journey through the heavens" (fr. 12). Its journey through the heavens is, of course, a journey in thought (*noein*). Numenius' phrase echoes Platonic passages like *Phaedrus* 246b6–c2, where soul governs the world by "circulating through the whole heavens." But the conception is older than Plato: Xenophanes' greatest god does not travel, but "exempt from toil, it agitates all things by the thought of its mind (*noou phreni*)" (fr. 25 DK). Numenius has divided this role between his first two gods: the first is exempt from toil; the second directs all things in the world below.

The relation between these two gods is further elucidated in fr. 18:

> A pilot, I suppose, traveling in the middle of the sea, steers the ship from his seat high above the rudder; his eyes and intellect are directed aloft, through the sky to the stars, and his path leads on high through the heavens, while he sails below on the sea. Similarly does the demiurge steer matter, established above it like the captain over the ship at sea, having bound it (sc. matter) in harmony that it may neither break loose nor wander away. The demiurge directs the harmony, steering by the Forms (*ideai*); instead of looking to the heavens it looks to the god above that attracts its eyes; and it takes its judgment (*to kritikon*) from contemplation, its impulse (*to hormêtikon*) from desire. (transl. after Des Places)

The first god thus occupies the place of the intelligible model in the *Timaeus*, by imitating which the second god constructs and orders the world. (In distinguishing the paradigmatic Forms from the demiurge, Numenius is more faithful to Plato's text than in the interpretation that locates the Forms in the mind of the demiurgic god.) We shall return to the theme of contemplation. But notice first how paradoxical is the situation of the second god. By looking down towards matter, it separates itself from the intelligible realm; but by looking up, it finds guidance for the ordering of the visible universe. Similarly paradoxical is Numenius' description of the highest principle: "Corresponding to the motion belonging to the second god, the rest (*stasis*) belonging to the first is an innate motion, from which the order of the cosmos and its eternal stability (*monê*) and preservation (*sôtêria*) are poured down upon all things" (fr. 15). The second god is here conceived simply as the channel by which stability and order are transmitted to the material world, which is itself intrinsically in flux.

The notion of an intelligible motion (*kinêsis*) within the eternal rest of the first principle will find an echo in Plotinus' account of his second principle, Nous or Intellect, which unfolds in its own vital activity and also serves as intelligible model for the sensible cosmos. And for Plotinus too Nous will be in a sense divided, as the second god is for Numenius. By looking up to the One, the Plotinian Nous will derive its rational structure; by looking down towards matter it becomes Psyche or Soul, which in turn provides the animating and organizing principle of the physical universe. Numenius' second god is also a psychic principle, the source of cosmic and personal life:

> Through the heavens is our journey also, when Nous is sent down in its excursion to all those who are assigned to share in it. When the god looks and turns to each of us, life and animation are then allotted to the bodies which are married to the beams (*akrobolismoi*) of the god. But when the god turns back to his own observation post (*periôpê*),[60] these (bodies) are extinguished but Nous enjoys a blessed life. (fr. 12, in continuation of the passage cited above, p. 124)

---

60 Numenius has taken the image of the pilot of the universe letting go of the tiller and withdrawing to his observation post (*periôpê*) from Plato's *Statesman* 272e.

As we shall later confirm, this text implies that human souls (and other souls as well) are parts of the cosmic Intellect, beamed down to receptive bodies on temporary loan. This has led some commentators to identify Numenius' second god with the world soul.[61] But in fact it is repeatedly called Nous, or Intellect. Numenius has thus accepted the traditional view of Plato's demiurge as a divine intellect, existing independently of the cosmic Receptacle (identified here with matter) and responsible for the rational structure of the physical world. (This is the demythologizing interpretation of the demiurge as cosmic Nous that appeals to so many modern commentators on the *Timaeus*.) Demiurgic causal action is represented by the metaphor, among others, of looking down (*blepein*). Answering to this is the gaze of *theôria*, contemplation turned upwards towards the first god.[62]

The imagery of sight here is, of course, to be understood in terms of intellectual activity or thinking. For it is by thought alone that things below participate in things above.

> The participants participate in it [Nous? or the first god?] only by thinking (*to phronein*) and by no other means. It is in this way and not otherwise that they (the participants) also enjoy congress with good. For thinking in fact encounters (or belongs to? *suntetuchêke*) only the first (god). By this do other things receive their color and their goodness. . . . If the second god is good not from itself but from the first, how could that by participation in which the second is good not be good itself? . . . It is by such reasoning that, for the sharp sighted, Plato concluded that the Good is One. (fr. 19)

The structure of this argument is obscure, but its intention is clear. Numenius has entitled his treatise *On the Good*, but he began it with a search for Being, which he argued must be located in the intelligible realm. Now the intelligible itself (*to noêton*) presup-

---

[61] See, e.g., Krämer (1967), 72.

[62] In fr. 18 (cited above), the term for contemplation, *theôria*, so central for Plotinus, refers to the gaze of the second *nous*, turned up towards the first god. That seems also to be the sense of *theôrêtikos* in fr. 16.

poses an Intellect (Nous), which is its superior and cause.[63] Furthermore, Numenius can take for granted that the intelligible realm is represented by the doctrine of three gods. It will turn out that the first and second gods are both described as *nous*. Whether the third god is identified with the created cosmos (as Proclus claims in fr. 21) or with the demiurgic world soul (on a plausible reading of fr. 11) does not seem to matter much to Numenius.[64] It is the first two gods and their action on the world that are his primary concern in the extant fragments. Both gods are intellects, and their action on the world is a form of thinking (*phronein, noein*).[65] In fragment 12 Numenius has made clear that this thinking is the source for all life in the corporeal world; in the text just cited (fr. 19), he maintains that it is also the source for everything good. But just as the source of intellectual activity must itself be an intellect, so the source of everything good must be itself good—in fact, it must be the Good itself. (Numenius thus accepts the usual transmission theory of causation which Plotinus will reject, since the One of Plotinus has none of the attributes that derive from it.) Numenius draws that conclusion more explicitly in fragment 20: "If the demiurge is good by participation in the primary good, the first *nous* will be a Form (*idea*), the Good itself,

---

[63] Compare fr. 16: "Since Being and the Form (*idea*) are intelligible, but it has been agreed that *nous* is elder and cause of Being, this Intellect itself alone has been found to be the Good." (The conclusion seems stronger than the premises, but Numenius' mode of reasoning is not strictly deductive.) There follow a series of proportions: as the demiurge is god of Becoming, so is the Good the principle of Being (*ousias archê*); as the demiurge of Becoming is good, so the demiurge of Being is the Good itself (*autoagathon*). The second god, as imitator (*mimêtês*) of the first, is double: "it self-makes its own Form (*idea*) and the world, and then it is (also) wholly contemplative (*theôrêtikos*). . . . There is one Being of the first god, another Being of the second; the beautiful cosmos is an imitation (*mimêma*) of this (second) Being, made beautiful by participation in the Beautiful."

[64] For an identification of the third god as both demiurge and world soul, see Frede (1987), 1068.

[65] The first god is called *auto-on* because it is the Idea of Being, the source of *ousia* for the intelligible realm. Thus in fr. 16, the Good is both *archê* and Demiurge of Being (*ousia*).

autoagathon." But the conclusion reached in fragment 19 is different: if all goodness comes from the first god, then there is only one entity that is intrinsically, nonderivatively good. So here the familiar Platonic doctrine of the Good merges with the more specifically Neopythagorean cult of the One. Numenius concludes that the first god must be not only a Nous but also the Good itself and the (first) One. He thus directly prepares the way for Plotinus' assumption that the highest principle can be conventionally named either the One or the Good. But for Plotinus these names of "One" or "Good" no longer have their usual descriptive content, since his highest principle has no positive attributes.

One of the most profound differences between Plotinus and Numenius is that in the latter we find no trace of the negative theology that is familiar from Alcinous and essential to Plotinus' conception of the One. On the contrary, where Plotinus denies all predicates of the One, Numenius tends to accumulate attributes for his first god. It is the principle of Being (*ousia*) as the demiurge is of Becoming; it is the Form of Good or the Good itself (*autoagathon*), and similarly the Form of Being or Being itself (*auto-on*). Above all, it is a Nous, an intellect. (Plotinus deviates from this Platonic tradition in refusing to identify the highest god with a divine Nous.) According to Numenius, because the first god "who is called Being itself (*auto-on*)" was unknown to mankind, Plato was obliged to exclaim, "Human beings, the Nous you know (the demiurge) is not the first, but there is another Nous before it, elder and more divine" (fr. 17).[66]

Furthermore, it is this first god, and not the demiurge, who is the true source and origin of the souls that the second god will distribute to bodies: "The One-who-is (*ho ôn*) sows the seed of every soul into all the things that share in it (the first god);[67] the demiurge, as lawmaker, plants and distributes and transplants into each one of us (the souls) that are previously cast down from above" (fr. 13).

---

[66] Fr. 17. For the apocalyptic form of this address Ω̃ ἄνθρωποι, see Norden (1913) 73, 191 n. 2.

[67] For the Biblical designation of the first god as ὁ ὤν, see Des Places (1973) 108 n. 2; cf. Philo's usage (above, p. 103). For doubts, see Dodds (1960), 15.

The second god is here assigned a role corresponding to that of the created gods in *Timaeus* 41–2. But whereas the lesser gods of the *Timaeus* are responsible for adding a mortal soul to the immortal, rational soul delivered to them by the demiurge, Numenius' second god is responsible only for the incarnation and reincarnation of immortal souls, which are themselves of higher origin. (It is the body, as matter shaped by elemental forms, that will provide the inferior or "evil" soul. See below.) Nothing shows better the originality of Numenius' scheme than this demotion of the demiurge, who in Plato's *Timaeus* had figured as the supreme deity, with only the model of the Forms above him. Since the Forms had long ago been absorbed into the demiurge as his Ideas, the Platonic scheme had, in effect, been reduced to two fundamental principles, God and matter, as logically prior to the world which they jointly produce. Numenius' innovation is, on the one hand, to insist that the demiurge is not the highest god, but that "there is another Nous before this, elder and more divine," while, on the other hand, maintaining the second, demiurgic god as essentially a transmission-belt, mediating between the first god and matter, and hence splitting into two in accordance with its double focus.[68]

The process of transmission is described in a striking passage quoted by Eusebius to show "how the second cause came into existence from the first":

> All things that, when given, pass to the taker and depart from the giver, . . . all these (gifts) are human and mortal; divine gifts, however, are such that, given from above, they are present here without departing from there, and they benefit the one without harming the other, but they add a further benefit by the recollection of things one knew. This noble thing is knowledge (*epistêmê*), where the taker is benefited but the giver is not deprived. It is like when a lamp is

---

[68] Proclus reports that, according to Numenius, the first god makes use of the second god in order to think (*noein*), as the second god makes use of the third in order to structure the world (*dêmiourgein*) (fr. 22). This latter claim is compatible with fr. 11, but I do not find anything in the extant fragments to support the former claim.

lit from another lamp; the light is not removed from the latter, but the matter in one is lit by the fire of the other. (fr. 14)

This model of knowledge as the mode by which life and form are
transmitted downwards from the first god is explained by Numenius' extraordinary claim that "the nature (*hexis*) and Being (*ousia*)
that possesses knowledge is the same in the god who gives and in
you and me who receive, and that is what Plato meant when he
said that wisdom was brought by Prometheus to mankind together with the brightest of fires" (fr. 14, citing *Philebus* 16c).

The Being that possesses knowledge is, of course, the soul, and
Numenius is in effect claiming that human souls are parts of the
divine Being of the highest god. We have met this doctrine before
in fr. 12, where bodies were said to be animated by the "beams
of the god," when Nous descends to our level. Now in the
Pythagorean tradition, as in Plato's own writings, the soul was always seen as immortal and hence as, in some sense, divine. But in
Plato it is only the rational soul, the soul made by the demiurge
himself and handed over to the lesser gods, that belongs to the intelligible realm: it is *nous* alone that comes to us from the *noêtos
topos*. Furthermore, although the human soul is made from the
same mixture of Forms as the cosmic soul, the human mixture is
less pure (*Timaeus* 41d). Although we do not have Numenius'
explicit statement on this point, the passages just quoted suggest
a much stronger view, a view that is also ascribed to him by several later authors. On this view, it is not a distinct rational part but
the entire soul that is *nous*, and that comes to us from the highest
god.[69] Thus Iamblichus reports that, according to Numenius, "incorporeal Being is all homogeneous and one and the same, so that
in each of its parts the whole is contained. Even in the individual
soul (these thinkers) establish the intelligible cosmos and gods
and daimons and the Good and all higher things, and thus all
things are in all, but in each according to the mode appropriate to

---

[69] Numenius' deviation here from the *Timaeus* may not be as great as it
seems, if the lower parts of the soul are explained by him in terms of
the mixture with matter. However, the implication in fr. 12 that all life
derives from the descent of Nous suggests a view rather different from
Plato's.

its essence (or Being, *ousia*)" (fr. 41). The force of the last clause is not entirely clear, since Iamblichus begins by asserting that the *ousia* of all soul is homogeneous. But probably *ousia* in the final clause should be taken more loosely, to refer not only to the intrinsic nature of soul as such, but also to its incarnate status. And this brings us to the role that matter plays in accounting for the doctrine of evil souls in the physical world.

Up to this point, in expounding Numenius we have made use almost exclusively of direct citations from his text. For Numenius' theory of matter, on the other hand, we are dependent upon later reports. However, the general lines of the theory seem to be well documented.[70] First of all, we must distinguish between precosmic, ungenerated matter, which is a fundamental principle prior to and independent of all divine action, corresponding to the precosmic Receptacle and the principle of Necessity in Plato's *Timaeus*, on the one hand, and postcosmic matter, on the other hand, which has been structured by the elemental forms and generated in determinate bodies. It is matter in the former sense that is bad and the source of all evil, whereas the generated bodies of the physical cosmos, as material products resulting from divine structuring, are a mixture of good and bad. Furthermore, it is essential to this view of precosmic matter that it is intrinsically ensouled, since it is by its own nature eternally in motion and change, and since (on one familiar Platonic principle) the soul is the source of all motion. It is by this reasoning that we get the conception of a bad world soul, namely, the soul that is innate in precosmic matter, and hence present within the material component in every body. This last consequence, that every body contains an evil soul as its inheritance from primeval matter, explains why Numenius seems to have claimed that human beings, and all living things, have two souls: a good soul (as a portion of divine Nous) and a bad soul, intrinsic to its body.[71]

The doctrine of a bad human soul, as well as an evil world soul,

---

[70] I am relying here on the report given by Chalcidius (Numenius fr. 52 Des Places), as interpreted by Frede (1987), 1052f.

[71] For the doctrine of two souls, see frs. 42–46a and Frede (1987), 1070–4. Gnostic influence is recognized here by Dodds and others; see Dodds (1960), 7f.

may seem to bring Numenius perilously close to Gnosticism, with which he obviously shares some tendencies.[72] But on the decisive point, he, like Plotinus, will reject the Gnostic position. For the Gnostics, the world is a bad place because it is the work of an evil demiurge. But Numenius is a true Platonist, and for him the demiurge is a good god who makes the world as good as possible. In Numenius' system, this cosmic optimism is guaranteed by the fact that his first god, who provides the intelligible model for creation, is identified with the Good itself. Like Plato, however, Numenius recognizes that the independence of matter sets limits to how good the cosmic product can be. The radical independence of pre-cosmic matter is thus an essential principle of Numenius' theodicy, and he reacts very strongly against a Neopythagorean tendency to monism that would undermine this independence.

> Numenius says that Pythagoras gave the name of Monad to god, the name of Dyad to matter; this indeterminate Dyad is by no means generated, but determinate (matter) has come into being. That is to say, before it was adorned with form and order, matter was without birth and origin, but its birth was its being adorned and embellished by the god who regulated it. . . . The ungenerated matter must therefore be understood as equal in age to the god who set it in order. But some Pythagoreans did not understand this doctrine and believed that even that indefinite and immeasurable Dyad was produced by the Monad withdrawing from its own nature and departing into the form of the Dyad—not correctly, as if the Monad which was should cease to be, and the Dyad which was not should come to subsist, and god would be changed to matter, and from Unity would come indeterminate and immeasurable Duality, an opinion which is unsuitable even for men of little education. (fr. 52, 5–24, from Chalcidius)

---

[72] The doctrine of an evil world soul had been presented earlier by Plutarch, who relied on this reading of *Laws* 896e. See *De Iside et Osiride*, 370F. Numenius seems to have followed Plutarch on this point: "Numenius praises Plato for proclaiming two world souls, one most beneficent, the other malicious, namely matter" (fr. 52, 64–7, from Chalcidius).

Numenius seems here to be criticizing not only the monistic trend among his predecessors but more specifically Moderatus, the only thinker reported to have generated the Dyad from the Monad by the latter's withdrawing from its own nature (above, p. 108). This radical dualism, which is distinctive for Numenius as for Plutarch and for some other second-century thinkers, can claim support not only from the Pythagorean Table of Opposites and the corresponding Monad-Dyad opposition in the Unwritten Doctrines, but also from dualist aspects of Plato's cosmology in the *Timaeus*.[73] And it is a nice question how far this metaphysical dualism has been eliminated even from the system of Plotinus, where so many other features of Numenius' thought have been preserved.[74]

6. It is no part of this study to pursue the transformation of Pythagorean themes in the great creative synthesis constructed by Plotinus in the third century A.D., or in the work of the Neoplatonic philosophers who follow Plotinus.[75] We must, however, take note of the fact that, after Numenius, the Neopythagorean tradition is fully absorbed into Neoplatonism. Perhaps the most striking piece of evidence for this continuity is the existence of two classic *Lives* of Pythagoras, composed in the late third and early fourth centuries A.D. by two major Neoplatonic philosophers: by Porphyry, the disciple and editor of Plotinus, and by Iamblichus, the pupil and rival of Porphyry. Unlike Plotinus himself (who tends to treat Pythagoras as one among other early predecessors, like Heraclitus or Empedocles),[76] both Porphyry and Iamblichus

---

[73] Most notably, the account of creation as a victory of Reason over Necessity at *Timaeus* 48a.

[74] Note Plotinus' hesitation at *Ennead* IV.8.6 as to whether or not matter is ungenerated. Ultimately, however, Plotinus seems to have rejected the metaphysical independence of matter.

[75] For a masterful survey of points of contact and contrast between Plotinus and Numenius, see Dodds (1960), 12–24.

[76] See *Ennead* IV.8.1, 21. Plotinus does, however, show considerable respect for the Pythagorean doctrine of the One. See *Ennead* V.1.9, 28 and V.5.6, 27. Compare J. H. Waszink "Porphyrius und Numenius," in *Porphyre*, Entretiens Hardt XII, (Vandoeuvres-Genève, 1966).

represent Pythagoras as a mythic figure, the paradigm of the sage as divine man. And both Porphyry and Iamblichus make use of the life of Pythagoras as a popular introduction to Platonic philosophy. Furthermore, the miraculous side of the Pythagoras legend is fully developed in both *Lives*, and it is natural to suppose that these accounts were composed with the implicit goal of providing a pagan competitor for the Christian gospels.[77] A similar anti-Christian motivation is often suggested in connection with Philostratus' hagiographical *Life of Apollonius* in the early third century A.D., as will be noticed in the next chapter.

Living in the generation immediately before the political triumph of Christianity, Porphyry (who died around 305 A.D.) was acutely aware of this threat to the classical-Platonic tradition, as he showed in his famous, largely lost treatise *Against the Christians*. And among Neoplatonists, it was Porphyry who first reinstated Pythagoras as the patron saint of Platonic philosophy, in the tradition of Nicomachus and Numenius. He did so in the context of a belief in the universal wisdom of primeval times, the *prisca sapientia*. [78] Like Numenius, Porphyry held that the ancient Indians, Egyptians, Hebrews, and other peoples had possessed the same original wisdom, of which Pythagoras was the earliest representative in Greece. Thus for Porphyry the Pythagorean and Platonic messages are essentially the same, but it was only with Plato (as interpreted by Plotinus) that this wisdom was fully articulated.[79] With his celebrated *Isagoge* or *Introduction to Aristotle's Categories*, Porphyry also introduced the great tradition of Neoplatonic commentaries on Aristotle. He recognized that Aris-

---

[77] The parallel to the gospels is emphasized in the case of Iamblichus' work by J. Dillon–J. Hershbell, *Iamblichus: On the Pythagorean Way of Life* (Atlanta, Ga., 1991), 25f. For a similar suggestion, see O'Meara (1989), 214.

[78] For the influence of Numenius on Porphyry's conception of *palaia sophia* among the barbarians, see Waszink (1966). For a classic account of the prestige of exotic wisdom in this period, see Festugière (1950) I, ch. 2: "Les prophètes de l'Orient."

[79] Compare the conclusion of J. Whittaker: "Clearly, for Porphyry the Pythagorean element was subsumed within the Platonic," in "Platonic Philosophy in the Early Centuries of the Empire," *ANRW* II.36.1

totelian science, and above all Aristotelian logic, was an essential part of the preparation for a full mastery of Platonic philosophy. Despite his ready acceptance of the miraculous in his life of Pythagoras, and despite his personal affinity for oracles and mystic cult, Porphyry was too much of a rationalist, and too close to Plotinus, to regard either revelation or ritual as a necessary condition for philosophical understanding and spiritual ascent.[80]

Iamblichus was a thinker of a different stripe, and much of his work took shape as a reaction to, or against, the writing of Porphyry, with whom he is reported to have studied. This is notably true of his treatise *On the Mysteries*, which aims to defend theurgy (invocation of the divine by supernatural tokens or *sunthêmata*) as the key to mystic union, in direct answer to the critical comments of Porphyry in his *Letter to Anebo*.[81] If on such matters Porphyry is hesitant, in the case of Iamblichus the break with Plotinian rationalism is clear-cut. Dodds quotes Olympiodorus to this effect: "Many, like Porphyry and Plotinus, prefer philosophy; others, like Iamblichus and Syrianus and Proclus, prefer theurgy (ἱερατική)."[82]

(1987), 119, commenting on *Vita Plotinou* 22.54f. This is the view explicitly formulated by Proclus in his commentary on the *Timaeus*: "Plato, who alone has preserved the character of the Pythagorean study of nature, has worked out the details (λεπτούργησε) in the present treatise" (*In Timaeum* I.1).

[80] On Porphyry's attitude to popular religion, see Zeller III.ii (1881), 668–77, and Dodds' comment: "Deeply religious by temperament, he [Porphyry] had an incurable weakness for oracles" (Dodds, 1956: 287). A balanced summary on this point in A. Smith, "Porphyrian Studies since 1913," *ANRW* II.36.2 (1987), 731–7.

[81] "The *de mysteriis* is a manifesto of irrationalism, an assertion that the road to salvation is found not in reason but in ritual," E. R. Dodds, *The Greeks and the Irrational* (Berkeley and Los Angeles, 1956), 287.

[82] Ibid., 301 n. 25, citing Olympiodorus *In Phaed.* 123.3. Compare A. Smith, *Porphyry's Place in the Neoplatonic Tradition: A Study in Post-Plotinian Neoplatonism* (The Hague, 1974), 88: "Iamblichus unlike Porphyry and Plotinus did not think that human νόησις could attain its pure united form without the aid of the gods."

In response to Porphyry's *Life of Pythagoras*, Iamblichus composed not another biography but a treatise *On the Pythagorean Way of Life* (*Peri tou Pythagorikou biou*), in which we find much the same narrative of Pythagoras' career, but embedded here in the larger framework of an account of Pythagorean institutions and doctrine.[83] Iamblichus composed this *Life* as introduction to a whole series of treatises, nine or ten volumes in all, under the general title *On the Pythagorean School*.[84] What Iamblichus presents in this vast work (only four volumes of which survive) is essentially a Neopythagorean view of the sciences, formally based on the work of Nicomachus but including copious paraphrases from Platonic dialogues and other authors. Book IV of the series is a systematic paraphrase of Nicomachus' *Introduction to Arithmetic*, and Books V to IX are entitled, respectively, Arithmetic in Physics, Arithmetic in Ethics, Arithmetic in Theology, On Pythagorean Geometry, and On Pythagorean Music. The whole series thus presents itself as a complete statement of Pythagorean philosophy. In addition to material from Aristotle and elsewhere, the three books on Arithmetic seem to have included a good deal of Pythagorean numerology, that is, a study of the numbers from one to ten as they apply to questions in physics, ethics, and theology. In particular, the theological treatise will have drawn elaborate parallels between these numbers and the traditional gods, in the style of the *Greater Arithmetic* or *Theologoumena* of Nicomachus. We have abundant evidence of this in the *Theologoumena arithmeticae* preserved under Iamblichus' name, even if he is not the author of the surviving text. (See above, pp. 115–7.)

Iamblichus' work can thus be seen as a wholescale "Pythagoreanizing of Platonic philosophy," and hence as a re-

---

[83] Burkert (1972, 98f.) has confirmed Rohde's argument that Iamblichus did not copy from Porphyry and that their common source was Nicomachus. But it does not follow, and seems in any case highly improbable, that Iamblichus was unaware of the fact that Porphyry too had written a *Life* of Pythagoras.

[84] Περὶ τῆς Πυθαγορικῆς αἱρέσεως. This is the title accepted by O'Meara (1989), 33, who translates it as *On Pythagoreanism*. The alternative title *Compendium of Pythagorean Doctrine* (Συναγωγὴ τῶν Πυθαγορείων δογμάτων) is preferred by Dillon-Hershbell (1991), 1.

turn to the tradition that sees Plato as the debtor to Pythagoras.[85] But this is only part of the story. Iamblichus' ten Pythagorean treatises represent the beginning but not the end of a training in philosophy. Higher philosophy is still represented by the works of Aristotle and Plato. We know that for Iamblichus as for later Neoplatonists, the curriculum proceeds beyond number theory to the study of Aristotelian logic and, finally, to the mastery of Plato's dialogues in a fixed order, culminating in the *Timaeus* and *Parmenides*.[86]

Iamblichus is the great systematizer of the Neoplatonic curriculum, and the form he gave to the tradition was decisive for later Platonists such as Syrianus and Proclus. As a result the Pythagorean component, with its emphasis on the importance of mathematics in general and numerology in particular, remained an essential feature of Neoplatonic philosophy in the following centuries. If Proclus in the fifth century A.D. could dream that he was a reincarnation of Nicomachus, the Neopythagorean author of the *Introduction to Arithmetic*, we may see this as a direct reflection of the importance assigned to number theory in the Neoplatonic tradition as determined by Iamblichus.[87] But beyond number theory, the Neoplatonic curriculum terminates in the study of the *Parmenides* and the *Timaeus*. Every Neoplatonist will read the *Parmenides* in the light of the Neopythagorean interpretation that sees the ineffable One as subject of the first hypothesis. And Proclus will begin his *Commentary on the "Timaeus"* by assuming that Plato has taken the core of his mathematical cosmology from the treatise *On the Nature of the Cosmos and the Soul* handed down under the name of Timaeus of Locri: "It is agreed by all that, since he acquired the book which the Pythagorean Timaeus composed

---

[85] This is the view presented in O'Meara (1989), 4 and passim.

[86] For the Pythagorean treatises as an introduction to philosophy, see B. D. Larsen, *Jamblique de Chalcis, Exégète et philosophe* (Aarhus, 1972) I, 69–71. For Iamblichus' philosophical curriculum, ibid., 318, 333f. Compare Dillon (1987), 872.

[87] Proclus' belief that he was a reincarnation of Nicomachus is reported in the *Life of Proclus* by Marinus, ch. 28.

On the Universe, Plato undertook to write the *Timaeus* in the Pythagorean manner."[88]

Thus Plato remains the supreme master, but from now on his philosophy will retain many traits from its Neopythagorean interpretation, and most of the Neoplatonists will draw no real distinction between Plato and Pythagoras. It is in this latest, Neoplatonic form, above all through the work of Proclus (and through his Christian imitator, pseudo-Dionysius, the author of *On Divine Names*) that Pythagorean thought survived into medieval philosophy and reemerged as a powerful influence in the Renaissance.

---

[88] Proclus *In Timaeum* I.7,18 Diehl. See also the Proclus passage cited above in n. 79. For the pseudonymous treatise ascribed to Timaeus of Locri, see above, p. 79.

IX

THE PYTHAGOREAN HERITAGE

IN THE PRECEDING CHAPTER, WE WERE CONCERNED WITH THE Pythagoreanism of the Roman period only as it concerns philosophy. In order now to trace the wider influence of Pythagorean ideas into late antiquity and down to the threshold of the modern age, it will be convenient to distinguish three different strands:

1. the tradition of the occult and the supernatural;

2. transmigration and vegetarianism;

3. the mathematical and musical traditions.

1. THE PYTHAGOREAN TRADITION OF THE OCCULT AND THE SUPERNATURAL

What does it mean to claim, as Cicero does, that Nigidius Figulus brought back to life the teaching (*disciplina*) of "those famous Pythagoreans who flourished for several centuries in South Italy and Sicily"? Presumably, those famous Pythagoreans include Empedocles from Sicily as well as Philolaus and Archytas from South Italy. Now as the Empedoclean papyrus from Strasburg has recently reminded us,[1] Empedocles was not only a natural

---

[1] A. Martin and O. Primavesi, *L'Empédocle de Strasbourg* (Berlin and New York, 1999).

philosopher in the style of Anaxagoras; he was also a godlike man or even, as he claimed, an immortal god, who travels from city to city, surrounded by crowds of admirers who hope to hear from him "the path to profit, prophetic advice and a healing word for all sorts of diseases" (fr. 112). The auditor of Empedocles' verses is promised remedies for ills and old age, power over wind and weather, and the ability to call a spirit up from the underworld (fr. 111). Thus, in Empedocles' world view, the lines between science and magic, philosophy and the occult, are nowhere drawn. In this respect, Empedocles may be an exception among the Presocratic philosophers. But he is much less exceptional when we consider him as a representative of the Pythagorean tradition. For here the uncanny and the arcane have been at home from the beginning. Their presence is reflected in Heraclitus' reference to Pythagoras as a trickster, in the superstitious element in the *akousmata* tradition, and in the miraculous stories concerning Pythagoras that were collected by Aristotle.[2] If Nigidius was a restorer of this *disciplina*, it was not only because of his vast learning and social prestige; it was also because of his mastery of occult knowledge, concerning "those subjects which nature seems to have kept hidden (*quae a natura involutae videntur*)," as Cicero says.

If Nigidius was the first genuine Pythagorean after so many years, where did he find his role model? For antecedents we must look to the Greek East, and more specifically to Egypt. It is in Alexandria that Pythagorean philosophy reappears, with Eudorus. But perhaps a closer parallel and precedent for this Roman senator of the first century B.C. is an earlier Egyptian figure, Bolus of Mendes, around 200 B.C.[3]

The works of Bolus are lost, but their influence was great and can still be detected in many extant works. Bolus seems to have

---

[2] Burkert (1972), 141–3.

[3] This is the date given by Burkert and Festugière, following Wellmann's later studies. The entry in the *Oxford Classical Dictionary*, which makes Bolus a contemporary of Callimachus some 50 years earlier, is apparently following Wellman's 1899 article in *RE* III, 676.

Burkert (1961: 233) recognized in Bolus one of the sources of Neopythagoreanism. (He is called a Pythagorean in the *Suda*.) For discussion, see Kingsley (1995), 325–7, 335–7, and passim.

combined elements from Greek philosophy with Eastern lore and with Egyptian craft knowledge in dyeing cloth and working with gold. His debt to Greek philosophy is marked by the fact that he is known as "Bolus the Democritean," and his major work was entitled *Physika dunamera*, "On the Natural Powers" or, alternatively, "On Antipathies and Sympathies." This work seems to have been a kind of encyclopedia devoted to the occult virtues of metals, plants, and animals, specifying the affinities and hostilities, attractions and dominations that relate all the powers of nature to one another. Bolus seems, in fact, to have been the founder of alchemy, in the form that was to endure down through the centuries until the creation of modern chemistry.[4] In addition to the "dyeing" of metals and the transmutation of less noble metals into silver and gold, Bolus' speculation covered the magical and medicinal virtues of various plants. His influence is plausibly traced in the pseudo-Pythagorean treatise on plants known to Cato, as well as in later collections such as Pliny's *Natural History*. So little is known about Bolus personally that we cannot be sure that he ever invoked the name of Pythagoras. But his influence on the Pythagorean tradition is well established. Bolus was, in short, the earliest known writer in the half-scientific, half-magical literary tradition represented in Rome in the first century B.C. by Nigidius Figulus.[5]

This occult side of the Pythagorean tradition was not presented only in literary form, in theoretical texts with practical applications, such as the writings of Bolus and Nigidius. The magical and miraculous aspects of this tradition are more dramatically illustrated in the lives of charismatic individuals who, like Empedocles in an earlier age, often seem to reproduce or reshape the pattern of Pythagoras' own life. In the Roman period, the most famous of these "divine men" was Apollonius of Tyana in Cappadocia, who was active in the second half of the first century A.D. and whose tradition was continued by Alexander of Abonuteichos in the following century.

It is a striking fact that for neither of these picturesque indi-

---

[4] Festugière (1950) I, 197–200, 222–38.
[5] Wellmann cited by Festugière (ibid.), 197.

viduals, Apollonius and Alexander, can we reliably distill an historical account from the magma of their legendary reputation, and in this respect again they recall the model of Pythagoras. Our limited knowledge of Alexander is almost entirely dependent upon the contemporary (and systematically hostile) satire of Lucian, and our much fuller information concerning Apollonius is largely derived from a fictionalized narrative of his life composed more than a century after his death.[6]

The *Life of Apollonius of Tyana* by Philostratus is an entertaining product of the literary movement known as the Second Sophistic, a kind of picaresque novel composed at the request of the empress Julia Domna (widow of Septimius Severus and mother of Caracalla) and apparently completed after her death in 217 A.D. Apollonius himself, however, lived under Nero and Vespasian and died under Nerva in 97 A.D. In the century separating him from his "biographer" Philostratus, Apollonius had become a figure of myth and cult. His prestige was most notably marked by the fact that, in about 215 A.D., the emperor Caracalla dedicated a temple to Apollonius in his native Tyana.[7] Reinforced by Philostratus' colorful literary portrait, Apollonius' fame lasted till the end of pagan antiquity and into Byzantine times.[8]

Philostratus depicts Apollonius as a Pythagorean saint, who repeats in his own person all the exotic travels in search of ancient wisdom that the tradition attributed to Pythagoras. Thus Apollonius first visits Babylon and India, and then travels to Egypt and throughout the Roman empire. Sitting at the feet of Brahman sages in India, Apollonius discovers the source of Pythagorean teaching and, in particular, the original doctrine of transmigration with a memory of previous incarnations (Book 3, chs. 19–26). In Egypt and Ethiopia, on the other hand, he finds that the Gymnosophists, or Naked Sages, have preserved only a decadent form of the Indian teachings. Apollonius' own philosophy is rather

---

[6] Lucian, *Alexander or the False Prophet*; Philostratus, *Life of Apollonius of Tyana.*

[7] J.-J. Flinterman, *Power, "Paideia" and Pythagoreanism* (Amsterdam, 1995), 24f.

[8] G. Anderson, *Sage, Saint, and Sophist* (London and New York, 1994), 107f., 194, with notes.

rudimentary: he preaches transmigration and does benevolent deeds, while practicing abstinence from meat, wine, and sex. In the course of his world travels Apollonius hobnobs with foreign kings, as well as with Roman emperors good and bad, whom he fascinates with his prophecies and predictions. His higher powers permit him to escape miraculously from persecution by both Nero and Domitian. Above all, he performs a long string of marvelous actions (including the revival of a maiden apparently dead) that anti-Christian polemic will later cite in pagan competition with the miracles performed by Jesus.

Philostratus is eager to protect his hero against the charge of witchcraft or magic; Apollonius' supernatural feats are attributed to his divine nature and to the extraordinary wisdom that has been perfected by his studies in India and elsewhere. But despite this explicit rejection of magic, Philostratus' rationalism is, from a modern point of view, extremely limited. It is clear that his own sense of "philosophy" and wisdom (*sophia*), as represented in the life of Apollonius, has been strongly contaminated by the rising tide of irrationalism that is characteristic of Roman society at the end of the second century A.D.

The historian who attempts to penetrate behind this elaborate third-century novel, in the hopes of retrieving a plausible account of the original miracle-worker, is at a serious disadvantage. We have no earlier record of Apollonius. It is true that Philostratus regularly refers to the memoirs of a certain Damis of Nineveh, who claims to have accompanied Apollonius on his travels. Scholars are, however, about evenly divided between those who believe that Damis is a fictional character, invented by Philostratus as a narrative device, and those who believe that Philostratus is actually relying on an earlier document preserved under this name.[9] More promising as an earlier source is the separate collection of letters ascribed to Apollonius.[10] Some of these letters are cited by Philostratus, but others present a rather different picture

---

[9] For a recent survey of scholarship on the highly disputed identity of Damis of Nineveh, see Flinterman (1995), 79–88. Of course, even if Philostratus is referring to an earlier document that actually existed under Damis' name, it might in turn be a fabrication.

[10] R. J. Penella, *The Letters of Apollonius of Tyana* (Leiden, 1979).

of their purported author.[11] We cannot be sure how many of the letters are authentic, if any. But Philostratus' defensiveness on the subject of magic strongly suggests that he is reacting against an earlier tradition in which Apollonius was credited with more occult powers. There seems to be a trace of such a tradition in a number of letters that are concerned to defend the close connections between a philosopher and a *magus*.[12]

More interesting than the letters from a philosophical point of view is a fragment from Apollonius' treatise *On Sacrifices*, preserved by Eusebius. If (as seems likely) the text is authentic, it shows that Apollonius' ascetic lifestyle must be understood as a regime of purification designed to release the spiritual or intelligible soul from the prison of the body. The fragment expresses the Neopythagorean conception of a transcendent god, "the god whom we call the first, who is one and separate from all things, after whom we must recognize the others. Anyone who takes a fitting care of the divine will make no sacrifice to this god, nor light any fire." Nothing from the sensible realm is pure enough to serve as an offering for him, who stands in need of nothing. "For him one can employ only the higher *logos*, I mean the one that does not pass through the mouth, and ask for good things from the finest of Beings by means of the finest thing in us: this is intellect (*nous*), which needs no organ."[13] This concluding echo of the

---

[11] The longest of the letters, no. 58, presents an eclectic philosophy with no trace of Pythagorean doctrine. If this letter is genuine, as some have suggested, Philostratus may have "over-Pythagoreanized" his hero. (Cf. Penella 1979: 28.) However, the letter seems less likely to be authentic than the Neopythagorean fragment from *On Sacrifices* quoted in the text. Both Porphyry and Iamblichus rely on a life of Pythagoras ascribed to Apollonius (Burkert 1972: 100, 104). And the connection with Alexander of Abonuteichos suggests an authentic Pythagorean tradition.

On the other hand, one has the distinct impression that the third century A.D.—the century of Porphyry and Iamblichus as well as Philostratus—is more profoundly Pythagorean than Apollonius' own period. The prestige of Pythagoras continually grows with the passage of time.

[12] Epistles 16 and 17, Penella (1979), 42–5. See comments in Flinterman (1995), 72.

[13] Quoted by Eusebius, *Praeparatio Evangelii* IV.13.

Aristotelian doctrine of incorporeal *nous* ("which needs no organ") is combined here with a Platonic distinction between a silent and a spoken *logos*. And we are reminded also of the passage in Alexander's *Pythagorean Notebooks* where the worship of the gods in pious silence is contrasted with the lower cult of the heroes or daimons (above, p. 83). All of this points to a close sympathy with the strand of Platonic theology developed by Moderatus and Numenius.

More tangible than Apollonius as an historical individual is a famous holy man from the second century, Alexander of Abonuteichos.[14] Our primary source is the hostile satire of Lucian, *Alexander or the False Prophet*. But Lucian is a contemporary who claims to have met Alexander personally, and his account clearly has an historical basis. Furthermore, many details can be independently confirmed. Thus the international prestige of Alexander's oracle is attested by contemporary coins with the figure and name of Alexander's serpent god Glycon, and Lucian's description of the god's appearance is confirmed by several statues, including one four-and-a-half meters tall from Tomi in Rumania. Lucian claims that the whole Roman Empire was deceived by Alexander; the archaeological evidence confirms the influence of his oracle as far as Dacia and Illyria.[15] By means of prophesy, Alexander succeeds in marrying his daughter to Rutilianus, an important ex-consul in Rome; and he is said to have exerted an influence on Marcus Aurelius himself on campaign against the Alemani.[16]

Lucian begins his story with a reference to a letter in which Alexander compares himself to Pythagoras (ch. 4), and Pythagorean echoes sound throughout the narrative. Thus when

---

[14] For Alexander's dates (approximately 110 to 170 A.D.), see C. P. Jones, *Culture and Society in Lucian* (Cambridge, Mass., 1986), 134 n. 6.

[15] Jones (1986), 138. Full documentation in L. Robert, *À travers l'Asie Mineur*, Bibliothèque des Écoles Françaises d'Athènes et de Rome, vol. 239 (Paris, 1980), 392–421; see 397–9 (with figures 7–8) for a description and photograph of the colossal statue of the god-snake Glycon.

[16] Lucian, *Alexander* ch. 48; Jones (1986), 144. For the social and political prestige of Alexander's connection with Rutilianus, see Anderson (1994), 120–3.

Alexander is asked to recommend a teacher for the son of a patron, he names Pythagoras and Homer (ch. 33). Lucian reports that when, in the performance of his mysteries, Alexander appears with a golden thigh, two of his associates debate whether this means that he has the soul of Pythagoras or that he has another soul similar to it (ch. 40). When this question is submitted to the oracle, Alexander responds with appropriate obscurity: "The soul of Pythagoras waxes and wanes, but prophesy comes straight from the mind of Zeus." In part this story reflects the popular prestige of Pythagoras' name, as the patron figure for holy men in the Roman Empire. But more specifically Pythagorean features appear both in the reference to Alexander himself as a possible reincarnation of Pythagoras, and in the account he gives of previous incarnations for his son-in-law Rutilianus (ch. 34). Finally, a link is established between him and his more famous predecessor by the report that one of his teachers was an associate of Apollonius from Tyana (ch. 5). So the Pythagorean credentials of Alexander are well attested, even though we hear nothing of his abstaining from meat. (This may be a peculiarity of our documentation, derived as it is primarily from Lucian.) His Pythagoreanism is in any case highly eclectic, and combined with a quasi-medical tradition. His god Glycon is presented as a "new Asclepius," and Alexander himself claims to be descended from Asclepius.

These two figures, Apollonius and Alexander, the contemporaries of Nicomachus and Numenius respectively, represent a version of Pythagoreanism that extends well beyond the more intellectual tradition of Neopythagorean philosophy. Apollonius and Alexander are not philosophers, but they are *sophoi*, sages, in the domain of religion and the occult. They represent one aspect of the continuing influence of Pythagoreanism, in rather diluted form, in the popular culture of the Roman Empire. Another aspect of that influence will be traced in the next section.

2. TRANSMIGRATION AND VEGETARIANISM

At the climax of his great poem the *Metamorphoses*, Ovid introduces Pythagoras as the preceptor of Numa, in accordance with the old Roman legend discussed in chapter VII. Pythagoras' long speech to Rome in the person of Numa, which occupies half of this concluding Book XV, begins and ends with a passionate appeal to abstain from animal food:

> Abstain! Preserve your bodies unabused,
> Mortals, with food of sin!
>
> Destroy what harms; destroy but never eat;
> Choose wholesome fare and never feed on meat![17]

This insistence on a vegetarian diet is grounded in a properly Pythagorean doctrine of transmigration:

> Our souls
> Are deathless; when they leave their former home,
> Always new habitations welcome them,
> To live afresh. (XV. 158–9)

But Ovid's Pythagoras is an eclectic philosopher, and his doctrine is framed within a broader pattern of elemental transformation and universal change: *cuncta fluunt, omnisque vagans formatur imago.*

> Nothing endures, all is in endless flux,
> Each wandering shape a pilgrim passing by,
> And time itself glides on in ceaseless flow.
>
> Nothing retains its form; new shapes from old
> Nature, the great inventor, ceaselessly
> Contrives. (XV. 77–9, 257–8)

These Heraclitean themes, enriched with poetic echoes of Lucretius' Epicurean epic, help to adorn Ovid's figure with the

---

[17] *Metamorphoses* XV. 75–6, 477–8, transl. A. D. Melville (Oxford, 1986). For secondary literature on the Pythagoras episode, see F. Bömer, *P. Ovidius Naso: Metamorphosen Buch XIV–XV* (Heidelberg, 1986), 268ff. The influence of Empedocles in this passage is emphasized by P. Hardie, "The Speech of Pythagoras in Ovid *Metamorphoses* 15: Empedoclean *Epos*," *CQ* 45 (1995), 204–14.

broad mantle of universal wisdom. He thus faithfully represents the popular, quasi-mythic image of Pythagoras as omniscient sage that predominates in late antiquity and again in the Renaissance. We note that in this popular image, as in Ovid's presentation, neither cosmic numbers nor cosmic music plays an essential part. What is distinctively Pythagorean here is the belief in transmigration and the avoidance of animal food.

For Xenophanes in the early days, Pythagoras' talk of reincarnation had been a subject of mirth. But Plato's myths had made metempsychosis respectable, and it became a school doctrine for the Platonic tradition. The doctrine remained popular throughout antiquity, both in literature and in philosophy. Among the Neoplatonists, transmigration was accepted in principle by Plotinus and, apparently, by Porphyry, but rejected by Iamblichus.[18] Some version of this view was maintained by the Manicheans and by Christian Platonists such as Origen, and there are traces of it in Jewish and Islamic tradition.[19] But belief in transmigration tends to disappear with the victory of Christianity and with a much more individual conception of personal survival and salvation. We can do no more than note here the persistence of different versions of metempsychosis both in Eastern religions and in various Western heresies.

Within the Pythagorean tradition, it was vegetarianism rather than transmigration that attracted wider attention and exercised greater popular appeal, presumably because of its immediate impact on everyday life. Thus the theme of vegetarianism predominates both in Ovid's presentation of Pythagoras and in Philostratus' account of the life of Apollonius. Ovid's Pythagoras does mention the grave danger of cannibalism (and worse—the feast of Thyestes!) for anyone who eats animal food (*Metamorphoses* XV. 459–62). But his primary appeal is to our sympathy for animal life and suffering (how can we cut the throats of kids and calves,

---

[18] Plotinus generally presupposes the standard Platonic version of metempsychosis, which he extends even to plants (in *Ennead* III.4.2; other passages are more equivocal). See the Neoplatonic texts with discussion in R. Sorabji, *Animal Minds and Human Morals: The Origins of the Western Debate* (Ithaca, N.Y., 1993), 188–94.

[19] See Sorabji (ibid.), 189, nn. 167–8. Reincarnation is still accepted in some Jewish traditions.

who cry out like children?) and to our moral solidarity with domestic beasts:

The ox whose meat you savor, whom you slew,
Worked, your own farmhand, in your fields for you.
   (XV.141–2)

For Apollonius, on the other hand, the vegetarian diet is less directly connected with respect for animal life. The avoidance of meat forms part of an ascetic lifestyle (including abstinence from wine and sex) that is primarily designed to guarantee access to the spiritual world and insight into the future. Apollonius' belief in metempsychosis, like his affection and sympathy for animals, seems to play only a secondary role in his devotion to a meatless diet.[20]

Vegetarianism had apparently become quite fashionable in some Roman circles in the first century A.D., as we can see both from Ovid and, later, from Seneca's report on his youthful experiment. This development is, of course, not unconnected with the Pythagorean revival in philosophy. But by then the Pythagorean ban on eating meat had been reinforced by a philosophical tradition going back to Theophrastus and Xenocrates, the heads of the Lyceum and Academy respectively in the late fourth century B.C. Theophrastus' work *On Piety* (much of which has been preserved in Porphyry's *On Abstinence*) presented a systematic argument against animal sacrifice, with an interesting theory of the prehistory of divine worship. Theophrastus cited Empedocles on the Golden Age (when Aphrodite ruled instead of Zeus, and "the altar was not drenched with the unspeakable slaughter of bulls"), and he claimed that the original offerings to the gods were made exclusively from the fruits of the earth.[21] For Theophrastus a re-

---

[20] This is the view of J. Haussleiter, *Der Vegetarismus in der Antike* (Berlin, 1935). See the passages concerning Apollonius collected there, pp. 308–12.

[21] See J. Bernays, *Theophrastos' Schrift über Frommigkeit* (Berlin, 1866/Olms reprint, 1979), 80. Full discussion in Haussleiter (1935: 237–44). Theophrastus explained animal sacrifice as a late development, replacing human sacrifice, which had been introduced by way of cannibalism in times of famine.

spect for animal life is grounded in the concept of community or *oikeiôsis*, the same principle that links human beings in families and communities, and that ultimately links all human beings together. Theophrastus emphasizes the anatomical and psychological features that we share with the animals, above all, sense perception and feeling.[22] He thus offers, for the first time, a philosophical basis for the notion of a moral community between us and the animals. On this view, we have the right to kill dangerous animals, but only in the same way that we have a right to protect ourselves against criminal human beings.[23]

Xenocrates, on the other hand, was concerned not only to protect animals but also to preserve the human being from contamination: animal food will assimilate the eater to the souls of irrational beasts.[24] In Xenocrates we recognize a forerunner of Neopythagorean asceticism. Xenocrates' successor Polemon defended a similar view, and abstinence from meat became characteristic of the Platonic school. The writings of Xenocrates and Polemon are lost, but the Platonist case for vegetarianism, on a wide variety of grounds, is abundantly preserved in the writings of Plutarch, notably *On the Eating of Flesh*, *Whether Aquatic Animals are more Intelligent than Land Animals*, and *On the Use of Reason by Brutes*.[25] The notion of "animal rights," so popular in our own time, can be traced back to these treatises on the intelligence of animals and to Plutarch's claim that respect for animal life is a requirement of justice.[26] These views of Plutarch are not necessarily original with him. Many of the arguments for respecting animals seem to have been originally developed by Carneades, in his

---

[22] Bernays (1866), 96ff.; Haussleiter (1935), 238f.

[23] Bernays (1866), 81; Haussleiter (1935), 239.

[24] This is Haussleiter's reading (p. 198) of fr. 100 (Heinze) from Clement. But Clement mentions both Xenocrates and Polemon in the same breath, and it is not clear whose view he is citing.

[25] See Haussleiter (1935), 212–33.

[26] However, as Sorabji (1993: ch. 11) points out, it is in one sense anachronistic to equate the modern notion of "animal rights" with the ancient view that our conduct towards animals must be regulated by justice, since the modern notion presupposes the "rights of man" as formulated in the eighteenth century.

skeptical attack on the Stoic dogma that animals are deprived of reason and therefore cannot belong to a moral community with human beings.[27]

As we saw in chapter VII, the Sextians in Rome in the first century A.D. also preached abstention from meat. In his *Letter to Lucilius* 108 Seneca reports Sotion's account of the reasons offered by Sextius and Pythagoras in favor of a vegetarian lifestyle. Sextius pleaded the cause on moral and hygienic grounds: one should reject meat in order to enjoy a sober and healthy diet and to avoid cruelty and bloodshed. But Pythagoras (according to Sotion) appealed to more general principles, including the kinship of all living things: no soul ever perishes, but it only disappears until it is infused in another body. By killing animals one runs the risk of murder and patricide. Seneca represents Sotion as pursuing this argument in a poetic style, apparently inspired by Ovid's Pythagoras: "Do you not believe that nothing perishes in this world, but only changes place? It is not only the heavenly bodies that turn in fixed orbits; souls and animals too return in regular cycles. Great men have believed this. Hence suspend your judgment, and leave the matter open. If these things are true, one avoids guilt by abstaining from meat; if false, you have gained in self-control."[28] In addition to an appeal to authority, we have here a neat precedent for the *pari de Pascal*. If you bet on abstinence, you win either way.

In this same period Musonius Rufus was active in Rome, as the teacher of Epictetus and younger contemporary of Seneca. Musonius is the only Stoic philosopher known to have defended vegetarianism, but, like the Sextians, he did so on grounds of health and moral self-improvement (*sôphrosynê*). The properly Pythagorean motives return with Musonius' contemporary, Apollonius of Tyana. As we have seen, for Apollonius abstinence from meat is only one component of an ascetic way of life that aims to escape from the bodily to a spiritual level, a level at which enhanced perception (including second sight) becomes available, and one is enabled to approach the highest divine powers. In this Neopythagorean view we can recognize a certain reading of the

---

[27] Haussleiter (1935), 209f.

[28] *Epist. ad Lucilium* 108.17–21.

Phaedo, according to which everything sensible and corporeal is regarded as a pollution, so that the pursuit of moral excellence comes to be identified with the practice of purification. And so also for the Neoplatonists, abstinence from meat forms part of a general *askêsis* of purification, a discipline that seeks to liberate the soul and its highest principles, *logos* and *nous,* from the chains of the body. This theme is most amply discussed in Porphyry's great treatise *On Abstinence,* which summarizes the whole ancient literature on the subject, including all the arguments for and against vegetarianism. The abstention from meat and animal sacrifice, which for Plotinus was a personal choice, became for Porphyry a defining feature of the philosophic life, an essential purification of the soul so that it becomes fit to approach the divine powers and to share in the higher life.[29]

Yielding to the influence of Iamblichus, both vegetarianism and transmigration tend to disappear from the Neoplatonic tradition after Porphyry,[30] and this fusion of Platonism with Pythagoreanism finally comes to a formal end with the closing of the pagan schools of philosophy in the early sixth century. The spiritual tradition of the *Phaedo* lives on in Christianity, but without the distinctively Pythagorean teachings on vegetarianism and reincarnation. When in early modern times, under the influence of Plutarch and Porphyry, there is renewed interest in vegetarianism and in humane attitudes to the animals, the name of Pythagoras is frequently invoked. Thus we find Voltaire describing Pythagoreanism as "the only religion in the world that was able to make the horror of murder into a filial piety and a religious feeling."[31] Today vegetarianism is again popular in many circles, above all among the young. But the new vegetarianism is based on moral and dietary considerations alone, and there is no visible connection with the Pythagorean tradition. The belief in metempsychosis also reappears in our popular culture, but contemporary associations are more likely to connect reincarnation

---

[29] See references to Plotinus and Porphyry in Haussleiter (1935), 315ff.

[30] Sorabji (1993), 184–94.

[31] *C'est que le pythagorisme est la seule religion au monde qui ait su faire de l'horreur du meurtre une piété filiale et un sentiment religieux,* cited in Haussleiter (1935), 359.

with Indian or Buddhist thought rather than with Pythagoras. It seems fair to say that this branch of the Pythagorean tradition has ceased to be productive, or that it lives on only in an obscure symbiosis with the mystical traditions of the East.

3. MATHEMATICS, MUSIC, AND ASTRONOMY

The case is quite different for that other cluster of Pythagorean ideas that descend not from Plato's *Phaedo* but from his *Timaeus*, and that center on the mathematical interpretation of nature. Here there was no conflict in principle with Christianity, and the Pythagorean-Platonic tradition of the *Timaeus* has, in a sense, retained its vitality down to our own day. We may even claim that Pythagorean cosmology achieved its greatest triumphs in the early modern period, with Copernicus and Kepler. But let us begin by tracing some lines of Pythagorean mathematical tradition in late antiquity.

Since the time of Philolaus and Archytas, the Pythagorean homeland had been established in the quadrivium, the "sister sciences" of arithmetic, geometry, music, and astronomy. These (together with the trivium of grammar, rhetoric, and dialectic) remained the basic school curriculum of late antiquity, and again of medieval times when schools were reestablished on the classical model. With Euclid geometry had achieved its classic form, in which it lost any distinctively Pythagorean features that it may once have had. (Of course some Pythagorean influence on geometry is at least symbolically retained in the legendary association of Euclid I.47 with the name of Pythagoras.) For arithmetic, on the other hand, the standard school text is that of an avowed Pythagorean, Nicomachus of Gerasa. We have seen in chapter VIII how his *Introduction to Arithmetic* was originally conceived as a preparation for Pythagorean numerology, including a numerical representation for the traditional gods. It was arithmetic and numerology in this Neopythagorean form that was transmitted to the Latin middle ages and to the Renaissance in the works of Augustine and Boethius. Augustine was exceptionally fond of the allegorical interpretation of Biblical numbers by reference to Pythagorean ideas. Thus, in the spirit of Philo, Augustine will point out that the six days of creation in Genesis 1 reflect the fact that six is a perfect number (*De trinitate* IV.7). Boethius' treatise on arithmetic was even richer in Pythagorean speculation, since he had in effect translated Nicomachus' *Introduction*. Such numerical Pythagoreanism remains popular in medieval thought; in the Renaissance, its influence will be reinforced by a combination with the Hebrew numerology of the Cabala tradition.

The most distinctively Pythagorean of the four arts of the quadrivium is music, or more exactly harmonics. In the Pythagorean tradition, this means the explanation of musical intervals and concordances in terms of numerical ratios. As we have seen in chapter IV, fundamental work on this subject was done in the fourth century B.C. by Archytas, who, as a mathematician of the first rank, gave a mature form to a harmonic tradition going back to Philolaus and beyond. Archytas' treatise is known only from a few fragments and testimonia. The first preserved work in this tradition is the *Sectio Canonis* attributed to Euclid, at the end of the fourth century B.C.[32] I quote Barker's summary:

> [The *Sectio Canonis*] consists of a short introduction and twenty propositions presented and argued in the manner of theorems . . . . The introduction sets out a theory of the physical causation of sounds and their pitches [by impact], designed to justify the treatment of pitches as relative quantities, and the intervals between them as numerical ratios. . . . There follow nine theorems that are purely mathematical, proving various propositions about ratios as such, and about the "intervals" . . . between terms in such ratios. At proposition 10, musical conceptions begin to be introduced. . . . Propositions 10-13 demonstrate the ratios of the principal musical concords, and that of the tone. . . . Finally, propositions 19–20 show how to divide the string of a monochord in ratios that give a system in the diatonic genus; this is the "division of the *kanôn*" from which the work gets its name.[33]

---

[32] Barker (1989: 190) is inclined to regard the attribution to Euclid as correct.

[33] Ibid.

Barker concludes that the author aims "to give systematic, formal proofs of propositions that are basic to the Pythagorean and Platonist tradition," that is, the tradition of analyzing musical sound in terms of numerical ratios, in contrast to the Aristoxenian tradition that takes heard intervals as a primitive concept. At the same time, Barker points out that Euclid's mathematical arguments do not operate entirely a priori but (like the work of Philolaus and Archytas before him) depend crucially upon empirical observation of the actual concords and discords.

The next text in this tradition is the *Enchiridion* of Nicomachus in the first century A.D. This is a rather pedestrian handbook, without any of the mathematical distinction of the *Sectio*.[34] The author claims that he is writing in haste and that he will produce a larger, more systematic work as soon as he finds leisure. (There is reason to believe that the promised work was completed, although it has not survived. The first three books of Boethius, *De institutione musica*, are apparently based upon the lost *Introduction to Music* of Nicomachus.)[35] From the *Enchiridion* we can see that, as we expect, Nicomachus' approach is systematically Pythagorean, "not only in the author's insistence on basing harmonics in physical acoustics, in his use of the language of ratios, and in his emphatic references to Pythagoras himself," but also in his assigning the notes of the octave to the heavenly bodies, so as to generate the music of the spheres (ch. 3).

By far the most important work in this tradition is the *Harmonics* of Ptolemy in the second century A.D., although Ptolemy regards himself as an independent thinker and feels free to correct the Pythagoreans' mistakes. He begins his treatise with philosophical reflection on the appropriate criterion for knowledge in music, insisting that both reason (mathematical theory) and perception (of heard sounds) have essential roles in the criterion. Accordingly, his own procedure combines a Euclidean form of mathematical reasoning with a broad concern for the actual musical phenomena, and he criticizes both Pythagoreans and

---

[34] "Like the *Introduction to Arithmetic*, it is not an intellectually distinguished or original piece, but it had an important influence on later writers," Barker (1989), 245, who provides a translation.

[35] See C. M. Bower (1989), xxvii.

Aristoxenians for emphasizing one aspect of this criterion at the expense of the other. Ptolemy's own work, however, preserves the essential features of Pythagorean harmonic theory: a concern with the physics of sound as well as with the mathematics of the octave, and above all, a sense that the whole cosmos is ordered in agreement with the musical numbers. Thus four chapters of Book III are devoted to the psychological consequences of harmonic theory, and the last nine chapters show how the theory applies to the zodiac and to planetary motions, in a detailed working out of the music of the spheres. As we shall see, this work by one of the greatest astronomers of antiquity was to prove a fateful influence on the astronomical researches of Johannes Kepler in the seventeenth century A.D.

For the sake of completeness, I mention here two more major works in the tradition of ancient harmonics. The *De musica* of Aristides Quintilianus (which may date from the end of the third century A.D.) is the latest, most detailed treatment of the subject, in part from a Pythagorean point of view.[36] Finally, Porphyry's *Commentary on Ptolemy's "Harmonics"* provides a kind of summa for the ancient tradition in harmonics. Porphyry's work is particularly important for identifying Ptolemy's sources, and thus for preserving information on early authors such as Archytas.

As an indication of the lasting influence of Pythagorean theory on musical practice, we may note the prevalence, until the Renaissance, of what is called Pythagorean intonation. This is a tuning of the scale in which all fifths and fourths are pure or untempered, so that the classical Pythagorean ratios (3:2 and 4:3) are preserved. Nearly all medieval theorists who discussed the arithmetic of musical intervals did so in terms of Pythagorean intonation, dependent as they were on Boethius, and hence ultimately on Nicomachus.[37] It was only in the fifteenth century that "tem-

---

[36] Translation by Barker (1989), 392–535.

[37] See J. M. Barbour, *Tuning and Temperament: A Historical Survey* (East Lansing, Mich., 1951), 2–4, on the persistence of Pythagorean musical theory into the eighteenth century. Hence the appropriateness of Pythagoras as the representative of music at Chartres; see the frontispiece.

pered" tuning (in which most or all of the concords are made slightly impure so that none will sound out of tune) became frequent. Since the Renaissance, such tempered tuning (as in Bach's "Well-tempered Clavichord") has been taken for granted by sophisticated musicians, but Pythagorean intonation persists in some folk traditions.[38]

We cannot follow any further the tradition of Pythagorean musical theory (although we will find the influence of Ptolemy's *Harmonica* returning with Kepler). For the history of philosophical thought, however, the fruitful use of Pythagorean ideas begins again with the rise of humanism and the renewed contact with Greek texts in the Renaissance. The preliminary stirrings are perceptible in Petrarch, who begins to learn Greek and quotes from Pythagoras as "the most ancient of all natural philosophers."[39] The humanists of the fifteenth century, such as Marsilio Ficino, Pico della Mirandola, and Johann Reuchlin, who were the first Europeans to gain full access to Greek philosophical literature, were immediately attracted to the Platonic tradition, and above all to the works of Iamblichus and Proclus in which Neopythagorean influence is so prominent. Ficino is responsible for making available in Latin translation all of Plato's works (with his own commentaries on the most "Pythagorean" dialogues, *Parmenides*, *Philebus*, and *Timaeus*); also the *Corpus Hermeticum*; some works by Porphyry, Iamblichus, and Proclus; as well as the writings of Plotinus and pseudo-Dionysius. After Ficino, the full literature of the Platonic tradition is open to the West. Both Ficino and his younger friend Pico della Mirandola accepted the viewpoint of the late Neoplatonists, according to which the philosophy of Pythagoras is scarcely distinguishable from that of Plato. Thus Pico, in his *Oration on the Dignity of Man*, can draw many teachings "from the ancient theology of Hermes Trismegistus, many from the doctrines of Chaldaeans and of Pythagoras, and many

---

[38] M. Lindley, "Pythagorean Intonation," in S. Sadie, ed., *The New Grove Dictionary of Music and Musicians* (London, 1980), Vol. 15, 485–7.

[39] Petrarch, "On His Own Ignorance," transl. in *The Renaissance Philosophy of Man*, eds. E. Cassirer, P. O. Kristeller, J. H. Randall, Jr. (Chicago, 1948), 94.

from the occult mysteries of the Hebrews."[40] But he will also refer more specifically to the "method of philosophizing through numbers" as known to "Pythagoras, Philolaus, Plato, and the first Platonists." In the case of Pico, Pythagorean numerology joins forces with the allegedly more ancient Hebrew texts of Cabalistic lore, where the words and numbers of holy Scripture are deciphered according to a mystical system. The first great German humanist, Reuchlin, shared Pico's passion for the Cabala and for the joint study of Hebrew and Greek as a guide in theology and philosophy. It was Reuchlin's idea to cover this enterprise with the name of Pythagoras. Reuchlin wrote to Pope Leo X that, as Ficino had made Plato known in Italy, and as a French scholar had restored Aristotle, "I will complete their work by the rebirth of Pythagoras in Germany." But this will require knowledge of the Hebrew Cabala, "since the philosophy of Pythagoras was drawn from the teachings of Chaldean science."[41] As the pagan Platonists of late antiquity had linked Pythagoras with the Eastern wisdom deposited in the Chaldean Oracles, so the Christian Platonists of the Renaissance could connect him with the Hebrew Bible as enriched by Cabalistic interpretation.

The humanists thus restored the image of Pythagoras as omniscient sage familiar from late antiquity. But it was left for the natural philosophers to make a truly creative use of Pythagorean ideas. Perhaps the first major Pythagorean thinker since Numenius or Iamblichus was Nicholas of Cusa in the mid-fifteenth century. As a Catholic cardinal working in the tradition of Christian Neoplatonism, Nicholas developed a profoundly original speculative system based upon mathematical conceptions, involving an infinite universe and a moving earth. Since all cognition was to be understood in terms of a relationship that involves both similarity and difference, Nicholas took as his paradigm for knowledge the form of numerical proportion. Scientific knowledge thus consists in the determination of ratios and cannot be attained without the help of numbers. As historians have observed, Nicholas' world view emerges from an authentic Platonic-Pythagorean

---

[40] Ibid., 245.

[41] Letter to Leo X, cited in A. E. Chaignet, *Pythagore et la philosophie pythagoricienne*, Vol. II (Paris, 1873), 330.

background, but at the same time it prefigures the new mathematical science of nature.[42] A century later Nicholas's ideas were taken over by Giordano Bruno, developed in the direction of pantheism and combined with an understanding of the Copernican system.[43] Important as was Bruno's work for the intellectual ferment of the age, however, it was not in speculative philosophy but in the technical domain of mathematical astronomy that the Pythagorean tradition was to make its greatest contribution.

We have already noted the fact that Copernicus repeatedly invoked Pythagorean antecedents for his thesis of the earth's motion. And there is more here than the usual Renaissance fashion of adorning one's work with classical allusions and ancient citations. In three respects, Copernicus's appeal to Pythagorean and Neoplatonic ideas reveals something essential about his own position. In the first place, his stubborn, almost pathological reluctance to publish a controversial theory was justified, in his own eyes, by Pythagorean precedent. We have mentioned his interest in the pseudo-Pythagorean "letter of Lysis," one of only two Greek texts that Copernicus is known to have translated into Latin. In his preface to *De Revolutionibus,* Copernicus seeks to explain his refusal to publish his work "not for nine years only, but to a fourth period of nine years," by citing "the example of the Pythagoreans and others who were wont to impart their philosophic mysteries only to intimates and friends, and then not in writing but by word of mouth, as the letter of Lysis to Hipparchus witnesses."[44] Copernicus had at one time thought to include his

---

[42] Ibid., 334. For Nicholas of Cusa and Bruno, see also E. Cassirer, *Individuum und Kosmos in der Philosophie der Renaissance* (Leipzig and Berlin, 1927/Darmstadt, 1963); A. Koyré, *From the Closed World to the Infinite Universe* (Baltimore, 1957), 6–24.

[43] According to Chaignet (1873: II, 336), Bruno is certainly "le plus grand des pythagoriciens de la Renaissance." (He does not consider Copernicus and Kepler.) Chaignet (ibid., 330–49) finds other traces of Pythagorean influence in European philosophy from the fifteenth century to Hegel.

[44] Dedicatory preface to *De Revolutionibus* as cited by Kuhn (1957), 137. (= *Gesamtausgabe* II [1984], 3). For the obsessive desire of Copernicus to avoid public disclosure of his system, see the colorful narrative of

translation of the letter as part of his own long-delayed publication of his astronomical work.

This temperamental sympathy for Pythagorean secrecy was reinforced by a second set of doctrinal considerations. In the same prefatory letter to Pope Paul III, Copernicus relates how he became dissatisfied with the traditional account of the heavenly motions, and hence began to peruse "the works of all the philosophers on whom I could lay hand" in search of an alternative view. He first found a mention in Cicero of Hicetas' hypothesis that the earth moves.[45] Copernicus says that he then found a fuller report in Plutarch's *Placita*; and he quotes the Greek text verbatim, in which Philolaus the Pythagorean is cited as claiming that the earth moves around the central fire, whereas Heraclides of Pontus and Ecphantus the Pythagorean are named for the thesis of the earth's diurnal rotation.[46] It is significant that both here in the preface and again in Book I, chapter 5, Copernicus chooses to mention his more obscure Pythagorean precursors rather than his greatest ancient predecessor, Aristarchus of Samos, with whose heliocentric hypothesis he was also familiar.

The third and final link between Copernicus and the Pythagoreans is more subtle and more profound. It has often been pointed out that, in practical terms, the heliocentric system as formulated by Copernicus did not produce more accurate predictions than its Ptolemaic rival, and that for purposes of observation and calculation, it achieved little if any simplification. Even its geometric detail, with epicycles and eccentrics, was almost as convoluted as Ptolemy's. The real advantage of the new system, both for Copernicus himself and for his later adherents such as Kepler and Galileo, is perhaps best described in aesthetic terms. There was something simple and harmonious in the Copernican conception, even if the details were unsatisfactory. Many diverse phenomena are explained by a single principle,

---

Arthur Koestler, *The Sleepwalkers: A History of Man's Changing Vision of the Universe* (New York, 1959), 148–58 and passim.

[45] This is Cicero's *Academica Priora* II.39.123.

[46] The text that Copernicus cites is [Plutarch] *Placita* III.13, published by Diels under the name of Aetius (*Doxographi graeci*, 378).

the movement of the earth around the sun. The relative size and sequence of the planetary orbits are so fixed that no change could be made in any one without altering the whole system. In addition, the position of the sun in the center was in accord with classical Neoplatonic representations of the sun as offspring and symbol of the Good. So in Book I, chapter 10, after summarizing the order of the planets, whose distance from the sun is determined in his system by the length of their periods, Copernicus continues: "In the middle of all sits Sun enthroned. In this most beautiful temple could we place this luminary in any better position from which he can illuminate the whole at once? He is rightly called the Lamp, the Mind, the Ruler of the Universe; Hermes Trismegistus names him the Visible God . . . . So the Sun sits as upon a royal throne ruling his children the planets which circle round him."[47] This symbolic role of the sun as a divine Father, ruling the planets as his children, will become even more important for Kepler, as we shall see.

Above all, however, the Copernican system as a whole has a naturalness that is lacking in earlier views. In Copernicus's own words, "we find underlying this ordination an admirable symmetry in the Universe, and a clear bond of harmony in the motion and magnitude of the Spheres such as can be discovered in no other wise."[48] As Thomas Kuhn has pointed out, the initial appeal of the Copernican system was to that small group of mathematical astronomers whose Neoplatonic or Pythagorean ear was attuned to the perception of mathematical harmonies.[49] Of these, the most important by far was Johannes Kepler, perhaps the greatest Pythagorean of them all. Copernicus's instinct was conservative, and his own conception of the solar system was only partially disengaged from the Aristotelian and Ptolemaic framework within which it had taken shape. The task of completing the Copernican revolution was left to astronomers who came later. It was Kepler, two generations after Copernicus, who finally

---

[47] *De Revolutionibus* I.10 (= *Gesamtausgabe* II [1984], 20–1), cited in Kuhn (1957), 131.

[48] Ibid., cited in Kuhn (1957), 180.

[49] Kuhn (1957), 181.

realized the Copernican vision of a heliocentric system of maximal harmony and simplicity.

The Pythagoreanism of Kepler was a deliberate, lifelong conviction. It is most eloquently expressed in the title of his last great work: *Harmonice Mundi*, "The Harmonics of the World."[50] (The title is clearly inspired by Ptolemy's *Harmonica*, which Kepler had planned to translate into Latin.) In this work, which contains a long Excursus discussing the Pythagorean *tetractus*, Kepler explicitly recognizes the *Timaeus* as his model. As if echoing Numenius, he construes the *Timaeus* as the best guide to understanding the Biblical creation story. "This work is, beyond all doubt, a commentary on the first chapter of Genesis, otherwise the first book of Moses, transforming it into Pythagorean philosophy, as will easily be apparent to an attentive reader who compares it with Moses' own words."[51]

Just as Plato's demiurge builds the world out of number series, elementary triangles, and regular solids, so Kepler's God is also a consummate geometer, whose plan for the world can be penetrated by the human mind only if it succeeds in discovering the mathematical relationships realized in celestial phenomena. Hence for Kepler, as for Nicomachus fourteen centuries earlier, the archetype for creation in the mind of God must be mathematical in form. But between these two there is a fundamental difference in the conception of mathematics. For Nicomachus the first science is arithmetic, and the deepest level of explanation is the symbolical account furnished by numerology. Kepler's Pythagoreanism is of a different stripe. Kepler's divine archetype is geometrical in form, and his preference for geometry is deeply motivated. He insists on an explanatory theory that can give results in terms of physical magnitudes to be measured in astronomical observation. Kepler has no patience with the significance

---

[50] *Harmonice* is Kepler's Latin transliteration of ἁρμονική (ἐπιστήμη), "the science of harmonics." The title *Harmonice Mundi* is frequently mistranslated (in both English and French) as "The Harmony of the World." In Caspar's German version, *Weltharmonik* is correct.

[51] J. Kepler, *Harmonice Mundi*, Book III, ch. 1, marginal notation, in *Gesammelte Werke*, ed. Max Caspar (München, 1940) Vol. VI, 221.

of numbers as such, as expounded in the occult practice of numerology. That is why he insists on the importance of *numeri numerati* rather than *numeri numerantes*, numbers as the measures of physical quantities rather than "counting numbers" or numbers in the abstract.[52]

This contrast between two different kinds of Pythagoreanism will be dramatically displayed in a famous polemic between Kepler and Robert Fludd. Fludd had published an elaborate cosmology that was also designed to disclose a Pythagorean harmony of the world order, but one in which the musical numbers make no serious contact with observational astronomy.[53] Fludd's work represents a paradigmatic example of the occult strand in the Pythagorean tradition, a strand that has not ceased to be active even today. The dispute between Kepler and Fludd is thus a clear marker of the parting of the ways, between a rational and an obscurantist version of Pythagorean thought, as it were a new division between the *mathêmatikoi* and the *akousmatikoi*. For Kepler, unlike Fludd, Pythagoreanism is not a vague theosophy but instead a philosophical approach to natural science.

The title of Kepler's first book, *Mysterium Cosmographicum* (published in 1597 when Kepler was twenty-five), presents his theory as the disclosure of a secret for deciphering the riddle of the universe, that is to say, for deriving a priori the underlying mathematical structure of the Copernican system of the heavens. Kepler's clue was to explain the spatial relations between the

---

[52] *The Harmony of the World*, transl. E. J. Aiton, A. M. Duncan, J. V. Field (Philadelphia, 1997), 150, 500, 506, = *Harmonice Mundi* Bk. III Prop.1. The English translation will be cited as *Harmony* (1997).

[53] R. Fludd, *Utriusque cosmi majoris scilicet et minoris metaphysica, physica atque technica historia* (4 volumes, Oppenheim, 1617–19). For Kepler's response to Fludd, see his Appendix to Book V of *Harmony* (1997), 503–8; full discussion by J. V. Field, "Kepler's Rejection of Numerology" in B. Vickers, ed., *Occult and Scientific Mentalities in the Renaissance* (Cambridge, 1984). See also the standard biography by Max Caspar, *Kepler*, Engl. transl. by C. D. Hellman (London and New York, 1959), 290–3. Abundant illustrations from Fludd's volumes are reproduced in S. K. Heninger, Jr., *Touches of Sweet Harmony: Pythagorean Cosmology and Renaissance Poetics* (San Marino, Calif., 1974), 184–90 and passim.

orbits of the earth and the other five planets by means of the five Platonic solids. This explanation is essentially Pythagorean in form: the discovery of a mathematical structure that can account for the empirical regularities, as the Pythagorean ratios account for the audible consonances. Thus the insertion between the planetary spheres of these five regular solids, "which have been so celebrated from the time of Pythagoras and Plato down to our own,"[54] would explain both why there are exactly six planets and also their relative distance from the sun and from one another. Kepler repeated essentially the same proposal twenty years later in the fuller statement of his cosmology in the *Harmonics of the World* (1619), and he confirmed it once again in the second edition of the *Mysterium* (1623). Despite Kepler's lifelong attachment to this theory, it turned out, of course, to be a scientific dead end and has now been forgotten. (A direct refutation came only in 1781, when the seventh planet Uranus was discovered.) Nevertheless, the book in which it was published was filled with brilliant ideas, and it established Kepler as one of the most promising young scientists of the day. Perhaps the most momentous result of this first book was the very favorable attention it attracted from Tycho Brahe.

Kepler's project in the *Mysterium* was to give (as the subtitle declares) "the true and proper reasons for the numbers, magnitudes, and periodic motions of the heavenly orbits." The proper reasons must lie in simple principles of mathematical order, which Kepler proceeded to exhibit in rigorous geometric demonstrations.[55] The general scheme was inspired by Plato's *Timaeus*, but Kepler's mathematics was derived from Euclid and Ptolemy. His account of the regular solids (pyramid, cube, octahedron, dodecahedron, icosahedron) was taken from Euclid XIII, the last

---

[54] *Mysterium Cosmographicum*, "Preface to the Reader"; the Latin text is reprinted with translation by A. M. Duncan in *Johannes Kepler, The Secret of the Universe* (New York, 1981). Kepler follows the Neopythagoreans of antiquity in attributing to Pythagoras the cosmology of the *Timaeus*, where the regular solids serve to construct the elements.

[55] For a full exposition of Kepler's ill-fated theory, see J. V. Field, *Kepler's Geometrical Cosmology* (London, 1988), chs. 3–5.

book of the *Elements*, and Kepler followed Proclus in believing "the goal of the *Elements* as a whole to be the construction of the so-called Platonic solids."[56] By way of Proclus, then, Kepler was, like Copernicus and other scientists of the Renaissance, directly dependent on the Greek scientific classics. Some fifteen centuries later, they were all prepared to begin their research precisely at the point that the best ancients had reached. What was new was not only the emphasis on testing theories against observation, but also the intense energy and competitive activity of an international scholarly community in incessant communication with one another, sending books and letters back and forth from Poland and Germany to Denmark, England, and Italy.

It was natural for Kepler to begin by seeking his mathematical principles in the five regular solids, since these were the perfect geometric forms utilized by Plato and studied by Euclid. But in his final attempt at unraveling the secrets of cosmic harmony and getting his scheme to match the best seventeenth-century measurements, Kepler was less Neoplatonic and more purely Neopythagorean. In the *Harmonice Mundi*, his attempt is based not only upon Euclidean geometry but also upon musical consonances. Even in the earlier *Mysterium*, he had sought for correlations between the perfect solids and the harmonic intervals in music. In his continuing effort to find a precise astronomical basis for the notion of cosmic music, Kepler had offered, jokingly, to pray to the ghost of Pythagoras for assistance, "unless the soul of Pythagoras has migrated into me."[57] More realistically, he made a careful study of Ptolemy's *Harmonica*. As we know, the great ancient astronomer had also produced a kind of Pythagorean tract in musical theory, in the tradition begun by Archytas and prefigured in Philolaus.[58] Like Kepler, Ptolemy first develops a

---

[56] *Proclus: A Commentary on the First Book of Euclid's Elements*, transl. G. R. Morrow (Princeton, 1970), 57. Kepler is full of admiration for Proclus, whom he cites often and refers to as "the Pythagorean" (*Harmony* [1997], 137).

[57] Cited in Caspar (1959), 96, and Koestler (1959), 277. Kepler is apparently alluding to the dream of Ennius (above, p. 87).

[58] See the translation of Ptolemy's *Harmonica* in Barker (1989). As we have pointed out (above, pp. 155f.), Ptolemy's general point of view on

mathematical theory of musical harmony and then applies it to ratios in the zodiac and in the movement of the heavenly bodies, in order to give an astronomical account of the music of the spheres (*Harmonica,* Book III, chs. 8–16). Kepler was delighted to discover that Ptolemy had anticipated his approach "one thousand five hundred years before," even though Ptolemy's results were quite unsatisfactory because of "the crudity of the ancient astronomy." But their general agreement on celestial harmonies showed that "the very nature of things was setting out to reveal itself to men, through interpreters separated by a distance of fifteen centuries."[59] But before composing his own work on cosmic harmony, Kepler had to learn more astronomy. Fortunately, as a result of his first book he had been invited to collaborate with Tycho Brahe, by far the finest astronomical observer in the age before the telescope.

Kepler's work with Brahe delayed his project on cosmic harmony, but it provided the observational data that permitted him to plot the true orbit of Mars. This task took him six years of hard work (1600–1605), and he may well have been disappointed to find that it was an ellipse rather than a perfect circle. In fact, this discovery really signaled the end of classical cosmology, which for two millennia, from the Presocratics to Copernicus, had been based on the circle and the sphere as the perfect celestial figures. Even Galileo never freed himself from this traditional assumption.

There was a great deal at stake. Aristotle had argued, and most natural philosophers had agreed, that uniform motion in a circle was the only form of change that could continue indefinitely, and therefore the only possible shape for the eternal movement of the

---

harmony is recognizably Pythagorean rather than Aristoxenian, even though he criticizes the more dogmatic Pythagoreans for ignoring audible consonances that do not conform to their preferred ratios. Ptolemy's criticism on this point is echoed and developed by Kepler in his introduction to Book III of *Harmonice* (= *Harmony* [1997], 137f.).

[59] *Harmonice Mundi,* Introduction to Book V = *Harmony* (1997), 391. Kepler discusses Ptolemy's *Harmonica* at length in the Appendix to Book V. He had originally intended to publish a Latin translation of Ptolemy's treatise, part of which was completed and finally published in the nineteenth century. See *Harmony* (1997), 499, n. 186.

heavenly bodies. Hence Kepler's new shape for celestial orbits required a new law for celestial motion. The elliptical orbit for the planets—what became known as Kepler's First Law—was thus supplemented by his Second Law, which specifies that the speed of the planet varies in such a way that the line connecting the planet to the sun sweeps through equal areas in equal intervals of time, so that the planet moves faster when it is closer to the sun, slower when it is farther away. With these two discoveries, Kepler definitively solved the problem of planetary motion, the problem that had caused Copernicus to abandon the geocentric system, but which Copernicus's own version of heliocentrism was not able to resolve.[60]

The discovery that the planets move more slowly when more distant from the sun led Kepler to posit a force in the sun that was responsible for pushing the planets forward in their orbit.[61] He was groping for Newton's principle of gravitation, but was not able to conceive it correctly. Nevertheless, Kepler's dynamic view of the sun added a new layer of significance to Copernicus's Neoplatonic conception of the sun as father and ruler of the planets. For Copernicus, the sun was only the source of light; for Kepler, it was also the cause of planetary motion:

> The sun, in the middle of the moving stars, himself at rest and yet the source of motion, carries the image of God the Father and Creator. . . . He distributes his motive force through a medium which contains the moving bodies even as the Father creates through the Holy Ghost.[62]

---

[60] For the significance of these discoveries, see Kuhn (1957), 212: "For the first time a single uncompounded geometric curve and a single speed law are sufficient for predictions of planetary position, and for the first time the predictions are as accurate as the observations." Kepler was apparently so reluctant to recognize the elliptical orbit that he was actually able to formulate the Second Law before the First. See Koestler (1959), 323–33; Casper (1959), 132–4.

[61] In the *Mysterium*, Kepler posited a Neoplatonic soul in each planet responsible for its movement, but he later spoke only of a "moving force" (*vis motrix*) in the sun.

[62] Letter to Mästlin, 3.10.1595, in *Gesammelte Werke*, Vol. XIII, eds.

Kepler thus blends his Neoplatonic reverence for the sun with his Lutheran notion of the Trinity in his own theory of planetary motion, where the sun as image of God the Father takes the place of Aristotle's Unmoved Mover.

Kepler's Third Law was discovered in the final stage of his work on cosmic harmony, when the *Harmonice Mundi* was almost complete. This is a law of an entirely different kind. It offers no direct advantage for observation and prediction, since it relates two magnitudes that are independently known. The Third Law states that the squares of the periods of revolution for any two planets are related as the cubes of their mean distance from the sun. The planetary periods had been known since Babylonian times, and the shape and size of the orbit can be calculated without this law, as Kepler demonstrated in the case of Mars. We know that Kepler's Third Law turned out to be of crucial importance for the development of celestial dynamics, since it provided the clue for Newton's formulation of the law of universal gravitation. Kepler, of course, could scarcely foresee this consequence. Nevertheless, for good Pythagorean reasons he had the sense that with this discovery he had finally deciphered the cosmic mystery that he had set out to interpret in his first book.

It is true that even without the Third Law, Kepler had succeeded in connecting the orbital speeds of the planets with concordant intervals of the musical scale, so that the planets as they revolve can generate musical consonances.[63] Even without this law, he could conclude with delight, "the heavenly motions are nothing but a perpetual song for several voices, perceived by the intellect, not by the ear."[64] So some historians, who do not share Kepler's delight in the music of the spheres, take care to

---

W. von Dyck and M. Caspar (München, 1945), 35. Cited in Koestler (1959), 261f.

[63] Summarizing the astral harmonies of *Harmonice* Book V, Field (1988: 143ff.) points out that the Third Law is only tangentially connected with the main astronomical argument but that it plays a decisive part in the cosmological deduction of the dimensions of the planetary orbits from Kepler's harmonic archetype.

[64] *Harmonice Mundi* V.7: *perennis quidam concentus (rationalis non vocalis) per dissonantes tensiones* (*Gesammelte Werke* VI [1940], 328 = *Harmony* [1997], 446).

emphasize the fact that the momentous Third Law is logically independent of those "elaborate and fantastic speculations on the mathematical harmonies constituted by the motions of the planets."[65] In the culminating deduction of Book V, chapter IX, on the harmonic motions of the planets, the very first axiom states that, wherever possible, "harmonies ought to have been established of all kinds, so that such variety should adorn the world."[66] The Third Law seems to add just one more kind of harmony, when the rest of the book had already been written. Why, then, should Kepler express so much enthusiasm over the discovery of this law, which he twice dates with precision on May 15, 1618?[67]

In the first place, the Third Law has the peculiarity that it applies to planets only in pairs and not to planets singly. Hence it is precisely the kind of regularity that Kepler had originally sought to find, when he went in search of the "true and proper reasons" for the orbital magnitudes and periodic motions: in this law the structure of the entire solar system is determined by a single numerical relation between the speed and size of the planetary orbits. Furthermore, and this seems to be what aroused Kepler's greatest excitement, the connection established in the law between planetary speeds and distance from the sun made it possible for Kepler to devise an empirical test for his old theory that the regular solids serve to separate the planetary orbits. Using the Third Law, Kepler was able to calculate the distance of a planet from the sun on the basis of the harmonies determined to match his theoretical polyhedra. "A part of my *Secret of the Universe*, put in suspense 22 years ago because it was not yet clear, is to be completed here," reports Kepler. The difference between the distances so calculated and those based on Tycho Brahe's observation was so small that "at first I believed I was dreaming, and assuming my

---

[65] E. J. Dijksterhuis, *The Mechanization of the World Picture*, transl. C. Dikshoorn (Oxford, 1961), 323.

[66] *Harmony* (1997), 452.

[67] *Harmony* (1997), 391: "nothing restrains me; it is my pleasure to yield to the inspired frenzy, it is my pleasure to taunt mortal men with the candid acknowledgement that I am stealing the golden vessels of the Egyptians to build a tabernacle for my God from them." The date of the discovery is repeated in detail on p. 411.

conclusion among my basic premises."[68] Thus the primary significance of the Third Law for Kepler was not simply the addition of
one more Neopythagorean harmony to ornament the cosmos. It
was rather the convergence between his original theory formulated in terms of Platonic solids and the precise empirical observations he had learned to make with Brahe. Or to put it differ-
ently, Kepler's extraordinary enthusiasm on May 15, 1618,
marked the long-delayed marriage between his Neoplatonic
speculation and his professional conscience as a meticulous observer. As Dreyer points out, it was in order to test his early theory that Kepler went to work with Brahe, and it was this theory
and the concern with cosmic harmony that motivated the work
that led to all three laws. "There is thus the most intimate connection between his speculations and his great achievements; without the former we should never have had the latter."[69]

In summary, we can understand how Kepler himself could see
his work, and above all his *Harmonics of the World*, as the realization of a Pythagorean dream: the natural order of the universe finally stands revealed as a tremendous exemplification of the musical numbers, and these numbers are now confirmed by precise
observations. It was in the course of pursuing this dream that Kepler laid the foundations for Newtonian mechanics and hence for
the new synthesis of classical physics. In one respect, Newtonian
physics is an even more complete realization of the enterprise
projected by the mathematical cosmology of the *Timaeus*, but in
another respect, it puts the Platonic-Pythagorean vision of the
cosmos hopelessly out-of-date. On the positive side, the new
physics is obviously compatible with the traditional conception
of God the Creator as a geometer. On the other hand, the laws of

---

[68] Book V, ch. 9; *Harmony* (1997), 411. A modern author observes that, by
contemporary standards of accuracy in cosmology, "Kepler's conviction of the confirmation of his theory by observation was an entirely
reasonable one" (Field 1988: 163).

[69] J. L. E. Dreyer, *History of the Planetary Systems from Thales to Kepler*
(Cambridge, 1906), 420. Dreyer gives a brief and lucid account of Kepler's cosmic harmonies (pp. 405–10). For a slightly different interpretation of the importance of the Third Law for Kepler, see Caspar
(1959), 287.

Newtonian mechanics rely not upon Euclid but upon the more complex mathematics of analytic geometry and the calculus. Kepler was thus the last scientist who could be a genuine Pythagorean in the strict tradition of the *Timaeus*, discovering the order of nature in the regular solids and the musical ratios. Furthermore, once Kepler's laws of planetary motion are explained by Newton's principle of universal gravitation, the "true and proper reasons" for the motions of the planets cannot be given in terms of geometry or number theory alone. What is required now is a causal theory involving physical forces, which neither Platonists nor Pythagoreans could provide.

In a sense, then, Kepler was the last Pythagorean; but a true Pythagorean he was. His success in uncovering mathematical regularities in the labyrinth of precise observations collected by Tycho Brahe was due in no small measure to his passionate commitment to a Pythagorean view of nature. It has been said that Kepler worshipped two deities, a Lutheran God and a Pythagorean God. He had, after all, started as a student of theology, and he paid a heavy price in later years for his loyalty to the Protestant creed. His scientific career was initiated almost accidentally, by his involuntary assignment to a mathematical teaching post. In the end, however, there was no conflict between his two vocations. Anyone who can read the *Timaeus* as a commentary on Genesis will have no difficulty in identifying the Christian with the Pythagorean God. And no scientist or theologian, before or since, believed more ardently than Kepler in the old axiom that God geometrizes. "Geometry existed before the Creation, is co-eternal with the mind of God, *is God himself* . . . ; geometry provided God with a model for the Creation, and was implanted in man, together with God's own likeness."[70]

In one sense, then, the tradition of scientific Pythagoreanism comes to an end with Kepler and with the half-modern, half-magical world of the late Renaissance.[71] After Newton's work and the

---

[70] *Harmonice Mundi* IV.1. (*Gesammelte Werke* VI [1940], 223 = *Harmony* [1997], 304). Transl. Koestler (1959), 262.

[71] Similarly Field (1988), 170: Kepler can be seen "as the last exponent of a form of mathematical cosmology that can be traced back to the shadowy figure of Pythagoras."

development of modern physics, a scientist can be a Pythagorean only in an extended, metaphorical sense. In this sense, many scientists today are still Pythagorean, if they believe that the laws of nature must be mathematical in form, and that the simpler and more general the mathematical relation is found to be, the more deeply it will penetrate into the nature of things. Einstein once wrote that the scientist is many things but that he may count also as "a Platonist or Pythagorean insofar as he considers the viewpoint of logical simplicity as an indispensable and effective tool of his research." If, as Whitehead and others supposed, Pythagoras and his followers had dimly divined "the possible importance of mathematics in the formation of science," then it is obvious that a modern scientist like Einstein is "following the pure Pythagorean tradition."[72]

---

[72] Whitehead (1925), 41f.

BIBLIOGRAPHY

This Bibliography makes no attempt at completeness. I list here only titles I have used and to which I refer in the footnotes. For a full scholarly bibliography see Centrone 1996. There is a more extensive but less critical bibliography in Navia 1990. For a full collection of relevant ancient texts in English translation, see *The Pythagorean Sourcebook and Library: An Anthology of Ancient Writings Which Relate to Pythagoras and Pythagorean Philosophy*, compiled and translated by K. S. Guthrie, new edition by D. R. Fideler, Phanes Press, Grand Rapids, Mich., 1987.

Anderson, G. (1994). *Sage, Saint, and Sophist*, Routledge, London and New York.

Annas, J. (1976). *Aristotle's "Metaphysics" Books M and N*, Oxford University Press, Oxford.

Barbour, J. M. (1951). *Tuning and Temperament: A Historical Survey*, Michigan State College Press, East Lansing.

Barker, A. (1989). *Greek Musical Writings, Vol. II: Harmonic and Acoustic Theory*, Cambridge University Press, Cambridge.

Barker, A. D. (1996). In S. Hornblower and A. Spawforth, eds., *The Oxford Classical Dictionary*, 3rd ed., Oxford University Press, New York.

Bernays, J. (1866). *Theophrastos' Schrift über Frommigkeit*, Grass, Barth und Comp., Breslau (Olms reprint, 1979).

Bömer, F. (1986). *P. Ovidius Naso: Metamorphosen Buch XIV–XV*, Winter, Heidelberg.

Bonazzi, M. (2000). "Plotino e la tradizione pitagorica," in *ΣΥΝΟΥΣΙΑΙ: Seminario di filosofica antica*, Vol. LIII Annali della Facultà di Lettere e Filosofia dell'Università di Milano, 38–73.

Bower, C. M. (1989). *Boethius, Fundamentals of Music*, Yale University Press, New Haven, Conn.

Boyancé, P. (1936). *Études sur le Songe de Scipion*, Feret & Fils, Bordeaux.

Bremmer, J. (1983). *The Early Greek Concept of the Soul*, Princeton University Press, Princeton.

Burkert, W. (1961). "Hellenistische Pseudopythagorica," *Philologus* 105, 17–28.

———. (1972). *Lore and Science in Ancient Pythagoreanism* (Harvard University Press, Cambridge, Mass. 1972), English transl. by E. L. Minar, Jr. of *Weisheit und Wissenschaft: Studien zu Pythagoras, Philolaos, und Platon* (Verlag Hans Tarl, Nürnberg, 1962), as revised by the author.

———. (1972a). "Zur geistesgechichtlichen Einordnung einiger Pseudopythagorica," in *Pseudepigrapha I*, Entretiens Hardt XVIII, Fondation Hardt, Vandoeuvres-Genève, 23–55.

———. (1982). "Craft versus Sect: The Problem of Orphics and Pythagoreans", in *Jewish and Christian Self-Definition* Vol. 3, B. F. Meyer and E. P. Sanders, eds., Fortress Press, Philadelphia.

———. (1998a). "Die neuen Orphischen Texte: Fragmente, Varianten, 'Sitz im Leben,'" in *Fragmentsammlungen philosophischer Texte der Antike*, W. Burkert et al., eds., Vandenhoeck & Ruprecht, Göttingen, 387–400.

———. (1998b). "Pythagoreische Retractationen: Von den Grenzen einer möglichen Editionen," in *Fragmentsammlungen philosophischer Texte der Antike*, W. Burkert et al., eds., Vandenhoeck & Ruprecht, Göttingen, 303–19.

Carcopino, J. (1927). *La basilique pythagoricienne de la Porta Maggiore*, L'Artisan du Livre, Paris.

Caspar, M. (1959). *Kepler*, C. D. Hellman, Engl. transl., Abelard-Schuman, London and New York.

Cassio, A. C. (1988). "Nicomachus of Gerasa and the Dialect of Archytas, Fr. 1," *CQ* 38, 135–9.

Cassirer, E. (1927). *Individuum und Kosmos in der Philosophie der Renaissance*, Teubner, Leipzig and Berlin (Darmstadt reprint, 1963).

Cassirer, E., Kristeller, P. O., and Randall, J. H., Jr., eds. (1948). *The Renaissance Philosophy of Man*, University of Chicago Press, Chicago.

Centrone, B. (1990). *Pseudopythagorica Ethica*, Bibliopolis, Napoli.

———. (1996). *Introduzione a i pitagorici*, Editori Laferza, Roma-Bari.

Chaignet, A. E. (1873). *Pythagore et la philosophie pythagoricienne*, 2 vols., Didier, Paris.

Cherniss, H. (1944). *Aristotle's Criticism of Plato and the Academy*, Johns Hopkins University Press, Baltimore.

———. (1945). *The Riddle of the Early Academy*, University of California Press, Berkeley and Los Angeles.

Copernicus, N. (1984). *De Revolutionibus Libri Sex*, in *Gesamtausgabe* Vol. II, H. M. Nobis and B. Sticker, eds., Gerstenberg Verlag, Hildesheim.

Cornford, F. M. (1937). *Plato's Cosmology*, K. Paul, Trench, Trubner, & Co., London (Hackett reprint, Indianapolis, 1997).

Cumont, F. (1929). *Les religions orientales dans le paganisme romain*, P. Geuthner, Paris.

Delatte, A. (1915). *Études sur la littérature pythagoricienne*, Champion, Paris.

———. (1922). *La vie de Pythagore de Diogène Laërce*, M. Lamertin, Brussels.

Des Places, E. (1973). *Numénius: Fragments*, "Les Belles Lettres," Paris.

Diels, H. (1879). *Doxographi graeci*, Reimer, Berlin.

Dijksterhuis, E. J. (1961). *The Mechanization of the World Picture*, transl. C. Dikshoorn, Oxford University Press, Oxford.

Dillon, J. (1977). *The Middle Platonists*, Cornell University Press, Ithaca, N.Y.

————. (1987). "Iamblichus of Chalcis," in *ANRW* 36.2, 862–909.

————, transl. (1993). *Alcinous: The Handbook of Platonism*, Oxford University Press, Oxford.

Dillon, J., and Hershbell, J. (1991). *Iamblichus: On the Pythagorean Way of Life*, Scholar's Press, Atlanta, Ga.

Dittmar, H. (1912). *Aischines von Sphettos*, Philologische Untersuchungen 21, Berlin.

Dodds, E. R. (1928). "The *Parmenides* of Plato and the Origin of the Neoplatonic 'One,'" *CQ* 22, 129–42.

————. (1956). *The Greeks and the Irrational*, University of California Press, Berkeley and Los Angeles.

————. (1959). *Plato: "Gorgias,"* Oxford University Press, Oxford.

————. (1960). "Numenius and Ammonius" in *Les Sources de Plotin*, Entretiens Hardt V, Fondation Hardt, Vandoeuvres-Genève, 3–32.

————. (1963). *Proclus: The Elements of Theology*, 2nd ed., Oxford University Press, Oxford.

D'Ooge, M. L. (1926). *Nicomachus of Gerasa: Introduction to Arithmetic* (transl. with historical introduction), Macmillan, New York.

Dreyer, J. L. E. (1906). *History of the Planetary Systems from Thales to Kepler*, Cambridge University Press, Cambridge.

Dunbabin, T. J. (1948). *The Western Greeks*, Oxford University Press, Oxford.

Duncan, A. M. (1981). *Johannes Kepler, The Secret of the Universe*, Abaris Books, New York (English transl. of *Mysterium Cosmographicum*).

Ferrero, L. (1955). *Storia del Pitagorismo*, Università di Torino, Turin.

Festugière, A.-J. (1945). "Les 'Mémoires Pythagoriques' cités par Alexandre Polyhistor," *REG* 58, 1–65.

————. (1950). *La révélation d'Hermès Trismégiste*, Vol. I: *L'astrologie et les sciences occultes*, Gabalda, Paris.

————. (1953). *La révélation d'Hermès Trismégiste*, Vol. III: *Les doctrines de l'âme*, Gabalda, Paris.

————. (1954). *La révélation d'Hermès Trismégiste*, Vol. IV: *Le dieu inconnu et la gnose*, Gabalda, Paris.

Field, J. V. (1984). "Kepler's Rejection of Numerology" in *Occult and Scientific Mentalities in the Renaissance*, B. Vickers, ed., Cambridge University Press, Cambridge.

———. (1988). *Kepler's Geometrical Cosmology*, The Athlone Press, London.

Flashar, H., ed. (1983). *Die Philosophie der Antike*, Vol. III: *Ältere Akadamie, Aristoteles-Peripatos*, Schwabe & Co., Basel and Stuttgart.

Flinterman, J.-J. (1995). *Power, "Paideia" & Pythagoreanism*, Gieben, Amsterdam.

Fludd, Robert. (1617–19). *Utriusque cosmi majoris scilicet et minoris metaphysica, physica atque technica historia*, 4 vols., Oppenheim.

Frank, E. (1923). *Platon und die sogenannten Pythagoreer*, Max Niemeyer, Halle.

Frede, M. (1987). "Numenius," *ANRW* II.36.2, 1034–75.

Fritz, K. von (1950). *Pythagorean Politics in Southern Italy*, Columbia University Press, New York.

Furley, D. J. (1987). *The Greek Cosmologists*, Vol. I, Cambridge University Press, Cambridge.

Gaiser, K. (1963). *Platons Ungeschriebene Lehre*, E. Klett, Stuttgart.

Giannantoni, G. (1991). *Socratis et Socraticorum Reliquiae*[2], Bibliopolis, Napoli.

Gottschalk, H. B. (1980). *Heraclides of Pontus*, Oxford University Press, Oxford.

Gruen, E. S. (1990). "The Bacchanalian Affair," in *Studies in Greek Culture and Roman Policy*, E. J. Brill, Leiden, 34–78.

Guthrie, W. K. C. (1962). *A History of Greek Philosophy*, Vol. I: *The Earlier Presocratics and the Pythagoreans*, Cambridge University Press, Cambridge.

Harder, R., ed. (1926). *Ocellus Lucanus, de rerum natura*, Weidmann, Berlin.

Hardie, P. (1995). "The Speech of Pythagoras in Ovid *Metamorphoses* 15: Empedoclean *Epos*," *CQ* 45, 204–14.

Haussleiter, J. (1935). *Der Vegetarismus in der Antike*, A. Töpelmann, Berlin.

Heath, T. L. (1913). *Aristarchus of Samos*, Oxford University Press, Oxford.

————. (1921). *A History of Greek Mathematics*, Vol. 1, Oxford University Press, Oxford.

Heinze, R. (1892). *Xenokrates*, B. G. Teubner, Leipzig (Olms reprint, 1965).

Heninger, Jr., S. K. (1974). *Touches of Sweet Harmony: Pythagorean Cosmology and Renaissance Poetics*, Huntington Library, San Marino, Calif.

Huffman, C. (1985). "The Authenticity of Archytas Fr. 1," *CQ* 35, 344–8.

————. (1993). *Philolaus of Croton*, Cambridge University Press, Cambridge.

————. (1999). "Limite et Illimité chez les premiers philosophes grecs," in *La Felure du Plaisir: Études sur le* Philèbe *de Platon*, Vol. II: *Contextes*, M. Dixsaut, ed., J. Vrin, Paris.

————. (forthcoming). *Archytas of Tarentum*.

Hussey, E. (1997). "Pythagoreans and Eleatics," in Taylor (1997), 128–74.

Isnardi-Parente, M. (1980). *Speusippo: Frammenti*, Bibliopolis, Napoli.

Johansen, K. F. (1998). *A History of Ancient Philosophy from the Beginnings to Augustine*, H. Rosenmeier, transl., Routledge, London and New York.

Jones, C. P. (1986). *Culture and Society in Lucian*, Harvard University Press, Cambridge, Mass.

Kepler, J. (1940–45). *Gesammelte Werke*, Vol. VI (*Harmonice Mundi*), XIII (Letters), W. von Dyck and M. Caspar, eds., C. H. Beck, München.

————. (1997). *The Harmony of the World*, E. J. Aiton, A. M. Duncan, J. V. Field, transl., American Philosophical Society, Philadelphia.

Keyser, P. T. (1998). "Orreries, the Date of [Plato] *Letter* ii, and Eudorus of Alexandria," *Archiv für Geschichte der Philosophie* 80, 241–67.

Kingsley, P. (1995). *Ancient Philosophy, Mystery and Magic*, Oxford University Press, Oxford.

Kirk, G. S., Raven, J. E., and Schofield, M. (1983). *The Presocratic Philosophers*, 2nd ed., Cambridge University Press, Cambridge.

Koestler, A. (1959). *The Sleepwalkers: A History of Man's Changing Vision of the Universe*, Macmillan, New York.

Koyré, A. (1957). *From the Closed World to the Infinite Universe*, Johns Hopkins University Press, Baltimore.

Krafft, F. (1970). *Dynamische und statische Betrachtungsweise in der antiken Mechanik*, Steiner, Wiesbaden.

Krämer, H. J. (1967). *Der Ursprung der Geistmetaphysik*, Grüner, Amsterdam.

——. (1990). *Plato and the Foundations of Metaphysics*, Engl. ed. and transl., John R. Catan, State University of New York Press, Albany.

Kroll, W. (1936). "P. Nigidius Figulus," *RE* XVII.1, 200–12.

Kuhn, T. S. (1957). *The Copernican Revolution: Planetary Astronomy in the Development of Western Thought*, Harvard University Press, Cambridge, Mass.

Laks, A. and Most, G. W. (1993). *Théophraste, Métaphysique*, "Les Belles Lettres," Paris.

——, eds. (1997). *Studies on the Derveni Papyrus*, Oxford University Press, Oxford.

Larsen, B. D. (1972). *Jamblique de Chalcis, Exégète et philosophe*, Aarhus University Press, Aarhus.

Lindley, M. (1980). "Pythagorean intonation," in *The New Grove Dictionary of Music and Musicians*, Vol. 15, S. Sadie, ed., Macmillan, London, 485–7.

Linforth, I. (1941). *The Arts of Orpheus*, University of California Press, Berkeley and Los Angeles.

Lloyd, G. E. R. (1990). "Plato and Archytas in the Seventh Letter," *Phronesis* 35, 159–74.

Marg, W., ed and trans. (1972). *Timaeus Locrus*, Brill, Leiden.

Martin, A. and Primavesi, O. (1999). *L'Empédocle de Strasbourg*, Walter de Gruyter, Berlin and New York.

Merlan, P. (1967). "The Pythagoreans," in *The Cambridge History of Later Greek and Early Medieval Philosophy*, A. H. Armstrong, ed., Cambridge University Press, Cambridge, 84–106.

Minar, E. L., Jr. (1942). *Early Pythagorean Politics in Practice and Theory*, Waverly Press, Baltimore.

Mueller, I. (1997). "Greek arithmetic, geometry and harmonics: Thales to Plato," in Taylor (1997), 271–322.

Navia, L. E. (1990). *Pythagoras: An Annotated Bibliography*, Garland Pub., New York and London.

Norden, E. (1913). *Agnostos Theos*, B. G. Teubner, Berlin.

O'Meara, D. J. (1989). *Pythagoras Revived: Mathematics and Philosophy in Late Antiquity*, Oxford University Press, Oxford.

Pearson, B. A. (1984). "Philo and Gnosticism," *ANRW* 21.1, 295–342.

Penella, R. J. (1979). *The Letters of Apollonius of Tyana*, Brill, Leiden.

Philo. (1953). *Questions and Answers on "Exodus"*, Loeb Supplement II, R. Marcus, ed. and transl., Harvard University Press, Cambridge, Mass.

Powell, J. G. F. (1990). *Cicero: On Friendship and The Dream of Scipio*, Aris & Philips, Warminster.

Proclus. (1970). *A Commentary on the First Book of Euclid's Elements*, G. R. Morrow, transl., Princeton University Press, Princeton.

Radhakrishnan, S. (1953). *The Principal Upanisads*, Allen & Unwin, London.

Rawson, E. (1985). *Intellectual Life in the Late Roman Republic*, Johns Hopkins University Press, Baltimore.

Robbins, F. E. (1921). "The Tradition of Greek Arithmology," *CP* 16, 97–123.

———. (1926). Introductory chapters on Nicomachus and Greek arithmetic, in D'Ooge (1926).

Robert, L. (1980). *À travers l'Asie Mineur*. Bibliothèque des Écoles Françaises d'Athènes et de Rome, vol. 239, Boccard, Paris.

Robin, L. (1908). *La théorie platonicienne des idées et des nombres d'après Aristote*, F. Alcan, Paris.

Rohde, E. (1925). *Psyche*, W. B. Hillis, English transl., K. Paul, Trench, Trubner & Co., London.

Ross, W. D. (1951). *Plato's Theory of Ideas*, Oxford University Press, Oxford.

Runia, D. T. (1995). "Why does Clement of Alexandria call Philo 'The Pythagorean'?" *Vigiliae Christianae* 49, 1–22.

Schibli, H. S. (1990). *Pherekydes of Syros*, Oxford University Press, Oxford.

———. (1996). "On 'The One' in Philolaus, Fragment 7," *CQ* 46, 114–30.

Smith, A. (1974). *Porphyry's Place in the Neoplatonic Tradition: A Study in Post-Plotinian Neoplatonism*, Nijhoff, The Hague.

———. (1987). "Porphyrian Studies since 1913," *ANRW* II.36.2, 717–73.

Sorabji, R. (1993). *Animal Minds and Human Morals: The Origins of the Western Debate*, Cornell University Press, Ithaca, N.Y.

Städele, A. (1980). *Die Briefe des Pythagoras und der Pythagoreer*, Hain, Meisenheim am Glan.

Szlezák, T. A. (1972). *Pseudo-Archytas über die Kategorien*, De Gruyter, Berlin.

Tarán, L. (1969). "Asclepius of Tralles' commentary to Nichomachus' Introduction to Arithmetic," *Transactions of the American Philosophical Society* n.s. 59.8.

Taylor, A. E. (1928). *A Commentary on Plato's Timaeus*, Oxford University Press, Oxford.

Taylor, C. C. W., ed. (1997). *Routledge History of Philosophy*, Vol. 1: *From the Beginnings to Plato*, Routledge, London and New York.

Thesleff, H. (1961). *Introduction to the Pythagorean Writings of the Hellenistic Period*, Åbo Akademi, Åbo.

———. (1965). *The Pythagorean Texts of the Hellenistic Period*, Åbo Akademi, Åbo.

Thom, J. C. (1995). *The Pythagorean "Golden Verses,"* E. J. Brill, Leiden, New York and Köln.

Turnau, C. (2000). "Die Prinzipienlehre des Moderatus von Gades," in *Rheinisches Museum für Philologie*, Vol. 143, 197–200.

van der Waerden, B. L. (1951). *Die Astronomie der Pythagoreer*, North-Holland Pub., Amsterdam.

———. (1988). *Die Astronomie der Griechen*, Wissenschaftliche Buchgesellschaft, Darmstadt.

Waszink, J. H. (1966). "Porphyrius und Numenius," in *Porphyre*, Entretiens Hardt XII, Fondation Hardt, Vandoeuvres-Genève, 45–62.

Wehrli, F., ed. (1944–53). *Die Schule des Aristoteles*: Heft I, Dikaiarchos; Heft II, Aristoxenus; Heft VII, Herakleides Pontikos. Benno Schwabe & Co., Basel.

West, M. L. (1983). *The Orphic Poems*, Oxford University Press, Oxford.

Whitehead, A. N. (1925). *Science and the Modern World*, Macmillan, New York.

Whittaker, J. (1987). "Platonic Philosophy in the Early Centuries of the Empire," *ANRW* II.36.1, 81–123.

Willi, A. (1998). "Numa's Dangerous Books: The Exegetical History of a Roman Forgery," *Museum Helveticum* 55, 139–72.

Zeller, E. (1880–92). *Die Philosophie der Griechen in ihrer geschichtlichen Entwicklung* I–III, Reisland, Leipzig.

Zhmud, L. (1997). *Wissenschaft, Philosophie und Religion im frühen Pythagoreismus*, Akademie Verlag, Berlin.

Zuntz, G. (1971). *Persephone*, Oxford University Press, Oxford.

INDEX OF ANCIENT AND EARLY MODERN NAMES

Note: Boldface indicates principal discussion of frequently cited authors

INDEX OF MODERN NAMES

INDEX OF SUBJECTS